The French Romantics

I

The French Romantics

VOLUME 1

edited by

D.G. CHARLTON

Professor of French in the University of Warwick

The right of the
University of Cambridge
to print and sell
all manner of books
was granted by
Henry VIII in 1534.
The University has printed
and published continuously
since 1584.

CAMBRIDGE UNIVERSITY PRESS

Cambridge

London   New York   New Rochelle

Melbourne   Sydney

Published by the Press Syndicate of the University of Cambridge
The Pitt Building, Trumpington Street, Cambridge CB2 1RP
32 East 57th Street, New York, NY 10022, USA
296 Beaconsfield Parade, Middle Park, Melbourne 3206, Australia

First published 1984

Printed in Great Britain at
the University Press, Cambridge

Library of Congress catalogue card number: 83–21010

British Library Cataloguing in Publication Data

The French romantics
Vol. 1
1. Romanticism – France 2. France –
Civilization – History
I. Charlton, D.G.
944.04   DC33.5
ISBN 0 521 24413 7 hard covers
ISBN 0 521 28673 5 paperback

SE

Contents

VOLUME ONE

Preface   *page* vii

Acknowledgments   x

I   THE FRENCH ROMANTIC MOVEMENT   I
     D.G. Charlton, *Professor of French in the University of Warwick*

II   RELIGIOUS AND POLITICAL THOUGHT   33
     D.G. Charlton

III   ILLUMINISM, UTOPIA, MYTHOLOGY   76
     Frank Paul Bowman, *Professor of French in the University of Pennsylvania*

IV   POETRY   113
     J.C. Ireson, *Emeritus Professor of French in the University of Hull*

V   PROSE FICTION   163
     D.G. Charlton

VOLUME TWO

List of illustrations   vii

Preface   ix

Acknowledgments   xii

VI   DRAMA   205
     W.D. Howarth, *Professor of Classical French Literature in the University of Bristol*

VII   CRITICISM AND THEORY   248
     Roger Fayolle, *Professeur à l'Université de la Sorbonne Nouvelle, Paris*

CONTENTS

VIII HISTORIANS   274
      Douglas Johnson, *Professor of French History at University
      College in the University of London*

  IX THE VISUAL ARTS   308
      William Vaughan, *Reader in History of Art at University
      College in the University of London*

   X MUSIC AND OPERA   353
      Hugh Macdonald, *Gardiner Professor of Music in the University
      of Glasgow*

  XI ROMANTICS ON THE FRINGE (*Les Romantiques*   382
      marginaux)
      Max Milner, *Professeur à l'Université de la
      Sorbonne Nouvelle, Paris*

Index   423

Preface

This work aims to describe and evaluate the collective achievements of the French Romantics and to reassess, some 150 years after their heyday and in the light of recently increasing scholarly attention, their significance and persisting value. To that end certain delimitations have been adopted, in part for reasons advanced in the introductory chapter. First, this is not a study of Romanticism and tries to eschew definitions of that much-defined abstraction; secondly, it seeks to examine the 'French Romantic movement' in itself, to the extent to which that is possible – in isolation from European Romanticism as a multi-national phenomenon and in isolation also from the numerous other developments within French culture during what has sometimes been rather over-inclusively termed 'the age of Romanticism'. The purpose, by contrast, is to focus upon the works of the French Romantics themselves and the movement they cumulatively created, and here a presupposition must be stated that explains the very design of the work (a view for which the editor alone is responsible, even though his collaborators may share it to a greater or lesser extent). This is that they and their movement have to be interpreted not only in the perspectives of literary history and criticism, as has quite often been the case in even the best and most helpful of previous studies, but, equally and much more broadly, of intellectual and cultural history in general. The Romantics' salons and *cénacles* included historians, painters and illustrators, men of politics, composers, critics and philosophers alongside poets, novelists and dramatists, and, furthermore, even the literary men themselves had far wider preoccupations than we today tend to connect with 'literature'. They lived at a time when works from Mme de Staël's *De la littérature* (1800) to surveys like Alfred Nettement's histories of French literature under the Restoration and under the July monarchy (1852 and 1854) commonly included under that term works of history, philosophy, even religious thought, as much as poems, novels and plays, and the Romantics themselves fully shared that range of interests, as the sheer diversity of their works readily illustrates.

As a consequence, this study of them contains chapters on the visual arts, music and opera, historians, religious and political thought, and criticism and theory, as well as on the main literary genres, and that in turn has entailed a practical conclusion. The present editor, at any rate, could not single-handedly write such a book (as kindly suggested by the Cambridge University Press initially); only a collaborative study, enriched by a variety of specialists, could hope to be adequate. I am most grateful to the distinguished scholars who accepted my invitations and pleased that, whilst most of them are by design British or American, the very considerable renewal of scholarly work on the Romantics in France is represented here by the chapters from Professors Fayolle and Milner. Another advantage may result: instead of a single, inevitably limited, interpretation the reader is offered several. The resulting differences of emphasis and judgment, the 'variations on a theme' played by my colleagues, will, I hope, make the total examination the more comprehensive and stimulating, not least where conflicting assessments are evident. We have not even sought complete agreement, indeed, as to *who* 'the French Romantics' *are* (a multi-sided problem discussed in chapter I), and each contributor is finally responsible for the dramatis personae of his own chapter, whatever pragmatic guide-lines the editor may have suggested. It may be tempting to appeal to Henri Bremond's well-known half-truth, salutary though it is for those seeking portable generalisations: 'Il y a autant de romantismes que de Romantiques.' Against that, my colleagues and I are agreed that there did exist, in the first half of the nineteenth century, a 'French Romantic movement' – slow though most of its rather loosely linked members were to become conscious of it and diverse as was their commitment in both duration and conviction. Our attempt is to reconsider it, but without ever attributing as much interest to the movement itself – finally an abstraction – as to individuals; the title, *The French Romantics* (*sic*), says what is intended.

The ordering of the following chapters is in good measure arbitrary, reflecting the claim that no aspect or genre has significant priority over any other, and so also is the division between the two volumes required by present publishing economics. Only the first chapter, surveying the movement as a whole and its rise, development and aims, fell naturally into place, and as well, to conclude, on chronological grounds, Professor Milner's chapter, which presents a final group of writers whom he describes as essentially 'les romantiques *marginaux*', translated here, with allusion to 'fringe theatre' and the like, as 'Romantics on the Fringe'. The chapters between have been re-ordered to the last, until choice became unavoidable. Chapter I is followed by two complementary chapters (II and III) on different aspects of what, in my view, was a fundamental intellectual commitment on the part of the French Romantics (whatever be true of their English, German and other counterparts), an intended *engagement* of which a recognition is basic for a full understanding of their concerns and works. Thereafter the literary genres are studied in turn: poetry (IV), prose fiction (V), drama (VI), literary criticism and theory (VII), and – seen as 'literature' by Nettement but perhaps not by Professor Johnson and other modern scholars – the work of the Romantic historians (VIII). (As to the specific ordering here a minor consideration should be mentioned; since the three chapters written by myself rest on a particular interpretation – which my colleagues may or may not share, though I naturally hope they do in good part – it seemed easier for the reader to judge it if they were placed in the same volume.) Chapters IX and X consider the other cultural forms prized by the Romantics as part of their belief in 'la fraternité des arts': the visual arts, and music and opera. Chapter XI, on the 'fringe' Romantics, completes the work, to which by intention there is no formal Conclusion. The current profusion of scholarly work on the Romantics, in France and abroad, would make conclusions more than normally premature at this time; secondly, any editor would be presumptuous, not to add hard-pressed, to attempt an agreed communiqué from his diverse colleagues. The worth-while conclusion, moreover, is really that the reader should eventually put aside this work and repair to the bookshelves, the concert halls and the art galleries. To help him to do so the more rewardingly, however, each chapter ends with a bibliographical essay, albeit firmly selective and biased in part to studies in English. Notes have been kept to the minimum needed, in the view of each separate contributor, in order, where thought desirable, to identify the sources referred to.

I feel greatly indebted to my fellow authors, and, for his frequent encouragement and advice, to Professor Garnet Rees, and equally so to the Syndics and to the Publisher and his colleagues at the Cambridge University Press; they have been especially generous, particularly in the present financial climate, in the length they themselves suggested, in agreeing to translation of chapters VII and XI from the original French and to the inclusion of illustrations, contained in the second volume, for chapters VI, IX and X, and in their constant helpfulness during the process of preparation and publication.

University of Warwick   D.G.C.
January 1983

Acknowledgments

The editor records acknowledgments from Professor J.C. Ireson to the British Academy for research grants which assisted the preparation of chapter IV, 'Poetry'.

Note

The place of publication of works cited is Paris unless otherwise stated.

I · *The French Romantic Movement*

D.G. CHARLTON

INTRODUCTION

The French Romantics collectively created one of the most prolific and wide-ranging movements in the history of any national culture. Mme de Staël once remarked: 'Dans tous les genres, nous autres modernes, nous disons trop.' It is easy to agree with her, but the sheer volume of their work was not only the consequence of a quite unusual energy and creativity. It followed in good part from the astonishing breadth of their concerns and the sheer diversity of literary, intellectual and artistic forms through which they explored and expressed them. Politics and history, ancient and modern alike; philosophy and religions of both past and present; the visual arts, music and opera: all these can be cited before one even considers the achievements in literature with which the Romantic movement is most often connected. There too their range was remarkable: a great enrichment of poetry, lyric, epic, political and philosophical all represented; a major transformation in the French dramatic tradition; a wide exploration of prose fiction in a variety of forms – personal, historical, and social novels, and the *conte* and *nouvelle* genres; literary theory and criticism.

The succeeding chapters of this work will attempt to describe and evaluate the Romantics in their intellectual and cultural significance understood in this very broad way, but one can at once note here that even an outline of the public careers and the works of leading Romantics indicates how extensive were their preoccupations. Chateaubriand, having received an army commission before the Revolution, returned from his American travels to fight with the Armée des Émigrés, being wounded at Thionville. After a period of exile in England, during which he published his first major work – his *Essai historique, politique et moral sur les révolutions anciennes et modernes dans leurs rapports avec la révolution française* (1797) – and started his apologia for Christianity, *Le Génie du christianisme* (1802), he began his diplomatic career under Napoleon in a post at the French Embassy in Rome. His political convictions, shocked

as he was by the execution of the duc d'Enghien and by other
Napoleonic actions and policies, quickly led him to resign, but his public
career was resumed very soon after the Emperor's downfall – first as a
Minister of Louis XVIII, later as French Ambassador in Berlin and
London and then in Rome. As to publications, *Atala*, *René* and his
autobiographical writings were only a minor part of his output. In
addition to his earlier intellectual works, he wrote a prose epic of early
Christianity, *Les Martyrs*, a number of political writings, including *De
Buonaparte et des Bourbons* and *De la monarchie selon la Charte*, his *Études
historiques* – four volumes in the Pourrat edition of his complete works –
not to add several travel books, critical essays, an *Essai sur la littérature
anglaise*, and a biography of the seventeenth-century Trappist Rancé.
Both his career and his *œuvres complètes* suggest a man of convictions in
religion and politics alike – the very reverse, one can note, of his
character René.

The same was true of his contemporaries Constant and Mme de Staël.
The latter was daughter of Louis XVI's chief minister Necker and thus
born into an environment that combined political activity and intellectual culture. First married to the Swedish Ambassador in Paris, she
herself created a salon of high distinction, and like Chateaubriand she
had the courage during the Revolutionary period to oppose political
régimes of which she disapproved – going into exile in England in 1792
and later to Switzerland. Under Napoleon too, most famously, her
liberalism brought her into conflict repeatedly with authority and led
again to her exile – in 1803, then in 1806, again in 1810. At her Swiss
home at Coppet she again created an intellectual centre, and by her
extensive travels, ranging from England to Russia and Sweden to Italy,
she established cultural contacts, notably with such German intellectuals
as the Schlegels, that were to be seminal through her mediation for
French thought over the next generation. As to her many writings, she is
remembered now less for her novels, *Delphine* and *Corinne*, than her
works of intellection: a pioneering study in cultural history and the
sociology of sensibility, *De la littérature considérée dans ses rapports avec les
institutions sociales* (1800); *De l'Allemagne* (1810), which both continued
the enquiries of the earlier book and offered a wide-ranging though
selective account of German literature, art, philosophy and religious
thought; and a number of philosophical, political and critical treatises,
including an *Essai sur les fictions* (1795), *De l'influence des passions sur le
bonheur des individus et des nations* (1796), *Réflexions sur le suicide* (1813), and
Considérations sur les principaux événements de la Révolution française (posth.,
1818). Her great friend Constant – described by contemporaries as one

of her few equals in intelligence – was even more emphatically involved in both scholarship and politics. Like her he was exiled by Napoleon for his liberal views but, although he attacked the Emperor in a celebrated essay *De l'esprit de conquête et de l'usurpation* (1813), his political career began during the Hundred Days. But his real work as a politician came during the Restoration when, as a *député* and by his writings, he established himself as a leader of the Liberal opposition. His political works form a substantial part of his published works, but even more important to Constant himself were his major scholarly studies of religious systems, especially Greek and Roman polytheism. He was preoccupied from his youth until his death by his work *De la religion considérée dans sa source, ses formes et ses développements* (5 vols., 1824–31), and it remains his greatest intellectual achievement. His most famous book, *Adolphe*, its unfinished companion-novel *Cécile*, and his *Journal intime* and *Le Cahier rouge* have a more minor place in his life and work than might appear from histories confined to literature.

If we turn to the succeeding generation, Lamartine provides a first illustration of a similar combination of thought, literature and action. His earlier career was as a diplomat – at Naples, Florence, and elsewhere – but after 1830 he moved into political activity, becoming in 1833 a *député* of independent and liberal views, popular and influential through certain of his speeches – on the death penalty, press freedom, and the abolition of slavery, for example – and in 1848, for a few months, he became the virtual ruler of France. His political writings and speeches are often ignored in favour of his poetry, yet a short essay like his *Politique rationnelle* (1831) is worth reading for its understanding of the more significant political issues of the day as well as for his own programme of reform. And though he has been criticised as a historian, especially for his later works, his *Histoire des Girondins* (1847) still warrants attention from students of the Revolution. It would be difficult to claim for him as acute an intelligence as a Constant, but even much of his poetry is less emotional, more intellectually involved, than such poems as 'Le Lac' which are commonly taken as most characteristic of him: epics like *Jocelyn* and *La Chute d'un ange*, or, earlier, the philosophical poem of 1823, *La Mort de Socrate*, inspired by Plato, not to add the philosophical poems of the *Méditations* themselves.

Vigny's life presents a less active picture – though certainly not by his own desire. As a youth he sought a career in action in the French army, in which he remained until 1827, but with the final fall of Napoleon all chances of military glory had disappeared. In later life he tried, briefly, to enter politics, but was unsuccessful. His existence was thus far more withdrawn and inactive than he wished. Yet he of all the Romantics had something of the philosopher about him, as his poems suggest, and his *Journal d'un poète* contains numerous references to thinkers – Kant, Pascal, Cousin and others – that reveal a mind that knew and could shrewdly judge the intellectual trends of his age. He was no less concerned as a writer with social issues: the role of the artist in society, as in *Stello* and *Chatterton*; the defects of capitalism, notably in this latter work; the rights of the soldier and the conflict of public duty and private conscience, as in the short stories in *Servitude et grandeur militaires*; the role of the aristocracy – a question underlying his historical novel *Cinq-Mars*.

Hugo perhaps came closest of all his contemporaries to being a universal man. Son of one of Napoleon's generals, his first career was none the less as a man of letters – poet, novelist and dramatist. Yet his earlier works already show fully his concern with politics – first as a royalist, then as a liberal – and with religious and other questions. His later role, it is all but needless to note, is almost as much political as literary. Supporter of Louis-Philippe and, after 1845, a *pair de France*, the Revolution of 1848 made him a republican and a representative in the Assemblée Législative and, as such, an ardent advocate of universal male suffrage, free education, and other progressive causes. Following Louis-Napoléon's accession to power, personally disappointed to receive no political office and shocked by the *coup d'état* of 1851, he chose exile in Belgium and the Channel Islands, refusing to return, despite the offer of an amnesty, for so long as the Emperor remained in power. He went back to France after the fall of the Second Empire and was elected first to the Assemblée Nationale and later as a senator, and though his influence on public policy appears to have been slight, he remained until his death almost a symbol of republican socialism, apotheosised as such by burial in the Panthéon.

Comparable involvement is seen in other Romantics. The historians treated in a later chapter were also philosophers of history and culture, and some of them became major political figures and statesmen: Guizot, Thiers, Michelet, and more minor writers like Duvergier de Hauranne. Mérimée too became Inspector-General of Historical Monuments from 1834 and achieved much to preserve the French architectural heritage, and during the Second Empire he would become a senator and a close friend of the Empress Eugénie. Even those Romantics who assumed no such public roles often became, by virtue of their social and intellectual commitments, revered public figures to an extent we now find hard to appreciate. Two instances must suffice here. So hard-headed a judge as Taine would see Musset as a major intellectual: 'Y eut-il jamais accent plus vibrant et plus vrai? Celui-là au moins n'a jamais menti... Il a imprimé sa marque dans la pensée humaine: il a dit au monde ce que c'est que l'homme, l'amour, la vérité, le bonheur.'[1] Or again, George Sand not only played a distinctive role in the diffusion of utopian socialism and the encouragement of *la littérature ouvrière*; her successive novels were eagerly awaited by readers from America to Russia, and admiring fellow writers included Dostoevsky, Flaubert, Matthew Arnold, Renan, Walt Whitman, and Henry James.

During the twentieth century, by contrast, the Romantics seem to have gradually but largely lost their former power to challenge and disturb. The tides of taste have flowed towards, for example, the symbolists and surrealists, the existentialists and the culture of absurdity, and as commonly presented (mainly in university departments of literature) they have often seemed of little more than historical interest and, stylistically, to be too rhetorical, even garrulous, for the undemonstrative, satirical, understated preferences of our time. Even now one senses in many older and younger readers alike a certain dissociation from the French Romantics, whatever be true of their counterparts in England, Germany and elsewhere. As recently as 1969 Henri Peyre could reasonably, if controversially, declare that 'of all the eras of French literature (and perhaps of other literatures), the romantic age has, for over half a century, been the least studied, the most misunderstood and distorted'.[2] That view may undervalue outstanding scholarship in the twenty years or so before the Second World War, to which we are still indebted – from Bray, Moreau, Martino, Souriau, Evans, Hunt, Guillemin, Flottes, Leroy, Van Tieghem, and others. But during the twenty years or more after the War, despite the expansion of university staffs over that period, the impression was one of comparative neglect, notwithstanding valuable studies and initiatives from a minority.

It had not been so even in the earlier decades of our own century. The fierce ideological attacks of Lemaître, Brunetière, Seillière, Maurras and Lasserre – astonished though one may be that they and Irving Babbitt's *Rousseau and Romanticism* could have been valued by young T.S. Eliot, T.E. Hulme and others – were none the less paying a more comprehending tribute to the Romantics than many of the more anodyne literary–historical surveys that were to succeed them. Pierre Lasserre's *Le Romantisme français* in 1907 attacked it as 'le torrent d'idées et de sentiments le plus subversif qui se fût jamais déchaîné parmi les hommes'; the Romantics purveyed 'la glorification, je dis plus, la déification de l'irrégulier, du paresseux, de l'impuissant, de l'insurgé et même du criminel'. By the following year Seillière was similarly diagnosing *Le Mal romantique* and linking it with neurasthenia, and soon Louis Reynaud would argue that this deplorable aberration had English and German rather than French sources. For Babbitt too it favoured 'every imaginable extreme' and was 'filled with the praise of ignorance'. However much we disagree, such views – and, at a higher level, the critical scrutiny of the Romantics' religious ideas in Auguste Viatte's *Le Catholicisme chez les romantiques* a little later – took the Romantic movement seriously as a major intellectual and cultural phenomenon. And in 1930, when the 'centenary' of the movement was acknowledged, criticism remained as evident as praise. To follow the account of twentieth-century evaluations of the Romantics prior to 1930 given by P. Mansell Jones's *Tradition and Barbarism* is to enter an atmosphere of ideological partisanship – on both sides of the debate, with their defenders as much as with their opponents – that refreshes one with its acknowledgment of the Romantics' living relevance.

The passionate involvement of those years is infrequent but not entirely absent in our own times. To take North America as example, a survey of 'recent research' could contend that 'Romanticism' has become almost a 'faith' for such scholars as Northrop Frye and Morse Peckham,[3] and Jacques Barzun in *Classic, Romantic and Modern* (1961), a revision of his earlier study, offered a most stimulating defence of the Romantics as 'first of all constructive and creative'. By contrast, M.Z. Shroder, in a work published in the same year (by Babbitt's former university indeed), could allege the Romantics' 'messianic pretension' and conclude that their 'image of the artist is ultimately an unrealizable megalomaniac ideal of personal omnipotence'.[4] Since then, moreover, there have been numerous illustrations of more dispassionate scholarship; it would be invidious to select particular individual studies here, but they are fully represented in the bibliographies to the following chapters. And at a more general and equally important level, the Société des Études Romantiques has been founded and its journal *Romantisme* (1971–), and various research centres in France and elsewhere have been created, as have such reviews abroad as *Studies in Romanticism* (1961–) and *Nineteenth-Century French Studies* (1972–). More specialist publications have also proliferated – devoted, for example, to Constant (from 1955), Chateaubriand (1957), Mme de Staël (1962), Vigny (1967), and others. So too have colloquia and special issues of other reviews devoted to the Romantics and to what can well be seen as a rediscovery of major but previously neglected authors such as (say) Mme de Staël, as in the cumulative work of the *Colloques de Coppet*, and as another straw in the wind, one can note that this present work offers the first overall study of the French Romantic movement to be published in English for many years.

This contemporary resurgence of interest has often been based, moreover, on most welcome perceptions of the multi-sidedness of the Romantics' collective achievements. The preface to *Romantisme*'s first issue affirmed views that others increasingly share. Romanticism, far from being literary alone, represents 'une période de l'histoire culturelle'; 'nous nous adressons donc aussi aux historiens de toutes disciplines, aux philosophes, aux sociologues, aux psychologues, aux linguistes, aux musicologues . . . A chacun d'allonger la liste!' Complexity too was stressed; in the review's very first paragraph the editor emphasised 'incertitudes sur la nature du phénomène, disparité de ses manifestations, contradictions dans ses effets, ambiguïté de ses formes spécifiques d'expression . . .' – 'le fait romantique échappe à toute prise sûre'.

Such warnings were fully warranted then – and may still be needed now. For half a century and more, one may well claim, study of the Romantics had not only been largely confined to literary scholars; above all it had been bedevilled by countless definitions purporting to sum up the essentials of Romanticism, not only in France but, very often, in Europe as a whole – in England, Germany, Italy, Spain, Poland, Hungary and elsewhere. Lovejoy's celebrated article of 1924, urging the need to discriminate between different 'Romanticisms' has often been quoted but rarely obeyed, and even less heeded has been his warning about the very use of the term itself: 'The word "Romantic" has come to mean so many things that, by itself, it means nothing. It has ceased to perform the function of a verbal sign.' Yet even Lovejoy himself, in 1941, would offer his criteria of Romanticism – the concepts of 'organicism', 'dynamism' and 'diversitarianism' – and others, notoriously, have produced numerous and usually conflicting definitions. Barzun's 'sampling of modern usage' gives one list amongst others – since when many more have flowed under the academic bridge. Amongst the competing adjectives equated with 'Romantic' he notes 'realistic' and 'unreal', 'conservative' and 'revolutionary', 'materialistic' and 'mysterious and soulful', 'formless' and 'formalistic', as well as 'unselfish', 'futile', 'heroic', 'stupid', 'nordic', 'bombastic', and many others. And a more recent study of Romanticism as a 'critical idiom' cites examples that range from 'the cult of the extinct', 'vague aspiration' and 'sentimental melancholy' to 'the renascence of wonder' and 'the fairy way of writing'. Well might its author refer elsewhere to 'the maze of Romanticisms' – prior to offering her own inclusive summary![5] Paul Valéry summed up both the confusion created and the abstracted irrelevance of all such attempts at definition in laconic sentences that are frequently cited by those about to disregard them: 'Il est impossible de penser – sérieusement – avec des mots comme Classicisme, Romantisme, Humanisme, Réalisme. On ne s'enivre ni se désaltère avec des étiquettes de bouteilles.'[6]

Such 'words', moreover, may all too easily come between ourselves and the works being studied. They may predispose us, for example, to stress in our interpretations those characteristics we have already defined as Romantic. They may also lead us to concentrate unduly upon those works within a given Romantic's total achievement that seem best to exemplify them and to treat others as less typical and thus peripheral – to focus above all (say) on Senancour's *Obermann*, with its depiction of Romantic *mal du siècle*, to the neglect of his *Libres Méditations*, even though he saw this later work as more important and definitive; on Chateaubriand's fictional and autobiographical writings rather than his religious, political and historical works; on Lamartine's lyric poetry more than his epics, and so on. Specific instances like these may in themselves be of minor significance, though symptomatic. More widely pervasive has been the influence of the most deeply fixed of all the definitions, underlying both such selectivity and many of the more partial summaries: that which isolates as the main features and criteria of Romanticism the twin cults of emotion and subjectivity.

In a valuable survey in 1951, J.-B. Barrère examined the statements of literary historians from Brunetière and Lanson to Jasinski and Castex and concluded: 'Ces définitions mesurées s'accordent à mettre l'accent, avec Croce, sur le sentiment, ou avec Goethe, sur la subjectivité: ce qui revient à peu près au même.' Since then similar assertions have continued. 'Romantic literature glorified strong passions, unique emotions and special deeds'; 'the Romantics emphasised individualism, imagination and emotion as their guiding principles'; 'Romantic doctrine sees poetry above all as the spontaneous expression of personal emotion': these are just three recent Anglo-Saxon instances of a persisting view – a view (it seems increasingly clear from much recent research) that mistakes the half-truth for the whole truth and distorts by extracting particular aspects from their far broader context. The starting point of at least the editor of this present work is nominalist revolt, and the purpose, even though never completely achievable, is to recapture the French Romantic movement in its complex totality and range. The ideal would be to look at the entire corpus of the Romantics' work and to do so without preconceived expectations.

'THE FRENCH ROMANTICS'

Who *were* 'the French Romantics'? To avoid abstract definitions highlights the more a question that is more difficult to answer than might at first appear.

Certain usages of 'romantic' and 'romanticism' are easily excluded here. Some scholars have applied the terms, entirely properly for their purposes, to writers, painters and others from the Ancients and the Middle Ages down to the twentieth century. They have had in mind what has been called 'intrinsic', 'perennial' or 'archetypal' romanticism, an age-long spiritual condition or set of attitudes of which they then give a more or less justifiable description. Others have adopted a more limited but partially related 'aesthetic' usage, often contrasting works that are more imaginatively or emotionally inspired with the more realistic or documentary, but likewise treating the terms as potentially applicable to the cultural achievements of all ages.

Here, by contrast, the 'historical' usage is intended: 'the Romantic movement', 'the Romantics', as in countless histories of literature, art and music in particular. Yet this usage above all has given rise to confusions, and not least where it is mingled with notions of 'archetypal' or 'aesthetic' romanticism or both. 'X is a lower-case romantic and lived between *c.* 1750 and *c.* 1870 and is thus properly to be considered as an upper-case Romantic': such is the invalid syllogism.

Some examples of the resulting confusion are relatively easy to resolve, however – notably where a scholar moves backwards or forwards in time in order to discern 'archetypal' or 'aesthetic' romanticism in the immediate predecessors or successors of the earlier nineteenth-century Romantics. Mornet's pioneering work on *Le Romantisme au 18e siècle*, for example, discerned in the period prior to 1800 so many detailed anticipations and influences that some were tempted – in the manner of Lasserre and Babbitt – to date the Romantic movement from Rousseau and others of his age. The concept of 'le préromantisme' served for a time as a convenient term of delimitation, as in the studies of Trahard, Monglond and others, but more recent criticisms have revealed such differences between 'préromantiques' and 'romantiques', alongside similarities, that its validity is largely undermined. Since a particularly trenchant colloquium devoted to it, only the boldest scholar would now rely on the notion, one may think.[7] An analogous movement forward in time has been equally or more frequently made. Thus, for instance, Mario Praz's celebrated study of *The Romantic Agony* traced its themes down to Huysmans and other *décadents* of the late nineteenth century, and it has been even more common, especially a few decades

9

ago, to consider various mid-century writers as in some sense Romantics, almost as a final generation of the Romantic movement – and not inexcusably so given its impact upon them, in their youth in particular. It was none the less surprising that the quite recent and distinguished multi-volumed history of French literature from Arthaud should have given to all three volumes on the nineteenth century – those covering 1843–1869 and 1869–1896 as well as 1820–1843 – the collective title of *Le Romantisme*.

Yet, despite implicit assumptions that we may distrust in such practices, few of us are seriously misled. Most present-day scholars would not name Rousseau, Greuze, Vernet, Bernardin de Saint-Pierre, and others in the eighteenth century as 'French Romantics', nor would Baudelaire, Leconte de Lisle, Flaubert and others of their generation be included as members of 'the French Romantic movement'. In practice, for the most part at least, the real difficulties in identifying who 'the French Romantics' were lie firmly within the first half of the nineteenth century. A not uncommon practice in some histories of French literature in particular has been to treat all the writers whose works fell within those fifty years as illustrative of 'the age of Romanticism'. This may be defensible if it amounts to no more than a substitute for dates (and *their* misleading restrictions), but it has proved easy to slip into Hegelian-type preconceptions about the spiritual unity of such an 'age' and even to attribute causal force to what is, finally, an abstract noun. A comparably over-extensive usage is based upon birth dates, linked with the notion (albeit not without its utility) of 'generations'. Thus Barzun, amongst other instances, defines 'historic Romanticism' as 'comprising those Europeans whose birth falls between 1770 and 1815, and who achieved distinction in philosophy, statecraft, and the arts during the first half of the nineteenth century'. This may be helpful in bringing out how diverse and wide-ranging were the achievements of this chronological generation, spread, moreover, over the very different countries of Europe. What is less clear is the validity or helpfulness of subsuming such multifarious activity under a single name.

All the same, to abandon such all-inclusiveness presents distinctive problems. If not all who were born or who produced their works within given dates are to be treated as Romantics, how do we select the 'real' Romantics from amongst their numerous contemporaries? The selection, furthermore, may carry major consequences for interpretation. It would be simple, for example – it would, indeed, be almost tautological – to demonstrate (say) the religious, philosophical, political and social importance of 'the French Romantics' by including in their ranks such writers as Bonald, Joseph de Maistre and Lamennais, Saint-Simon and his followers, and other socialistic thinkers of the age. There are distinguished precedents for such inclusions. Viatte treated the Catholic Traditionalists as examples of 'le catholicisme chez les romantiques'; but in what ways are 'les romantiques' being defined if even the age's outstanding proponents of Roman orthodoxy illustrated a regrettable 'romantic' heresy? Talmon in his *Political Messianism: The Romantic Phase* relied heavily on the left-wing thinkers of the time in order to validate his critical thesis and, moreover, omitted all the writers most commonly classed as Romantics except for Constant and Lamartine (whom he rightly presented as liberal opponents of the authoritarian views under attack); in what sense is 'Romantic' being used within the title, we may therefore ask, even where we agree with the basic interpretation of the other thinkers discussed?[8] And to give a final and present-day instance, may not many an illuminist minor writer – currently wandering between his transmigratory incarnations or between planets – be surprised to observe himself conscripted to the 'Romantic' camp, even in the distinguished pages of *Romantisme*?

Such questions point to the adoption of a perhaps more pedestrian definition, more circumscribed to those who were actually members of the *cénacles* and salons of the 1820s in Paris – where 'the French Romantic movement', if anywhere and to the extent that it existed at all as other than a convenient generalisation for historians since, was hammering out new doctrines and aims and quarrelling about new social and intellectual problems. To equate 'the French Romantics' with those who attended such friendly and disputatious meetings is certainly tempting, and a full enquiry on that basis might well throw unaccustomed light on numerous adherents who have fallen into oblivion except for their names as recorded by the scholarship of Bray, Eggli or Martino. We may know something of such frequenters of Nodier's salon as Émile Deschamps and Alexandre Guiraud, but even specialists may be more ignorant of Saint-Valry, Rességuier, Victor Pavie, Francis Wey, Dauzats, and Droz, or, at Hugo's *cénacle* in 1827, enthusiasts like Turquéty, Pauthier de Censay, and Alcide de Beauchesne. Yet by this yardstick they were amongst the 'French Romantics' for whom Hugo and a few others were the more fortunate and self-advertising 'frontmen'. However, there would be distinct difficulties if one used this criterion: first, to establish a reliable and comprehensive listing; secondly, to distinguish between deeply-involved and short-lived membership; thirdly, to decide which of the succeeding, conflicting, and constantly changing groupings should be taken as most representative of the whole 'movement'. One could perhaps settle upon Hugo's *cénacle* of 1827, since it, as Bray notes, 'constituera vraiment l'École romantique';[9] one would thereby illuminate a fascinating moment in French cultural history, yet it would none the less show no more than a moment in the longer story of the French Romantics and their achievements.

Scholarly usage has in fact usually understood 'le mouvement' to be much wider than 'l'école' (or even 'les écoles') – and has done so without adding 'le préromantisme' or the generation of Baudelaire and Flaubert. Most especially it has included within 'movement' (but not in 'school') a first generation that includes Chateaubriand, Mme de Staël, Constant, Ballanche and Senancour in particular. True, they lacked the cohesion, the sense of mutual purpose, that would unite some of the next generation. Moreover, although the concept of 'romantic' was (we shall see) already 'in the air', Chateaubriand, for example, denied that it applied to him, and his *Atala* and *Le Génie du christianisme* and Mme de Staël's *De la littérature* too were not really felt by contemporaries to challenge existing traditions. Yet this retrospectively dated attribution is not only almost universally made but is surely justifiably made, and above all with Staël and Constant from whom came the first explicit theoretical challenges to older views and, with them, the first formulation of ideas which the Romantics of the 1820s would adopt and develop. The case is as with Wordsworth, Coleridge or Shelley – who never saw themselves as 'romantics' and yet are surely sensibly subsumed under that head. In France too the contrary view would produce some quixotic results. Hugo in the *Préface des nouvelles odes* of 1824 refused the title of 'romantic' and presented himself as a conciliator between classical and romantic; is he then not a 'Romantic' until a later date? Lamartine's *Méditations* were judged by many readers of the day to be within the bounds of poetic orthodoxy, and he would later be attacked by *Le Globe*, organ of the Romantics as it then was; is he too not a 'Romantic' at that time? Musset, most famously, satirised the very use of the term, and his heroes defined it to mean merely a mania for adjectives; is the author of *Les Nuits* to be omitted, and likewise Delacroix who proclaimed himself a 'classic'?

One is led, in short, to adopt the most commonplace scholarly usage, fully accepting that this will give no more than practical definitions for present purposes. Even so, differences will persist at the margins between different observers – as they do, indeed, between the contributors of the various chapters of this work, each of whom has been given a freedom he could in any case hardly have been denied to identify for his own subject those whom he sees as 'Romantics'. Nor is that apparent discrepancy indefensible. The Stendhal who wrote *Racine et Shakespeare* must surely appear in any chapter on French Romantic theory; it need not follow that his novels should be included as part of the Romantic movement's contribution to prose fiction. What, similarly, of Balzac? In his youth he frequented the Romantic *cénacles*, remained friendly with various Romantics throughout his career and was eulogised by Hugo at its end, and an early work like *Les Chouans* has usually been treated as one of the Romantics' historical novels. Yet his maturer work, like Stendhal's, is commonly felt to overflow, to transcend, the category of 'Romantic prose fiction'. The ambivalent position of both novelists is well illustrated by the one-time literary–historical placing of them as 'les grands réalistes romantiques': the chapter later on 'Prose fiction' largely excludes them, giving precedence, so to say, to noun over adjective – but a different contributor of that chapter might have decided otherwise. Similar 'demarcation disputes' arise with the other literary genres and with history, art, music and opera likewise. Finally, pragmatic decisions in varying cases are inevitable in judging who 'really belongs' to (say) a particular religious or political movement – even a membership card may not establish commitment – and likewise with cultural movements.

PHASES OF THE MOVEMENT

The French Romantic movement, understood in these ways, spanned a very considerable period. Mme de Staël was born in 1766, Constant in 1767, and Chateaubriand in 1768. Victor Hugo died in 1885 and Liszt in 1886. Staël's first remembered work, her *Lettres sur les ouvrages et le caractère de J.-J. Rousseau*, was published in 1788 (and in English translation in 1789), whilst two of Hugo's best-known poetic works, *La Fin de Satan* and *Dieu*, did not appear until 1886 and 1891 after his death. Such basic dates only underline the need to distinguish the various phases of the movement as a whole, not least to avoid any unconscious assumption that what may be characterised as 'Romantic' in one phase will be equally dominant in some other phase. For the German Romantics the division was clearer-cut: between *Frühromantiker* like the Schlegels, Novalis, Tieck, Schelling and others and *Hochromantiker* such as Heine, Hoffmann, Arnim, Chamisso and Eichendorff later – though even they were all born within the eighteenth century and were thus noticeably earlier in time than all but the first of the French Romantics. With the French movement the divisions are more blurred, and yet are distinct enough for normal purposes. Some have adopted a separation based upon generations, without necessarily invoking any wider theory of literary generations. They have noted that Staël, Constant, Chateaubriand and Senancour were all born between 1766 and 1770 (and Ballanche in 1776) and were thus mature adults well before the new century began. Nodier (1780) and Stendhal (1783) chose their birth dates less conveniently, as did Guizot (1787) too, but have usually been treated as elder members of the new generation born between 1790 (Lamartine) and 1805. This included Vigny (1797), Michelet (1798), Balzac (1799), Dumas and Hugo (1802), Mérimée (1803), Sainte-Beuve and George Sand (both 1804), to whom one should add Géricault (1791), Augustin Thierry (1795), Thiers (1797), Delacroix (1798), the Devéria brothers (1800 and 1805), and Berlioz (1803). A little late on their historical cue were Nerval (1808), Musset and Chopin (1810), and Gautier and Liszt (1811). Some historians thus classify them as late arrivals in this same generation; others see them as a fresh generation, linked with the 'Bohemians' of the 1830s and beyond, who were formerly described as 'les petits romantiques'. A different separation, based upon divisions within French history, has been favoured by other scholars. Thus J.-B. Barrère proposed we should distinguish between *le Romantisme Empire*, *le Romantisme Restauration*, and *le Romantisme Louis-Philippe*. This has the advantage of being founded upon historical realities; in contrast, the 'generations' of 1800, of 1820, and of 1830 are only convenient fictions, whilst a term like Moreau's 'la génération de René' may be positively tendentious in isolating Chateaubriand's melancholy solitary as symbolic of an entire phase of the Romantic movement. The only disadvantages of a division like Barrère's may be, first, to imply an even closer link with political events than undoubtedly existed and, secondly, to conflate, for the years from 1830, the quite separate developments found in the maturer works of Hugo, Lamartine, Vigny and others, on the one hand, and, on the other, in the works of a mainly younger group.

Yet another alternative one may adopt, interlocking though it largely is with both generations and historical periods, rests upon the rise and development of the Romantic movement itself in terms of both theory and practice. On this basis one may perhaps discern four separable phases, preceded by *le préromantisme* and followed by a largely neglected period in the careers of many of the principal Romantics. A brief sketch here may help any reader unfamiliar with the history of the movement as a whole.

The eighteenth-century years which have been described by Trahard, Monglond and others as the period of pre-Romanticism and of the rise of sensibility are being excluded here, as already noted. Yet in one way at least this period must enter our story – because it witnessed the first usages of the term 'romantique' itself. The Romantics did not invent it, nor was it first applied to them, it is important to appreciate. The term was being defined, discussed, criticised, well before most of them were adults and even before some of them were born. Moreover, even when their careers had begun, it was only very gradually and with many disclaimers and disputes that they came to connect their own aims with current talk about 'le romantique', a notion that had already gathered several accretions of meaning.

'Romantique' was first applied in France to external nature – to landscapes and to gardens of the newly appreciated, more informal and less controlled kind known as 'le jardin anglais'. The best-known instance is in Rousseau's fifth *Rêverie d'un promeneur solitaire*, written in the last year before his death in 1778: 'Les rives du lac de Bienne sont plus sauvages et romantiques que celles du lac de Genève, parce que les rochers et les bois y bordent l'eau de plus près . . .' This linking had already been made a year or two earlier by Letourneur and by the marquis de Girardin (Rousseau's host during his final weeks at the Parc d'Ermenonville). It was to be consecrated in the fifth edition of the dictionary of the Académie Française in 1798 – with a speed unusual in that body: 'Il se dit ordinairement des lieux, des paysages qui rappellent à l'imagination les descriptions des poèmes et des romans.' One finds here a reflection of an earlier equating of 'romantique' and 'romanesque', but this was soon to end. In 1801, for example, L.-S. Mercier would distinguish the two words, and in 1802, in the second edition of *Les Jardins*, the abbé Delille would replace 'romanesque' in his first edition of 1782 by 'romantique'. But the Académie's definition also implied the word's connections with wilder nature, imagination, feeling and literary reveries – connections that have never been severed during its devious fortunes since. Other lasting implications were added at the same time. Mercier, for example, declared what so many others have reiterated, even if so rarely obeyed: 'On sent le Romantique, on ne le définit point.' And Senancour, in *Obermann* in 1804, deepens the concept of romantic emotion: 'romantique' is now linked with 'la véritable sensibilité' as found in '[des] âmes profondes' and also – as others including the young Chateaubriand had suggested a little earlier – with the 'awe' provoked by such 'sublime' scenery as the Alps. An accompanying noun would arrive a little later: first, under German influence, as 'la romantique' (*sic*), then 'le romantisme' – probably first in 1816 in a review of Saint-Chamans's *L'Anti-Romantique* and used pejoratively. By now, indeed, the confusion of meanings was such that the Académies at both

CHARLTON

Toulouse and Dijon would, around 1820, offer prizes for essays defining 'romantic literature'. Already, too, one of the greatest members of the first phase of the movement, Mme de Staël, had died – and not before adding, very influentially for the future, new layers of theoretical significance.

Against that background one can now turn to the French Romantic movement itself and suggest, as a convenient scheme, that it falls into the phases that follow. The first comprises the period to about 1817, the date of Staël's death and by which time both Constant and Chateaubriand were preoccupied mainly by political affairs. It witnessed the publication or at least the composition of many of their major works and also Ballanche's *Du sentiment* (1801) and Senancour's *Obermann* (1804) – though in every case other important works would appear later, even, posthumously, from Mme de Staël. These were also the years of 'the first controversies' (in Bray's words) around theoretical issues, arguments that were particularly stimulated by German influences upon Staël and Constant, and that led to the linking of the notion of 'the romantic' with, firstly, the medieval and Christian in contrast to the Ancient, secondly, the northern European in contrast to the Mediterranean, and, thirdly, the national and modern in opposition to the classicist doctrines (though some critics contended that precisely these should be preserved and defended as representing the true national tradition). Such, broadly, was the notion of 'le romantique', usually used by critics rather than friends, that was in the public arena of dispute by the time of Saint-Chamans's polemical *L'Anti-Romantique*.

A second phase, covering the years from about 1818 to about 1829 or 1830 saw the first successes achieved by the next generation, successes which drew more public attention to a new spirit at work. Géricault's *Radeau de la Méduse* in the Salon of 1819; Lamartine's *Méditations poétiques* (1820), of which eighteen editions would appear by 1830; Hugo's three collections of 'odes' (1822, 1824, and 1826); Vigny's *Poèmes antiques et modernes* and *Cinq-Mars* (both 1826) and his version of *Othello* (1829); Delacroix's controversial *La Barque de Dante* in the Salon of 1822 and *Scènes des massacres de Scio* in that of 1824 – followed in the Salon of 1827 by a veritable exhibition of 'romantic' paintings by him (notably, *Le Christ au jardin des Olives*) and others like Eugène Devéria and Ary Scheffer: these are the main examples. One may add Hugo's *Les Orientales* (1829), *Dernier Jour d'un condamné* (1829), and (so often used as a symbol of the coming-of-age of the Romantic movement) *Hernani* (1830), and also the first poetry of Sainte-Beuve (1829) and Musset (1830), or alternatively one could choose – it hardly matters – to place them as early achievements of their maturity and of the succeeding phase of the movement as a whole.

These years also included the major disputes about theories and aims, the formation (and dissolution) of various salons and *cénacles*, and the emergence by about 1827 or 1828 of a relatively coherent and self-conscious set of 'Romantic doctrines'. This was, in short, the period of what has long been termed 'la bataille romantique'. Nodier's three important articles of 1818 (collected in his *Mélanges de littérature* in 1820), not to add in the same year one of the first and best-known of his fictions, *Jean Sbogar*; early friendships and groupings – around the journal *Le Conservateur littéraire* in 1820 and the conservative Société des Bonnes-Lettres in 1821, whose political and royalist views in turn provoked a counter-grouping by such liberals as Delécluze and Stendhal; the creation of *La Muse française* in 1823, which, though seeking to be literary rather than political, stimulated the liberals nevertheless to start a counter-journal, *Le Mercure du XIXe siècle*, in the same year: these are well-known episodes in the early history of the debates. Nodier's appointment as librarian at the Bibliothèque de l'Arsenal in January 1824 and the group of young enthusiasts, mainly royalists and Christians from *La Muse*, whom he welcomed there represented a more emphatic step forward; he played 'an essential role' in this way in the creation of the movement, as Bray remarks. And partly as a liberal counter-measure there was started a journal of marked importance in the movement's consolidation: *Le Globe*.

Edited by Paul Dubois, who had recently lost his teaching post on account of his political opinions, it began in September 1824 as a *journal littéraire* with liberal tendencies. But its collaborators were already wide-ranging in their commitments and included philosophers, historians, and politically involved intellectuals as well as literary men. Its sub-title became *Recueil philosophique et littéraire* in 1826, and the full span of its concerns was made all the clearer when, in 1828, that was expanded to *Recueil politique, philosophique et littéraire*. Politics and philosophy, indeed, were the main *raison d'être* of *Le Globe* during these years as much as when, from 1830, under Pierre Leroux, it developed into a Saint-Simonian journal. In philosophy it favoured the Eclecticism of Jouffroy (a collaborator) and Cousin, not then the force for educational conservatism he became later and in fact much admired as a liberal by several of the Romantics, and it was also linked with *doctrinaires* like Royer-Collard and Guizot. In politics it was opposed to both royalism and Catholic power: hence, in particular, its attacks on Lamartine at this time, and it is no surprise to find one of the team, Vitet, even defining

Romanticism as 'le protestantisme dans les lettres et les arts'. To read the
editor's 'profession de foi' is to realise just how extensive he wished to
be in his coverage: 'Donner toutes les nouvelles étrangères, littéraires,
industrielles ou morales . . . voilà ce qui remplacera dans notre feuille le
compte rendu des théâtres et les esquisses parisiennes.'[10] 'Ne craignons
de devenir Anglais ni Germains', added Dubois. Scott and Byron were
already admired, but Shakespeare above all became an emotionally
revered model for Delacroix, Berlioz, Hugo, Vigny, Dumas and many
others, and a symbol of the 'Romantic' as against a 'dead' classicism –
under the impact especially of Stendhal's two *brochures* of 1823 and 1825
on *Racine et Shakespeare*.

On Shakespeare at least the liberals of *Le Globe* were in agreement
with erstwhile Catholic royalists like Hugo and Lamartine from *La Muse
française*. And not only did liberals and royalists meet at Nodier's and
find other areas of agreement; some of the latter were now moving into
opposition to the Restoration monarchy. The libertarian implications of
(say) Hugo's odes on 'La Liberté' and 'La Guerre d'Espagne' might
have been ambivalent; his commitment to liberty and a changed view of
both Napoleon and the Bourbon monarchy became ever more apparent
in later poems, culminating in his 'Ode à la Colonne' in February 1827.
To the consensus on literary and artistic matters already emerging
between the two groups was now added sufficient political agreement to
remove the last and hitherto most serious obstacle to their achieving
unity. The first meeting and rapid friendship, begun a few weeks earlier,
of Hugo and the young liberal Sainte-Beuve helped in the same
direction, and so – in practical terms – did even Hugo's removal from his
small flat in the Rue de Vaugirard to a larger home in the Rue Notre-
Dame-des-Champs! At last the members of both political camps were
brought together in the final *cénacle*, with a leader, a physical centre, and a
broadly common doctrine. Well-known manifestos followed: Hugo's
Préface to his Shakespearean play *Cromwell* (1827); Sainte-Beuve's
Tableau de la poésie française et du théâtre français au XVIe siècle (1828); and
the *Préface des Études françaises et étrangères* (1828) by Émile Deschamps,
one of the most persistent members of the Romantic groups throughout
this decade, one of the most active in bringing about this new 'école
romantique française'. With its controversial successes in the theatre in
1829 and 1830 the Romantic movement may be said to enter now upon a
further phase.

This third phase in the years after 1829–30 coincided with a different
situation in various ways. The Restoration monarchy was replaced in
1830 by the new government of Louis-Philippe, with new political and

economic policies, new attitudes to the Church and to personal freedoms. During the same years the impact of the industrial revolution, later by far to develop in France than in England, was becoming ever more disturbing in terms of poverty, unemployment, urbanisation, factory exploitation of women and children as well as men, and other signs of the capitalism of the age. And from this came different political and economic doctrines – most notably, the development (already anticipated by Saint-Simon earlier) of numerous socialistic and utopian doctrines, challenging the older attitudes. The Church and the old Christian assumptions were also being increasingly questioned, before 1830 by the *idéologue* thinkers, by Saint-Simon, by Eclectic philosophers like Jouffroy, after 1830 by many more from Comte and his fellow Positivists onwards. And for the Romantics the situation was different in another way also. They were now established in their aims and successful in their achievements; they had moved into the period of their creative maturity and of many of the works to be discussed in later chapters.

Yet these same years after 1830 also witnessed – and very quickly after unity had apparently been secured – a new turn in the story, a breakaway by a minority. Soon, for instance, Gautier would accuse the Hugo of *Les Feuilles d'automne* (1831) of betraying his former principles in the cause of social and political involvement and would reaffirm against his former comrades the standpoint of 'art for art's sake' and attack all 'utilitarian' preoccupations in literature and art. Cousin had declared in 1818: 'L'art n'est pas plus au service de la religion et de la morale qu'au service de l'agréable et de l'utile.' By 1830 and earlier some of the major French Romantics were abandoning this conviction or, indeed, had never held it even in their youth (as we shall shortly note). Now, against them, in his Preface to *Albertus* (1832) and, most famously, in the Preface to his novel *Mademoiselle de Maupin* (1835), Gautier stood for *l'art pour l'art*: 'Il n'y a de vraiment beau que ce qui ne peut servir à rien; tout ce qui est utile est laid . . .' Around him were to gather other enthusiasts for 'art', and by the mid 1840s a new *école de l'art pour l'art*, with Théodore de Banville, Arsène Houssaye, and others, would be emerging. Normal practice by historians of poetry is, understandably, to see this as an innovation separable from the Romantic movement itself – and that is the practice followed here. Yet one can also distinguish even before that, both around Gautier and independent of him, a loosely-linked collection of engagingly eccentric, Bohemian, writers and artists – of whom Gérard de Nerval in his later years has become the chief symbol. Gautier and Nerval excepted, they have sometimes been treated as outside the

Romantic movement – or were largely ignored, apart from a few admirers like Asse. More recently, however, and especially since a major collective study in 1949, edited by F. Dumont, they have gained markedly more attention and appeal and have been seen as illustrating a distinctive new phase of the Romantic movement – initiating within it, not just inheriting from it.[11] In time it is concurrent with the mature careers of Hugo and his fellows, with the third phase suggested above, but in other ways it is separable and is separately discussed in a later chapter. The very title of that chapter reflects an increased appreciation in recent decades of what may be thought a 'new wave' in the movement's development. 'Les petits romantiques' was acceptable in 1949; over thirty years later a less pejorative term is required. Since Professor Milner's treatment stresses the notion of 'la marginalité' as of central and positive relevance, the no less positive implications of 'the fringe' in present-day Anglo-Saxon culture have been invoked in choosing the title of his chapter.

To divide the French Romantic movement broadly into these four phases is merely to suggest one convenient way amongst others of ordering what was in reality a continuing, confused cultural situation. As postscript one may wonder also whether there was not a final period, calling for more attention, in the careers of many of the leading Romantics themselves – a few like Hugo excepted, whose energies remained to the end. It has rarely been studied, other than incidentally, and yet it might be of deep interest to look more at the Romantics' activities and works and at their reactions to newer ideas and literary and artistic practices during what might be distinguished as a fifth phase – the old age of the French Romantics.

The decline of the Romantic movement has sometimes been dated, though rather arbitrarily, from the unsuccessful theatrical performance in 1843 of Hugo's *Les Burgraves*. But if so, it is noteworthy that most of the Romantics survived for a surprisingly long period afterwards. More broadly, a popular image of the 'romantic' writer or artist suggests, first, that he struggled for long years but in vain to win the appreciation of a materialistic, uncultured, bourgeois society, secondly, that he was of lower-class and unconventional background and lived in poverty in some chilly garret, and, thirdly, that he died, often of consumption and malnutrition, at a sadly early age. This picture only slightly applies to the 'fringe Romantics' – Petrus Borel lived to fifty and Xavier Forneret to seventy-five, for example – and the truth about the major Romantics is even less moving, and largely the reverse of this image in all three respects. First, they found publishers for their books or Salon space for their paintings at a quite early age by our present-day standards, usually by their late twenties, and they had mostly attained fame by the age of thirty or earlier. Secondly, they mainly came from upper-class families and enjoyed the particle of nobility, and, although they inherited financial problems and needed to earn a living from their art, they were quite quickly successful and several of them received sinecures and 'pensions' at a relatively early age. Thirdly, far from dying before their promise could be fulfilled, as the image requires, they mostly survived to a ripe old age. Géricault, exceptionally, died by an accident at the age of 33 (or in his 33rd year, as for all these figures), and Musset and Nerval alike died at 47. Mme de Staël and Balzac survived to 51 and Stendhal to 59, but all others, in a representative listing, entered their sixties. Gautier and Augustin Thierry (both 61), Constant (63) and Nodier (64) did not reach our own normal retirement age, and Delacroix and Sainte-Beuve (both 65) only barely so, but the surviving Romantics could have formed an old persons' home of intriguing diversity: Vigny and Berlioz (66), Mérimée (67), and Dumas (68); Ballanche (71), George Sand (72), Senancour and Michelet (76), Lamartine (79); and the octogenarians. These included Chateaubriand and Thiers (80), Hugo (83), and, heading the list at 87, Guizot. An observant insurance company might even equate longevity with being a French Romantic and enjoying its alleged unconventialities and financial gains. No less striking as regards the later Romantics and 'le déclin du romantisme' are their dates of death. Nerval died in 1855, Thierry in 1856, Musset in 1857, Delacroix and Vigny in 1863, and Berlioz, Lamartine and Sainte-Beuve in 1869. But the remainder outlived the period of Louis-Napoléon: Dumas and Mérimée hardly so (1870), Gautier (1872), Michelet and Guizot (1874), George Sand (1876), Thiers (1877); Hugo (1885), finally, died over half a century after the notional high-point of the Romantic movement around 1830. Great cultural movements are normally and naturally studied in their heyday; the French Romantics offer in addition an unusual and extensive chance to examine the twilight of such a movement.

Here, however, our concern is with the heyday; we must now, in the final section of this introductory chapter, return to their youthful and most innovative years in order to ask how they then conceived of their work and role.

AIMS AND INTENTIONS

Declared aims and intentions carry no guarantee of fulfilment, obviously enough, and no less evidently they develop and change with time. Yet to look at the Romantics' most recurrent affirmations, as found in their prefaces, theoretical statements and elsewhere, may at least be suggestive and point to those aspects of their work which they themselves judged central. Whilst a later chapter discusses their significance in theory and criticism, this introductory survey seeks only to outline their conception of the wider tasks they set themselves and their approach to them. And in this regard it is the literary writers amongst the Romantics who especially call for discussion, not only because they predominated within the movement numerically speaking but also because misconceptions (if that is what they are) still prevail about them far more than about the Romantic historians, artists or composers. In particular, as already suggested, their unquestionable concern with the individual self and their valuation of emotion and imagination need to be seen within a broader context, as a part only – albeit a highly significant part – of far wider, more reasoned and more objective concerns.

The first of these is expressed in their recurrent contention that theirs should above all be a literature of their own age and society. Bonald's celebrated formula, 'La littérature est l'expression de la société', was widely accepted and led the Romantics to conclude that their own work should both express and seek to modify contemporary society. This emphasis was clear from Mme de Staël onwards and was influentially explored in her first major book, *De la littérature considérée dans ses rapports avec les institutions sociales* (to stress its full title). 'Les ouvrages qui appartiennent à la haute littérature [she there affirms] ont pour but d'opérer des changements utiles, de hâter des progrès nécessaires, de modifier enfin les institutions et les lois.' And *De l'Allemagne* reiterated the view that literature and especially poetry have throughout the ages been determined by 'toutes les circonstances politiques et religieuses' of their time.[12] One can also note a related standpoint in Chateaubriand when he argues that 'tous les grands talents politiques et militaires . . . ont été aussi de grands talents littéraires' – a dual role he clearly linked with himself.[13] Nodier – a 'father' of the Romantics – took up the same theme, as when he wrote in 1821: 'Convenons que le romantique pourrait bien n'être autre chose que le classique des modernes, c'est-à-dire l'expression d'une société nouvelle . . .'[14] Lesser critics too affirmed the close connection. Aignan declared in *La Minerve française* as early as 1818 that Romanticism expresses 'l'ordre nouveau d'idées et de sentiments, né des nouvelles combinaisons sociales'; Alexandre Guiraud's article on 'Nos Doctrines' in *La Muse française* in 1824 would write of 'la société, et la littérature qui en exprime les goûts et les besoins'; and Desprès a little later would refer in *Le Globe* to 'cette civilisation moderne dont le romantisme serait l'expression littéraire'. Likewise, Émile Deschamps could declare in well-known words: 'Il n'y a réellement pas de romantisme, mais bien une littérature du dix-neuvième siècle.'[15] Repeatedly, moreover, they stressed, like Mme de Staël before them, that literature should seek to influence and form current social and intellectual ideas as well as to reflect them.

The leading Romantics of the post-1820 years fully shared these convictions. Hugo, by 1824 – well before the date of 1830 sometimes assigned to the birth of social Romanticism – was asserting 'cette liaison remarquable entre les grandes époques politiques et les belles époques littéraires', was noting that 'un mouvement vaste et profond travaille intérieurement la littérature de ce siècle', and was urging the poet to 'marcher devant les peuples comme une lumière et leur montrer le chemin'. 'La littérature actuelle [he declared] . . . est l'expression anticipée de la société religieuse et monarchique qui sortira sans doute du milieu de tant d'anciens débris, de tant de ruines récentes.'[16] And in the *Préface de 'Cromwell'* also he was to argue at length that changes in literature follow from changes in society and in religious beliefs, instancing especially the Homeric age and the period since the establishment of Christianity. Vigny expressed parallel conclusions in his 'Réflexions sur la vérité dans l'art' : 'L'étude du destin général des sociétés n'est pas moins nécessaire aujourd'hui dans les écrits que l'analyse du cœur humain . . .'[17] Lamartine took a similar view in his famous essay 'Des destinées de la poésie'. Following the very early years of the nineteenth century, when literature was inhibited by scientific materialism, by 'une ligue universelle des études mathématiques contre la pensée et la poésie', he argued that 'la poésie était revenue en France avec la liberté, avec la pensée, avec la vie morale que nous rendit la Restauration'.[18] And even Musset, in 'Un mot sur l'art moderne', favoured a contemporary literature – 'tenant au siècle qui la produit, résultant des circonstances, quelquefois mourant avec elles, et quelquefois les immortalisant'.[19]

The Romantics stressed not only the social relevance of their writing but also, secondly, its philosophical and religious significance. Of Romantic literature Mme de Staël claimed in *De l'Allemagne*: 'C'est notre religion et nos institutions qui l'ont fait éclore'; 'elle exprime notre religion; elle rappelle notre histoire'. The next generation shared her view. Desprès identified Romanticism with 'le transport du spiritualisme dans la littérature' and argued that 'le christianisme devrait être le principe fondamental de la littérature'.[20] Ballanche, perhaps not surprisingly, expressed a similar commitment: 'C'est toujours une vérité religieuse que le poète est chargé de transmettre. Religion et poésie ne font qu'une seule et même chose.'[21] Hugo especially agreed: the poet 'doit ramener [les peuples] à tous les grands principes d'ordre, de morale et d'honneur'; 'le drame . . . doit donner à la foule une philosophie, aux idées une formule . . .' And in the *Préface de 'Cromwell'* he was even more far-reaching when he related his theory of the *drame*'s fusion of the *sublime* and the *grotesque* to the Christian idea of man as a combination of spiritual and bodily. 'Le point de départ de la religion est toujours le point de départ de la poésie. Tout se tient.'[22] Vigny took a similar stand in regard to the drama: 'Si l'art est une fable, il doit être une fable philosophique'; in 'Dernière Nuit de travail' commenting on *Chatterton* he even identified his own age as 'le temps du DRAME DE LA PENSÉE'. And one finds him affirming more widely still in his *Journal d'un poète*: 'Il y a dans les œuvres d'art deux points de vue. L'un philosophique, l'autre poétique. – Le point de vue philosophique doit soutenir l'œuvre, drame ou livre, d'un pôle à l'autre . . .' It is in line with this claim that he should describe his own *Poèmes antiques et modernes* as '[des] compositions . . . dans lesquelles une pensée philosophique est mise en scène sous une forme Épique ou Dramatique'.[23] Lamartine likewise, predicting in 1834 the likely evolution of poetry, envisaged something quite unlike the lyric genre in the normal sense: 'La poésie sera de la raison chantée . . .; elle sera philosophique, religieuse, politique, sociale . . .; elle doit se faire peuple, et devenir populaire comme la religion, la raison et la philosophie.'[24]

The French Romantics thus tended less to the particular and private than to the general and impersonal. They did so in virtue, firstly, of the social significance they attributed to their art and, secondly, by their conviction that (in Coleridge's words) 'no man was ever yet a great poet without being at the same time a profound philosopher'. They did so, thirdly, in a rather different manner, in their view of poetic experience. This for them was not confined to emotion but was a cognitive process including intellectual and sensory components and bringing the whole personality into play. The Romantics in general rejected eighteenth-century rationalism, but that should not be confused with a rejection of reason. Their attack was not upon the intellect (nor on science itself[25]), but upon the exclusive reliance placed on it, and on the scientific method associated with it, by some of the *philosophes*. They were fully aware that scientific rationalism played a large part in the thought of their day – in the *idéologues* and the Positivists, for example – and they therefore naturally stressed the rights of intuition, feeling and the individual conscience: this last was, indeed, a part of their religious and political liberalism. Yet their intention was not to abandon the intellect but to complement it, to invoke a more complete epistemology that could find a place for the promptings of spiritual and occult experience, for the intuitive wisdom (as some of them believed) of primitive peoples and their mythologies, for the *esprit de finesse* as well as for reason and empirical knowledge.

This is a notion already implicit in their German precursor, A.W. Schlegel, who identified the *mélange des genres*, later propounded by Hugo, with Romantic literature. Mme de Staël, the leading French mediator of the thought of the Schlegels, shared his conviction. 'La poésie est de tous les arts celui qui appartient de plus près à la raison', she affirmed in *De la littérature*, and in the Preface to *Delphine*, developing a notion of imagination that partially resembles Coleridge's distinction between Fancy and Imagination, she rebutted any notion that there is 'une sorte d'opposition entre la raison et l'imagination'. On the contrary, 'l'imagination qui a fait le succès de tous ces chefs-d'œuvre [she says of the works she is discussing] tient par des liens très forts à la raison'. Her successors would take a similar view, and Lamartine of all the Romantics gave it fullest expression in his famous definition of poetry:

C'est l'incarnation de ce que l'homme a de plus intime dans le cœur et de plus divin dans la pensée, de ce que la nature visible a de plus magnifique dans les images et de plus mélodieux dans les sons! C'est à la fois sentiment et sensation, esprit et matière; et voilà pourquoi c'est la langue complète, la langue par excellence qui saisit l'homme par son humanité tout entière, idée pour l'esprit, sentiment pour l'âme, image pour l'imagination, et musique pour l'oreille![26]

Parallel with this there goes Hugo's description of the triple inspiration of the poet in the Preface to *Les Voix intérieures*:

L'auteur a toujours pensé que la mission du poète était de fondre dans un même groupe de chants cette triple parole qui renferme un triple enseignement, car la première s'adresse plus particulièrement au cœur, la seconde à l'âme, la troisième à l'esprit.

As for Vigny, if his view were not evident from his philosophical poems, it would be clear from comments in his *Journal*. 'La poésie doit être la synthèse de tout', he wrote, and of 'the heart' he declared its need to be enlightened by 'the head': 'La mémoire et la pensée l'illuminent et y font paraître les sentiments. Sans la tête, ils s'éteignent.'[27] Others of their statements emphasised, undeniably, the expression of emotion, but most of these refer specifically to lyric poetry; since 'lyricism' carries with it, as the dictionary confirms, the notion of 'high-flown sentiments', it is little more than tautologous to note the sensibility behind such poetry.

Their broader view – manifest in their philosophical, political and epic as well as their lyric poems – strikingly resembles that of Wordsworth: 'Poetry is the most philosophic of all writing: . . . its object is truth, not individual and local, but general, and operative.'[28]

His stress upon the 'general' – found likewise in Friedrich Schlegel's conception of 'eine progressive Universalpoesie' – points us to a further aspect of the French Romantics' approach. Literature as they conceived it is to call upon and fuse all the ways to knowledge available to the writer and to do so in order to explore the great social and religious questions of their age, but its purpose is also to examine the personal aspects of human life – a commitment so often stressed as to require no substantiation here. They wished to defend the full reality of the self, a reality far transcending man's need for economic well-being and social order, as their studies of the 'mal du siècle' and its causes underlined. They lived in an age threatened by authoritarianism in religion and politics alike, whether from the Catholic Right or from the new socialistic and Positivist prophets. In reaction the Romantics almost all stood for personal rights, and whilst some began as Catholic royalists, they all ended as political and religious liberals. At the same time and to the same end, on the philosophical front, they resisted the concept of man as 'l'homme–machine' propounded by certain of the *philosophes* and their *idéologue* successors – externally determined in all he does and without a soul, a creature whose main desire is claimed to be for a happiness that can be ensured by suitable social and educational engineering. Although Lamartine, Sainte-Beuve and others would condemn 'l'odieux individualisme' – as manifest in *laissez-faire* economic practice, for example – they repeatedly praised the pursuit of 'l'individualité', an important distinction in their thinking.[29]

This second type of 'individualism' has quite often been linked by critics with egotistic self-preoccupation and with a cult of the exceptional individual, but their theoretical statements strongly suggest, to the contrary, that they aspired to move from the personal as starting point towards the general and even universal. Georges Poulet has observed that their withdrawal into the 'centre' of the self is followed by a return to the 'circle' of the external world, and this is confirmed by at least their declarations of intent.[30]

A first example is offered by Mme de Staël in *De la littérature*. Having developed her contention that poetry should 'suivre, comme tout ce qui tient à la pensée, la marche philosophique du siècle', she then goes still further: '[L'imagination] peut exalter les sentiments vrais; mais il faut toujours que la raison approuve et comprenne ce que l'enthousiasme fait aimer . . . La philosophie, *en généralisant davantage les idées*, donne plus de grandeur aux images poétiques.'[31] A similar purpose is seen in Chateaubriand and Constant, in their statements about *René* and *Adolphe* respectively. *René* seeks as its first aim to depict a widespread passion of the age, 'le vague des passions' as analysed in *Le Génie du christianisme*. *Adolphe* explores likewise 'une des principales maladies morales de notre siècle'. The autobiographical element in both novels, in so far as it exists, is explicitly subsumed within far more universal concerns.

Their successors in the Romantic tradition expressed a parallel insistence that was especially emphatic in Hugo. Thus in the Preface to *Les Chants du crépuscule* he could declare: '[L'auteur] ne laisse même subsister dans ses ouvrages ce qui est personnel que parce que c'est peut-être quelquefois un reflet de ce qui est général.' A few years later in the Preface to *Les Rayons et les ombres* he reiterated the point when writing of 'cette profonde peinture du moi qui est peut-être l'oeuvre la plus large, la plus générale et la plus universelle qu'un penseur puisse faire'. And in 1856 – the year before Baudelaire would address himself to his 'hypocrite lecteur, mon semblable, mon frère' – Hugo asserted to his reader in the Preface to *Les Contemplations*: 'On se plaint quelquefois des écrivains qui disent moi. . . . Hélas! quand je vous parle de moi, je vous parle de vous.' Vigny is similar in his poetic aims. Depiction of man and his time should be lifted to 'une puissance supérieure et idéale', and earlier he had claimed that 'l'imagination donne du corps aux idées et leur crée des types et des symboles vivants qui sont comme la forme palpable et la preuve d'une théorie abstraite'. Later in life too he makes the same preference plain: 'Il y a plus de force, de dignité et de grandeur dans les poètes *objectifs* épiques et dramatiques tels qu'Homère, Shakespeare, Dante, Molière, Corneille, que dans les poètes *subjectifs* ou élégiaques se peignant eux-mêmes et déplorant leurs peines secrètes, comme Pétrarque et autres.'[32] Musset, likewise, analyses in the *Confession d'un enfant du siècle* 'une maladie morale abominable' that in his view afflicts many others as well as Octave – as the very opening paragraph stresses: 'comme il y en a beaucoup d'autres que moi qui souffrent du même mal, j'écris pour ceux-là . . .'

It is noteworthy, finally, that this frequent movement from personal to general was a feature singled out by contemporary critics favourable to the Romantics. Already in 1817, in the *Archives philosophiques, politiques et littéraires*, the sources of 'the new poetry' are defined as the ideas and feelings that are rooted in 'le coeur de l'homme *ordinaire*'; 'tous les matériaux de la poésie se tirent de la nature commune à tout homme doué des facultés de l'homme'. Charles de Rémusat, writing in *Le Globe* a little later about the new lyric poetry, praises 'son caractère de généralité' as well as its personal emotion; 'l'univers et un seul homme, l'infini et l'individu, tel est le contraste qui fait le fond de la poésie lyrique comme de la pensée humaine'. Or again, in the *Mercure du XIXe siècle* in 1830, Sainte-Beuve's *Consolations* are admired because their author 'part d'un incident de la vie privée et domestique pour arriver aux régions les plus élevées du déïsme, de la morale et de l'éclecticisme'.[33] And the reference to Eclecticism may remind us that Cousin expounded precisely this link of personal and general in his influential lectures on aesthetics of 1817–18 and later: 'Le beau réel se compose donc de deux éléments, le général et l'individuel, réunis dans un objet réel, déterminé.'

The Romantics' central preoccupation was with 'truth', they often declared. 'Il faut le dire et le redire [wrote Hugo in 1824], ce n'est pas un besoin de nouveauté qui tourmente les esprits, c'est un besoin de vérité, et il est immense.'[34] Vigny agreed: 'Cette *vérité*, toute belle, toute intellectuelle . . . est comme l'âme de tous les arts.'[35] To judge from their declarations of intent, this truth was to be sought through an appeal to every human faculty of knowledge and through a painstaking attention to past history and thought. Above all this truth was to be concerned with the whole range of human life – political and social, religious and philosophical, personal and moral – and most especially as it related to men in their own contemporary world, in a nation just emerging from the ravages of the Revolution and the Napoleonic wars and now undergoing the further upheaval of the industrial revolution, and in a time when the old religious certainties were crumbling and when political controversy was increasingly sharp and strident. They were acutely aware, indeed, that theirs was an age of both social and intellectual disintegration and crisis. Hugo's Preface to *Les Feuilles d'automne* sums up what Vigny, Musset, Nerval and other Romantics also felt with intensity. 'Au dedans, toutes les solutions sociales remises en question . . . Au dehors, çà et là, sur la face de l'Europe, des peuples tout entiers qu'on assassine, qu'on déporte en masse ou qu'on met aux fers.' And on the intellectual plane, likewise, he attests to what Vigny would shortly term 'le naufrage universel des croyances': 'au dehors comme au dedans, les croyances en lutte, les consciences en travail'. The 'dominant problem' for the Romantics, Barzun remarked, was 'to create a new world on the ruins of the old'.[36] Their reactions and solutions naturally differed, as later chapters will show, but were rarely despairing or escapist in the manner of their alleged 'héros romantique'. Hugo spoke for other Romantics as well as himself when he later declared: 'Les écrivains et les poètes du dix-neuvième siècle ont cette admirable fortune de sortir d'une genèse, d'arriver après une fin de monde, d'accompagner une réapparition de lumière, d'être les organes d'un recommencement.'[37] The challenges of renewal in a situation of controversy and ferment, of a new beginning – intellectual, social and political, literary and cultural – are the essential context for the attempts and achievements surveyed in the following chapters.

NOTES

1. H. Taine, *Histoire de la littérature anglaise* (4 vols., Hachette, 1864), IV, 479–82.
2. H. Peyre, 'The originality of French Romanticism', *Symposium*, 23 (1969), 333.
3. H.H. Remak, in H. Eichner (ed.), '*Romantic' and Its Cognates: The European History of a Word* (Manchester UP, 1972), pp. 480–1.
4. M.Z. Shroder, *Icarus: The Image of the Artist in French Romanticism* (Cambridge, Mass., Harvard UP, 1961), p. 247.
5. L.R. Furst, *Romanticism* (London, Methuen, 1969) and *Romanticism in Perspective* (London, Macmillan, 1969), p. 26.
6. P. Valéry, *Mauvaises Pensées* (Gallimard, 1943), p. 35.
7. Cf. P. Trahard, *Les Maîtres de la sensibilité française au 18e siècle* (4 vols., Boivin, 1931–3); A. Monglond, *Le Préromantisme français* (2 vols., Grenoble, Arthaud, 1930); and, for several colloquium essays critical of the concept, P. Viallaneix (ed.), *Le Préromantisme: hypothèque ou hypothèse* (Klincksieck, 1975).
8. A. Viatte, *Le Catholicisme chez les romantiques* (Boccard, 1922); J.L. Talmon, *Political Messianism: The Romantic Phase* (London, Secker and Warburg, 1960).
9. R. Bray, *Chronologie du romantisme* (Nizet, 1963), p. 160.
10. P. Trahard, *Le Romantisme défini par 'Le Globe'* (Les Presses Françaises, n.d.), p. 6.
11. E. Asse, *Les Petits Romantiques*, original edn 1896 (Geneva, Slatkine Reprints, 1968); F. Dumont (ed.), *Les Petits Romantiques français* (Cahiers du Sud, 1949). On the link between these writers and the 'Bohemian' image more widely attributed to the Romantics, cf. M. Easton, *Artists and Writers in Paris* (London, Edward Arnold, 1964). Cf, in particular, chapter XI below and its bibliography.
12. Mme de Staël, *De la littérature* (2 vols., Geneva, Droz, and Paris, Minard, 1959), II, 318, and *De l'Allemagne* (5 vols., Hachette, 1958–60), II, 134. The interpretation of the Romantics' intentions in the following pages is more fully developed in my essay on 'The personal and the general in French Romantic literary theory', in *Balzac and the Nineteenth Century: Studies . . . presented to Herbert J. Hunt* (Leicester UP, 1972), pp. 269–81.
13. Chateaubriand, *Préface*, 1836, *Poésies diverses, in Œuvres complètes* (36 vols., Pourrat, 1836–9), XXIV, 6.
14. Cited from *Mercure du XIXe siècle*, 2 (1821), in C.M. Desgranges, *Le Romantisme et la critique: La Presse littéraire sous la Restauration, 1815–1830* (Mercure de France, 1907), p. 214.
15. Émile Deschamps, *Préface des Études françaises et étrangères*, ed. H. Girard (Les Presses Françaises, 1923), p. 6.
16. Hugo, *Œuvres poétiques* (3 vols., Bibliothèque de la Pléiade, Gallimard, 1964–74), I, 273–4, 272, 277 and 274.
17. Vigny, *Œuvres complètes* (2 vols., Bibliothèque de la Pléiade, Gallimard, 1948–50), II, 19 and 22.
18. Lamartine, *Premières Méditations poétiques* (Hachette, 1903), pp. xxvii and xxxiii.

19. Musset, *Œuvres complètes en prose* (Bibliothèque de la Pléiade, Gallimard, 1960), p. 884.
20. Staël, *De l'Allemagne*, II, 134 and 139; Desprès, in *Le Globe*, 1 October 1825.
21. Ballanche, *Orphée*, in *Œuvres complètes* (6 vols., Encyclopédie des Connaissances Utiles, 1833), VI, 96.
22. Hugo, *Œuvres poétiques*, I, 277, and *Théâtre complet* (2 vols., Bibliothèque de la Pléiade, Gallimard, 1963–4), II, 556 and I, 416.
23. Vigny, *Œuvres complètes*, II, 379; I, 770; II, 1082; and I, 3.
24. Lamartine, *Premières Méditations*, pp. lix and lxi.
25. On the Romantics' attitude to science itself, cf. D.L. King, *L'Influence des sciences physiologiques sur la littérature française de 1670 à 1870* (Les Belles Lettres, 1926); C.A. Fusil, *La Poésie scientifique de 1750 à nos jours* (Scientifica, 1918); and Nina Smith, *L'Accord de la science et de la poésie* (Ligugé, 1928).
26. Lamartine, *Premières Méditations*, p. xxxiv.
27. Vigny, *Œuvres complètes*, II, 1223 and 1127.
28. Wordsworth, *Poetical Works* (vol. II, Oxford, Clarendon Press, 1944), p. 394.
29. For a discussion of this distinction, cf. K.W. Swart, 'Individualism in the mid-XIXth century', *Journal of the History of Ideas*, 23 (1962), 77–90.
30. G. Poulet, *Les Métamorphoses du cercle* (Plon, 1961), ch. VI and especially p. 138.
31. Staël, *De la littérature*, II, 361–3, my italics.
32. Vigny, *Œuvres complètes*, II, 22, 880 and 1121.
33. Cited in Desgranges, *Le Romantisme et la critique*, pp. 248, 288 and 310.
34. Hugo, *Œuvres poétiques*, I, 274.
35. Vigny, *Œuvres complètes*, II, 21.
36. J. Barzun, *Classic, Romantic and Modern* (London, Secker and Warburg, 1961), p. 14.
37. Hugo, *William Shakespeare* (Albin Michel, 1937), p. 210.

BIBLIOGRAPHY

There are numerous surveys of the French Romantics written in French. The best of these include: M. Milner, *Le Romantisme, I: 1820–1843* (Arthaud, 1973), with a particularly wide and helpful bibliography; P. Moreau, *Le Romantisme*, 2nd edn (Gigord, 1957); and H. Peyre, *Qu'est-ce que le romantisme?* (PUF, 1971). P. Moreau, *Le Classicisme des romantiques* (Plon, 1932) was a major reappraisal whose lessons, one may think, are still not fully learned; much the same is true of R. Canat, *L'Hellénisme des romantiques* (3 vols., Didier, 1951–5).

Other literary histories include: J. Giraud, *L'École romantique française*, 4th edn (Colin, 1942); G. Michaud and Philippe Van Tieghem, *Le Romantisme* (Hachette, 1952); and M. Souriau, *Histoire du romantisme en France* (2 vols., Spes, 1927). For the earlier decades, B. Didier, *Le XVIIIe Siècle, III: 1778–1820* (Arthaud, 1976) is very useful (with full bibliographies).

In English comparable surveys are almost non-existent; the last such work written in English known to me is N.H. Clement, *Romanticism in France* (New York, MLA, 1939), but a most stimulating interpretation, even where one may disagree, is J. Barzun, *Classic, Romantic and Modern* (London, Secker and Warburg, 1961). M.B. Finch and E.A. Peers, *The Origins of French Romanticism* (London, Constable, 1920) included only the first generation. Interesting collective discussions are 'Romanticism revisited', in *Yale French Studies*, 13 (1954), and *Symposium*, 23 (1969), and in J. Cruickshank (ed.), *French Literature and its Background* (vol. 4, London, Oxford UP, 1969).

Earlier controversies around the French Romantics are best described in English by P. Mansell Jones, *Tradition and Barbarism* (London, Faber, 1930). To sample the attacks upon them in the earlier twentieth century, one could look especially at P. Lasserre, *Le Romantisme français*, new edn (Garnier, 1919); E. Seillière, *Le Mal romantique* (Nourrit, 1908); and I. Babbitt, *Rousseau and Romanticism* (Boston and New York, Houghton Mifflin, 1919) – but very few would now accept their interpretations. A more recent and helpful critique within its declared area is M.Z. Shroder, *Icarus: The Image of the Artist in French Romanticism* (Cambridge, Mass., Harvard UP, 1961). An early defence is H. Bremond, *Pour le romantisme* (Bloud et Gay, 1924), and a full bibliography up to its date is given by H. Girard and H. Moncel, *Pour et contre le romantisme* (Les Belles Lettres, 1927).

On Romanticism as a European movement there are numerous works, many in English, although – as a generalisation – they give more attention to the English and German than to the French Romantics; some of them tend to be in search of definitions, and some are restricted to the perspectives of comparative literature or of intellectual history. In addition to Barzun's study one may note, amongst more recent works, L.R. Furst, *Romanticism in Perspective* (London, Macmillan, 1969) and *The Contours of European Romanticism* (London, Macmillan, 1979); J.B. Halsted (ed.), *Romanticism* (London, Macmillan, 1969); M. Peckham, *Beyond the Tragic Vision* (New York, Braziller, 1962) and 'Towards a theory of romanticism', *PMLA*, 66 (1951), 5–23; A.K. Thorlby (ed.), *The Romantic Movement* (London, Longmans, 1966); M.H. Abrams, *Natural Supernaturalism* (New York, Norton, 1971); and H.M. Jones, *Revolution and Romanticism* (Cambridge, Mass., Harvard UP, 1974). Paul Van Tieghem, *Le Romantisme dans la littérature européenne* (Albin Michel, 1948) remains a useful survey from a French viewpoint.

On the words 'Romantic' and 'Romanticism' and their foreign equivalents and on problems of definition there are several useful studies. These include: J. Aynard, 'Comment définir le romantisme', *Revue de littérature comparée*, v (1952), 641–58; F. Baldensperger, '"Romantique", ses analogues et ses équivalents', *Harvard Studies and Notes in Philology*, 19 (1937), 13–105; A. François, 'Où en est romantisme?', in *Mélanges offerts à F. Baldensperger* (2 vols., Champion, 1930), I, 321–31; J.B. Halsted (ed.), *Romanticism: Problems of Definition, Explanation and Evaluation* (Boston, Mass., Heath, 1965); A.O. Lovejoy, 'On the discrimination of Romanticisms', *PMLA*, 39 (1924), 229–53, and 'The meaning of Romanticism for the historian of ideas', *Journal of the History of Ideas*, 2 (1941), 257–78; J.-B. Barrère, 'Sur quelques définitions du romantisme', *Revue des sciences humaines*, 62–3 (1951), 93–110; R. Wellek, 'The concept of Romanticism in literary history', and 'Romanticism re-examined', reprinted in *Concepts of Criticism* (New Haven, Yale UP, 1963). Particularly helpful is M.Z. Shroder, 'France', in H. Eichner (ed.), '*Romantic' and Its Cognates: The European History of a Word* (Manchester UP, 1972), pp. 263–92.

The development of the French Romantic movement and the quarrels of theory involved are described in several authoritative books: most notably, R. Bray, *Chronologie du romantisme* (Nizet, 1963); E. Eggli and P. Martino, *Le Débat romantique en France (1813–1830)* (vol. I, Les Belles Lettres, 1933); J. Marsan, *La Bataille romantique* (2 vols., Hachette, 1912–25); P. Martino, *L'Époque romantique en France, 1815–1830*, 4th edn (Hatier, 1944); and, more specialised in their interest, C.M. Desgranges, *Le Romantisme et la critique: La Presse littéraire sous la Restauration, 1815–30* (Mercure de France, 1907); P. Trahard, *Le Romantisme défini par 'Le Globe'* (Les Presses Françaises, n.d.); and Émile Deschamps, *Préface des Études françaises et étrangères*, ed. H. Girard (Les Presses Françaises, 1923), an important manifesto published in 1828.

The reader interested in recent and current research on the French Romantics should above all consult the successive issues of *Romantisme*, journal of the Société des Études Romantiques, as well as the standard bibliographies and journals devoted to a single author. Surveys in English are given by H.H. Remak, 'Trends of recent research in West European Romanticism', in H. Eichner (ed.), '*Romantic' and Its Cognates*, pp. 475–500, and L.M. Porter, 'The present directions of French Romantic studies, 1960–1975', *Nineteenth-Century French Studies*, 6 (1977–8), 1–20. A most helpful annual survey is provided by *The Year's Work in Modern Language Studies* (Cambridge UP), in the chapters on the earlier nineteenth century.

II · *Religious and political thought*

D.G. CHARLTON

INTRODUCTION

The intellectual and political contexts within which the Romantic movement developed were marked by turmoil, uncertainty and an exceptional polarisation of ideas. Following Rome's Concordat with Napoleon, the Catholic Church had regained something of its pre-Revolutionary position, and Traditionalist theologians like Bonald, Joseph de Maistre and the younger Lamennais were powerfully re-stating the old Christian doctrines. On the other side, however, *idéologue* philosophers like Cabanis were reiterating the anti-Christian arguments of eighteenth-century *philosophie*, and their attack was being extended by appeals to new scientific, historical and philological knowledge. More widely influential still, Saint-Simon and later socialistic radicals were sharply criticising the social and political record of the Churches, accusing them of betraying Christ's message of charity and fraternity. Comte too, in *opuscules* in the 1820s and definitively in his *Cours de philosophie positive* from 1830 on, roundly condemned the theological and metaphysical 'states' of human thought as unscientific and thus. outdated. Typical of the sceptics, Stendhal in 1822 could confidently predict that the Roman Church had a mere twenty-five years to live, and similar expectations were entertained by Michelet, Quinet, Heine, Auguste Barbier and others a little later. The political battle-lines were no less sharply drawn: between the conservatism of the Restoration monarchy and its mainly Catholic supporters and, on the other hand, the liberalism of opposition leaders like Constant and the quasi-socialism of the Saint-Simonians, Fourier, Proudhon, Leroux and others – including eventually Lamennais himself, moving from the opposing party. And the ideological conflicts were the more aggressively waged as indus-trialisation brought to France, as earlier to Britain, blatant economic hardship and urban squalor. The clash between those who wished to re-establish the *ancien régime* and those who wished a thoroughgoing transformation of society extended even to the analysis of the past; the two camps invoked widely opposed interpretations of French history, most especially as to the significance of the Revolution and the Terror and of France's defeat in 1815. It has even been argued that the whole explosion of historiography at this time was politically motivated.[1] Nor were these deep divisions regarded by any of the protagonists as merely academic; all of them were convinced that it is ideas above all which govern history. To restore the old society one must restore the old religious truths; to create a new order in a new society requires as foundation a new intellectual synthesis: these assumptions gave to all the arguments a momentous, practical relevance.

The first generation of French Romantics was actively involved in these disputes, and the second generation, coming to maturity during the 1820s when the disputes were becoming ever more strident, rapidly became involved too. During the formative years of the Romantic movement even its various groupings and journals (as was noted in chapter 1) were separated by religious and political differences more than by aesthetic disagreements, and its unity was achieved only with a reconciliation of political attitudes around 1827. Their theories likewise (we saw then) stressed repeatedly the centrality within literature and art as they conceived them of both religious and social ideas. Even more fundamentally, that very *mal du siècle* with which they were so often concerned derived in good part, on their own analysis, from these same concerns and the uncertainties about them that were so widespread in their own time. For Constant, Adolphe suffers 'une des principales maladies morales de notre siècle', and what is manifest in his relations with Ellénore has far wider consequences, he stresses in the second preface to his novel. 'La fidélité en amour est une force comme la croyance religieuse, comme l'enthousiasme de la liberté . . . Nous ne savons plus aimer, ni croire, ni vouloir.' Musset's analysis in his *Confession d'un enfant du siècle* traces Octave's 'malady' back to the same sources: disillusionment with contemporary society and unbelief as to the old religion, a 'désespérance' that has led him to 'l'abîme du doute universel'. Nerval too evokes, in *Sylvie*, a similar 'mélange d'activité, d'hésitation et de paresse, d'utopies brillantes, d'aspirations philosophiques ou religieuses . . .' – as do other Romantics like Hugo and Lamartine in writing of the 'crisis' they felt to be overshadowing their age.

The Romantics' approach to these great issues has sometimes been presented by their critics as primarily emotional, but in reality they were painstakingly wide-ranging in their search for solutions. They aspired to little less than 'totality' in the sources they explored, enquiring into every past religion and philosophy, undertaking laborious historical studies of earlier ages, intrigued by occultist and illuminist beliefs. Their theory of knowledge mirrored that eclecticism, moreover. Reason, observation, emotion, imagination in an almost Coleridge-like sense, as well as exceptionally wide reading: all these were invoked in aid, as their works (and a private record like Vigny's *Journal d'un poète* also) amply illustrate. It may even be, as this present chapter will argue, that they were still more deeply eclectic – in the very aims of their religious and political thought. There were distinct affinities, it would seem, between the Romantics and certain of the thinkers who, as between the religious and political polarities of their day, were striving for 'a middle way': in politics such proponents of the *juste milieu*, of 'middlingness', as Guizot; in philosophy such Eclectics as Cousin and Jouffroy.[2] Guizot and Jouffroy attended Romantic salons in the 1820s, we saw, and, beyond that, several Romantics were affected by the ideas of Cousin in particular, at that date the inspiring young leader and teacher, banned from lecturing for most of the 1820s, not yet the educational administrator he would become. Stendhal wrote of 'son influence sans bornes sur la jeunesse', and that his Sorbonne lectures in 1828 'électrisent tous nos jeunes gens'; Sainte-Beuve claimed that his earlier lectures from 1818 to 1820 left an 'almost legendary memory' and created 'a revolution in French philosophy'; young Balzac returned from those same lectures 'la tête en feu'; and young Renan and his fellow students were 'enchanted' by the later ones. Other individuals too were specifically marked by him, whatever their later disclaimers. Young Michelet declared his counsels 'excellents pour ma vie entière'; for young Quinet he was the 'très vénéré et très cher maître'; Sainte-Beuve found him 'très-bien pour moi et de très-bon conseil pour ma destinée et mes travaux à venir'. Leroux and Montalembert were others inspired by him, whilst Émile Deschamps could assert in his celebrated Romantic manifesto of 1828, the *Préface des Études françaises et étrangères*: 'Les besoins philosophiques et historiques du siècle sont admirablement bien servis par les cours de MM. Cousin et Guizot.' Cousin's direct influence perhaps extended – though further study is needed – even to Vigny (as the outlook of Libanius in *Daphné* suggests) and Lamartine, but of at least resemblances between Romantics and Eclectics there can be little doubt.

It follows from their eclecticism, whether Cousin-inspired or not, that any survey of their thought has to be no less wide-ranging, and all the more so since, in addition, the individual Romantics were far from agreeing with each other. Consequently, several chapters of this present work discuss their ideas, from different viewpoints and within various areas. Thus the present chapter seeks to describe their intellectual responses to, first, the crisis of religious faith and, secondly, the political and social problems of their time. Chapter III examines a significant area of their thinking which some critics have too readily dismissed as 'irrationalist': their deep interest in occultism, illuminism and mythologies of various kinds, and, linked with that, their attempts to express their ideas not only in the staider language of intellectual discourse but also in myths and symbols that fuse imagination with reason and aspire to transcend the limitations of each alone. Chapter VIII discusses the Romantics' historiography and their ideas about history, and whilst pride of place must naturally go to Thiers, Guizot, Michelet and others, writers like Chateaubriand, Mme de Staël, Lamartine, and the historical novelists and dramatists are also directly relevant. Chapter VII surveys their views on literary criticism and theory – a further substantial area within their intellectual interests. Their ideas, finally, about the individual's 'existential' and moral situation are explored above all through their literary and other creative works: it follows that the remaining chapters also are inevitably pertinent, and chapter V in particular includes a brief explicit discussion in its survey of their *romans personnels* and their depictions of what has been sometimes too simply summed up as 'le héros romantique'.

THE ROMANTICS AND RELIGION

All the Romantics were keenly aware of the conflicts between Christian orthodoxy and growing unbelief, and all of them experienced the torments of 'honest doubt'. Not for them a calm, optimistic or aggressive scepticism; they valued religion for both personal and social reasons and their uncertainties became a mainspring of inner crisis. 'Que nous reste-t-il de sacré?': thus Vigny in *Servitude et grandeur militaires*; 'on croirait que l'égoïsme a tout submergé'. Musset's *L'Espoir en Dieu* captures the anguished tension which most of them knew:

> Que me reste-t-il donc? Ma raison révoltée
> Essaie en vain de croire et mon cœur de douter.
> Le chrétien m'épouvante, et ce que dit l'athée,
> En dépit de mes sens, je ne puis l'écouter.

And his poem goes on to survey a variety of alternatives to Christianity – theism, Spinozism, Platonism, the philosophies of Locke, Kant, and others – reminding us of another salient element in the context within which the Romantics' own ideas evolved: the proliferation of multifarious 'secular religions' during this period. Some were predominantly social creeds, as witness Saint-Simon's 'nouveau christianisme', developed by Enfantin and others into a complete Église Saint-Simonienne, or Comte's Positivist 'religion de l'humanité', or the various new systems of belief proposed by Pierre Leroux, Charles Fourier, Étienne Cabet and their followers. Others of these religious substitutes were primarily metaphysical, such as Cousin's 'spiritualism', not to add the pantheism that appealed in various forms to so many nineteenth-century writers. Yet others sought to revive the teachings of other world-religions or to appeal to occultist and illuminist notions to provide the core of a new faith. What, we must now ask, were the responses of the Romantics to this whole ideological situation?

It has been alleged – notably by Lasserre, Seillière, Viatte, and other critics in the earlier twentieth century – that the Romantics' religious outlook manifested a common feature. All were dominated by what Seillière called an irrationalist 'mysticism', by an increasingly exclusive trust in feeling. Thus, in the best of these studies, Viatte's *Le Catholicisme chez les romantiques*, it is argued that each of them – from Bonald and Maistre (whom he classifies as Romantics) onwards – was marked by the same trait: 'Un seul élément reste permanent et stable'; 'cet élément unique, le *sentiment*, fondement du courant romantique, a servi seul de base tant à ses affirmations qu'à ses négations religieuses.'[3] In sharp contrast to this once widely-held assertion, nothing has become clearer in the light of further scholarship than the diversity of their individual responses to the religious question. Not only was their approach based upon an eclectically wide theory of knowledge, but above all their conclusions, albeit often tentative and changing, could hardly have been more differing – within their single common assumption that the central question as to the truth or falsity of religion was of paramount importance.

The first generation

The first generation illustrated this diversity as clearly as the later Romantics. The new 'secular' alternatives, it is true, were not yet announced as they formed their own views; even Saint-Simon's new Christianity came at the end of his career. Knowledge of other world-religions was already growing, however, thanks to Creuzer and other German philologists, and, in France, Constant himself had long been studying in depth the polytheistic faiths he would analyse in *De la religion* and other works. Moreover, 'les sources occultes du romantisme', in the title of Viatte's major study, were already powerful influences in contemporary thought. All of the earlier Romantics faced the 'religious crisis' with as preoccupied a concern as their successors, and, like them, ended with widely different conclusions.

Even Chateaubriand underwent a period of scepticism during his early career, and his first published work, the *Essai sur les révolutions* (1797), opposed the very Catholicism he would shortly re-embrace and posed the problem the later Romantics would confront in their turn: 'Quelle sera la religion qui remplacera le christianisme?' He provided no answer, and indeed he dismisses here some of the alternatives that would attract others. Thus he argues that 'la doctrine de Swedenborg ou des Illuminés ne deviendra point un culte dominant': so much for Ballanche, Hugo and others! Again, 'la Religion naturelle n'offre plus de probabilité' and 'un culte moral, où l'on personnifierait seulement les vertus . . . est absurde à supposer': so much for Cousin, Lamartine, Vigny and others! His own road lay towards reconversion to Catholicism and his renewal of Christian apologetics in *Le Génie du christianisme* (1802). Yet his arguments were primarily emotional and utilitarian: the Roman faith heals our sufferings and offers us true happiness; it is the most poetical and aesthetically inspiring of religions and has inspired the sublime beauties of such works as the Bible, *The Divine Comedy* and Racine's tragedies, and of church architecture and ceremonial over the centuries; it has made major contributions to the growth of human civilisation as a whole. It was Senancour who first challenged his essential pragmatism: '[Les choses que vous annoncez] sont belles sans doute; elles sont morales et poétiques, mystérieuses et pittoresques. Mais ce n'est pas du tout de cela qu'il s'agit: prouvez qu'elles sont vraies.'[4] Most of the later Romantics were in effect to follow this criticism: to question Catholicism's truth whilst accepting the appeal of religion as such. What they will reject are thus the specifically Christian themes of *Le Génie* – a work Lamartine later dismissed as 'le reliquaire de la crédulité humaine' – and also Chateaubriand's contention here and in later works like his *Études historiques* that Christianity has been a bastion of human liberty and of social justice and equality. The impact of his apologia was therefore perhaps to heighten religious yearning without convincing his fellow Romantics that his own faith could assuage it.

Some scholars have queried the orthodoxy and even the sincerity of Chateaubriand's Catholicism.[5] Yet it clearly illustrates one pole of thought amongst the earlier Romantics, that of a convinced supernaturalism. Ballanche was hardly less influential in expressing broadly the same conclusions in *Du sentiment considéré dans ses rapports avec la littérature et les arts* (1801) and in later works, but with a distinctive addition from occult and related thought. His mystical concepts of a universal religion and of 'harmonies' are described in Chapter III; here, however, we may just note that Ballanche, albeit remaining relatively orthodox, was motivated by a profoundly reconciling, synthesising impulse that is analogous with that 'eclecticism' of later Romantics already mentioned.

If Chateaubriand and Ballanche retained a Catholic conviction, their contemporaries Mme de Staël and Constant were more ambivalent in their relation to their Protestant background – though space only allows this to be briefly suggested. Mme de Staël, descendant of a line of Calvinist pastors, was always certain throughout her life of what her father, Necker, had declared to be 'l'importance de la morale et des opinions religieuses'. Though familiar with the anti-religious views of *philosophes* like Diderot and Grimm (some of whom she heard as a girl in her mother's salon), she was far closer in her outlook to Rousseau – as her very first book (*Lettres . . . sur J.-J. Rousseau*) of 1788 already shows – and to his 'Confession de foi du vicaire savoyard'. Her belief in God, immortality, and religious commitment rarely wavered, and if actions speak louder than words, one can notice that she continued to attend the Protestant church at Coppet, and took her guests with her, during the years she lived there. Simone Balayé's authoritative study of her thought points to a counter-preoccupation – 'la peur du néant' – that haunted her to the end, but in other ways she does not appear an anguished doubter.[6] Yet in two respects at least she was less than wholly orthodox. First, her primary concern was with morality. As Delphine asks: 'La vertu fondée sur la bonté, ces principes ne doivent-ils pas suffire à tous les cœurs?' Religion, she came to think, was a firmer basis for morality than even Kant's moral will and categorical imperative – a view reflected in *Corinne* – but its theological doctrines remained subsidiary in her mind. For, secondly, she was suspicious of both priests and dogmas, committed to free enquiry, drawn to 'enlightened' religion more than to any organised Church. It would also seem that religion's more mystical dimensions appealed to her only in later life, under the influence of Zacharias Werner especially, and even in *De l'Allemagne* her definition of them remains vague and general – 'une manière plus intime de sentir et de concevoir le christianisme'. Corinne defends Catholicism against Oswald's rather Kantian Protestantism, but this juxtaposition in her novel hints at an ambivalence, and *De l'Allemagne*'s exposition of German religions favours the freedom of thought of the latter rather than the faith of the former. What of her deep belief in 'l'enthousiasme'

– in religion as in literature, art and the moral life – as she expounds it in the work's last three chapters? This famous notion has sometimes been interpreted as predominantly emotional, illustrative of a final irrationalism, but her definition reveals that it includes but also far transcends feeling alone. 'Enthusiasm' is not only alien to passion, fanaticism and selfishness; it is essentially 'contemplative' and tolerant, essential to 'la pensée' as well as to imagination, needed in the search for abstract truths and even in danger of favouring 'l'esprit de système'. Nor should we follow it alone: it requires to be reunited with 'le caractère', and it is their union that constitutes 'la vraie gloire humaine'. Yet, finally, it sometimes seems, enthusiasm is needed by Mme de Staël in order to transcend reason as much as emotion, to quieten her remaining intellectual doubts. In well-known words, 'c'est l'amour du beau, l'élévation de l'âme, la jouissance du dévouement'; it is even, following the Greeks, 'Dieu en nous'. But perhaps these deeply-held convictions were almost unwittingly prerequisite if she was (in words from *De la littérature* earlier) to '[transporter] l'espérance au-delà des bornes de notre raison'.

A similar attitude, mingling conviction and reservation, was developed by Constant, and with outstanding intellectual sophistication and a profound learning in the history of religions. His life-long elaboration of the ideas finally presented in *De la religion* (1824–31) and in lesser studies of polytheism defies summary here. He moved steadily away from an initial scepticism and even atheism in the manner of the *philosophes*. 'Forced back into religious ideas' under the impact of German scholars like Creuzer – and of Mme de Staël too – and by an interest thereafter in Quietism, he refined his mature outlook, ever revising his work, of which there had already been some 600 or 700 pages as early as 1794, as he did so. His religious evolution is of fascinating complexity and has rightly received close scholarly attention, not least in recent years. Here only a few aspects of his final attitude, much simplified, can be noted in order to point to both his commitment and his ambivalence towards the religious.

The 'religious sentiment' is innate and fundamental in man, he affirms, 'une loi fondamentale de sa nature'.[7] Over the centuries it has progressively attained ever truer insights – a contention advanced with overwhelming erudition as he traces the evolution from fetishism to polytheism and beyond. But it has been distorted and even falsified by 'sacerdotal organisation', by controlling 'forms' being imposed upon its essentially personal and free characteristics. Priesthoods, dogmas, intolerance, vested self-interest – these constant features of institutionalised religion over the ages have almost always proved deleterious. Constant thinks 'forms' are desirable and even inevitable, but yet are usually inimical to true religion. The title of the final chapter in the entire work is 'Combien est funeste à la religion même tout obstacle opposé à sa perfectibilité progressive': the greatest of obstacles, he was convinced, were the 'sacerdotal corporations'; hence his approval of Greek polytheism – one of the few religions to be 'independent of the priests', unorganised and free. This is not to say that he was opposed to Christianity, as his article on 'Christianisme' in the *Encyclopédie moderne* in 1825[8] makes especially clear: he warmly praises the Gospels, for example, and can even argue in his *Principes de politique* that the State should subsidise religion, provided it leaves it free of governmental control. Yet he was clearly not committed to Christianity as a permanent faith: the religious sentiment must eventually move on – through an almost Hegelian dialectical process – to some future 'form', and, moreover, he asserted that the religious sentiment was not incompatible with intellectual doubt.

What of Senancour, the final representative of the earlier Romantics who calls for comment? He was clearly at the opposite pole to Chateaubriand, in the earlier part of his life at least; the contrast is amply illustrated by his *Observations critiques sur le Génie du christianisme* (1816). Well before that polemic, however, Senancour – child of Jansenistic parents – had been deeply preoccupied with questions of religious faith. In the outcome, one may think, he prefigured the search by later Romantics for a 'purer' religion, freer of dogmas, priests and ceremonies than orthodox Christianity with what he felt to be its defects and irrationalities. In him were combined an Epicurean disciple of Condillac and a Platonist mystic, and readers who have concentrated only on his famous *Obermann* (1804) and its disenchantment may well lose sight of a continuing tension between these two sides of his mentality. The *philosophe* in him is most evident in his early works. *Sur les générations actuelles* (1793) attacks theology and mystical 'enthusiasm' alike and especially such aspects of Christianity as the doctrines of Original Sin and of the Atonement in its substitutionary form, the papacy, and monasticism. His *Rêveries sur la nature primitive de l'homme* (1799) reiterate these views, less sardonically but no less firmly, and go further. The work expresses a Vigny-like rebellion against the deity who created man only for a life of suffering and doubt, against the vast 'disproportion' between the world as it is and the eternal world to which we are fated to aspire, against the 'determinism' that rules us and thus undermines in reality all choice, morality and would-be objective knowledge. *Obermann* explores the saddened stoicism which is all, at this stage, that the mystic in Senancour can accept and gives a classic statement of the *mal du siècle* that would especially affect later, after re-publication in 1833 and 1840, such different minds as George Sand and Matthew Arnold. Drawn to both Boulanger and Rousseau, he yet achieved the faith of neither: social action or a deistic trust in however sublime a nature around us are contemplated only to be finally rejected as valueless. The *Observations* revealed no change from this nihilistic conclusion: *Le Génie du christianisme* is dismissed as a monument to Chateaubriand's 'credulity'.

But these were not Senancour's last words on religion, as is sometimes assumed by those who overlook a later work which he himself saw as the summation of his mature thought and his major achievement: his *Libres Méditations d'un solitaire inconnu*. First published in 1819, it was to be extensively revised by him in the quarter-century during which he lived on, praised by the Romantics and others, and he left his definitive version in manuscript form when he died in 1846.[9] It is this, and an intermediate work on *Traditions morales et religieuses* (1825) as well, which give us his later ideas on religion.

From far earlier he had been interested in such occultist thinkers as Saint-Martin, in the theosophical views of his friend Ballanche, and in other world-religions. This is reflected in the first version of the *Libres Méditations*, along with a continued attention to the Gospels and St Paul, but its God remains somewhat abstract and even negative – the reality that is beyond our understanding but that, we may believe, exists. Senancour remains more certain of man's religious aspirations than that they and the demands of his reason correspond with any transcendent truth. How far beyond this tentative spiritualism he went in the work's final form may be variously assessed. There is an undoubted 'will to synthesis'; some may think it is unfulfilled, whereas others have discerned both 'idealism' and 'mysticism'.[10] Fuller study of a neglected book is needed; pending that, only a personal view is offered here – and is perhaps best based on neither the first edition nor the unpublished final version of his old age but on the second edition of 1830, reflective of his maturer but not yet declining years.

The Senancour of 1830 has persisting doubts, but he no longer insists on certainty, still less on a comprehensive certainty. 'Qu'on ne dise point que, s'il me reste des doutes sur quelques sujets, je dois me taire sur tous', he asserts, and again: 'il n'est pas indispensable de regarder toujours comme certain ce qu'il est raisonnable et juste de désirer'. Uncertainties may themselves be part of the intentions of 'la Divinité'. Clear as to the advantages of a positive faith, he is none the less prepared now to settle for something less assured; he even advances arguments he had earlier rejected in Chateaubriand or Pascal. His God is that of the deist, with an admixture of the pantheist's also, and remains shadowy but firmly present for him. 'Ce qui est illimité est divin. L'infini ne saurait être mauvais, ou défectueux: l'infini, sous tous les rapports, ne peut se distinguer de la Divinité.' This adaptation of the Cartesian argument from a 'perfect being' seems to persuade him, and so does his sense of a principle of general harmony in the world. He even concludes a chapter on death by declaring: 'Dieu est magnanime: Dieu est Dieu, et nous sommes à lui.'[11] On immortality – the aspect of religion that most preoccupied him – he appears similarly convinced, though again on grounds he would earlier have dismissed. He invokes something not unlike 'le Pari de Pascal': 'la sagesse prescrit de tout faire pour mériter une durée perpétuelle, et de ne point balancer entre la vie et l'éternité'. Moreover, what he terms the supreme power is benevolent, and we would thus surely not aspire to a future life if it were non-existent – another reminiscence of Pascal. He even suggests a version of the Day of Judgment: since God is just, it is reasonable to think that survival is granted only to those who have made 'un sage emploi de leurs forces'.[12] As to ethics – and he remarks that 'la religion est la morale dans l'infini' – he still advocates stoicism, but it is now based on confidence, not on his earlier despair. Since the joys of this world lack all permanence, 'attachons-nous aux biens invariables'. The passions are useful and natural but should be followed in moderation and be controlled by reason and an almost Kantian concern for moral duty.

The work is not very orderly or lucid and will certainly not persuade every reader. Nor is the old Obermann entirely dead, as one sees in its criticism of 'superstitions and popular religion', and senses in the slightly desperate arguments he adduces. He can still observe that 'l'état le plus habituel de mon âme est un paisible renoncement, une espérance indéfinie, un doute favorable, une tristesse heureuse'.[13] Yet his system here is markedly removed from his earlier nihilism and warrants more attention than it normally receives.

The second generation

The successors of the earlier Romantics were almost all convinced Catholics in their youth and, even later, valued religious commitment far above the negations of atheism – of those Voltairean 'démolisseurs stupides' whom Musset would attack in *Rolla*. Yet their liberalism and the intellectual trends of their time would lead them – sooner or later –

away from the Roman faith. Orthodox doctrine and irreligion would be equally repugnant to them, and hence the problem overshadowing their thinking was to find a belief that was both genuinely spiritual and religious and yet also intellectually and, as well, morally acceptable. Can there be a reasonable Christianity – or any other reasonable religion that is truly a religion? Can both 'head' and 'heart', in Musset's terms, be satisfied? Such were the underlying questions in their minds as they went to Cousin's Sorbonne lectures or Lacordaire's sermons in Notre-Dame, as they frequented Saint-Simonian meetings, argued with Leroux, or followed Lamennais's fateful debates with the Vatican, as they delved into the Buddhist, Muslim and other religions. And as they faced such questions, far from retreating emotionally into purely subjective concerns, they were anticipating the arguments of our own century – or so one may claim. They were surely prefiguring in their anxious questionings the modernist controversies of the 1920s and beyond, and Girard is surely right to claim that 'l'âme du modernisme était en puissance dans la pensée religieuse de nos grands romantiques'.[14] They may even be thought a century and more ahead of those thinkers who have sought and still seek to demythologise and to reinterpret God.

To discuss in any detail the ideas of those major Romantics who came to maturity from around 1820 is beyond the space available here. It is thus preferable to concentrate for the most part upon two illustrations of two rather different reactions to the religious debate – for diversity is as characteristic of them as of their predecessors: Vigny and Lamartine. They can indeed be thought to work from opposite starting points. Lamartine, after a short period of youthful scepticism, regained his Catholic faith; Vigny lost his Christian beliefs by about 1815 and never regained them – prior at least to his death-bed conversion, if such it was. The former began from belief and was searching to know how far, in the light of modern knowledge and attitudes, belief must be attenuated; the latter began from unbelief and was searching to know how far unbelief can be attenuated.

Vigny's approach to religion was predominantly ethical – an emphasis already inculcated in him in childhood by his mother, it appears – and certainly his religious doubts sprang much less from the scientific and philosophical arguments that weighed with some of his contemporaries than from a moral revolt. If God exists, He is a cruel and unjust tyrant who merits hatred, not worship. Already in 1820 'La Fille de Jephté' depicts a jealous deity:

> Seigneur, vous êtes bien le Dieu de la vengeance:
> En échange du crime il vous faut l'innocence.

44

Similar moral questioning is, around that date, implicit in 'La Femme adultère' and 'Le Déluge' and explicit in 'La Prison' and 'Satan Sauvé':

> – Un mal universel accable la nature,
> Une douleur profonde est dans la créature.

This rejection of the idea of a morally perfect God was reinforced by Vigny's abhorrence for certain notions added by the Christian Churches – as witness his rejection of the doctrine of Hell, of divine punishment for sins that derive from the very nature that God has given to man; of the substitutionary view of the Atonement (as in *Stello*) whereby an innocent victim pays for the sins of others; of Joseph de Maistre's treatment of the problem of unmerited suffering (again in *Stello*). Vigny, as is well known, even turns men's religious doubtings into an argument against God, as when, in 'Le Mont des oliviers', he depicts Christ Himself deserted by His Father:

> Mal et doute! . . .
> C'est l'accusation
> Qui pèse de partout sur la Création . . .

And the conclusion of this poem is a deservedly familiar re-statement of the poet's basic attitude:

> Si le Ciel nous laissa comme un monde avorté,
> Le juste opposera le dédain à l'absence
> Et ne répondra plus que par un froid silence
> Au silence éternel de la Divinité.

Vigny does also criticise the record of the Christian Churches – particularly the intolerance illustrated by the wars of religion, the Calvinists' burning of Michel Servet, the massacre of the American Indians, and the history of the Inquisition and the Jesuits. But even without this evidence, it is clear, Vigny would have rejected Christianity's claims to moral supremacy.

For the rest he was a metaphysical agnostic and remained so throughout his life, in a state of unhappy ignorance comparable to the 'anguish' of modern existentialism and, even more, to the condition of 'l'homme sans Dieu' of Pascal – a writer whose name and whose very images of man's lot recur throughout his *Journal* in particular.

Is the religious agnostic to settle, then, for an explicitly secular moral code? Some students of Vigny's stoicism have suggested that he does so, and he was clearly drawn at many times in this direction. And yet, if morality is the central element of religion, perhaps metaphysical ignorance need not destroy all hope of religious commitment. Perhaps our religious aspirations will be fulfilled if religion can be redefined as, in Matthew Arnold's later words, 'morality touched with emotion'. Hence, for example, Vigny's respect – expressed in 'Paris', at the end of *Daphné* and elsewhere – for the Saint-Simonian religion, a creed which drastically reinterprets Christianity as a primarily moral doctrine. Vigny's description of this cult indicates some of his own desiderata – for example, the rejection of ecclesiastical rites, an emphasis on a practical religion inspired by charity, his desire for a 'universal', unifying creed, the unacceptability of the Christian doctrine of Election and his adherence to the notion of universal salvation.

His most explicit attempt to base religious devotion upon an ethical principle is seen a few years later in the conclusion to *Servitude et grandeur militaires*. In 'le naufrage universel des croyances' around him he finds one 'faith' intact, 'une dernière lampe dans un temple dévasté' – the faith of 'honour', based on an innate feeling in man, 'indépendant des temps, des lieux et même des religions', and which attracts us without any promise of reward in an after-life. And so closely does Vigny link the religious and the moral that, without any apparent sense of linguistic strain, he can baptise this ethic as 'la Religion de l'Honneur'. His description of it also reiterates and expands the conception of religion found in 'Paris'. 'C'est une Religion mâle, sans symbole et sans images, sans dogme et sans cérémonies, dont les lois ne sont écrites nulle part . . .'

He regards this cult as 'la plus pure des Religions', and the same quality is attributed to the beliefs of the Quaker in *Chatterton*: 'Je suis chrétien et de la secte la plus pure de la république universelle du Christ.' (This notion of purity constantly recurs in Vigny's thought in fact – finding a last expression in his poem 'L'Esprit pur'.) The Quaker's Christianity is a humanitarian doctrine of charity, but free of the materialism and the cult of pleasure Vigny came to associate with the socialistic doctrines of his day; he combines a deeply contemplative and spiritual faith with a concern for practical action motivated by pity, and though he manifests a Vigny-like pessimism about his society he is never tempted by the despair of Chatterton. 'J'ai passé tous mes jours avec mes frères dans la méditation, la charité et la prière", he claims; one may well think that Vigny aspired to follow him in all three respects.

The Quaker believes in the reality of God and human immortality, however, unlike Vigny himself, and in the long-planned *Deuxième Consultation du docteur Noir*, entitled *Daphné*, written mainly in 1837 (though not published until 1912), the author is concerned again with the preoccupying question: without those beliefs, what ethic, if any, can fulfil man's religious need? The work evokes the stoic beliefs of Julian the Apostate, with whom Vigny especially identified himself, and his greatness in the author's eyes lies partly in his courage and honour and above all in the fact that though opposed to Christianity he strove none the less to preserve a spiritualistic faith.

The creed Julien establishes for the Empire is centred upon 'l'amour de Dieu et des hommes' and stresses 'le soin de faire du bien à tous'; he himself can claim: 'J'ai passé ma vie entière à supplier le Dieu souverain et tout-puissant, Créateur du ciel et de la terre, de diriger . . . le cours difficile de ma vie.' Yet at bottom, though he speaks of the Roman gods, his belief is in abstract principles, in a philosophical spiritualism and not in a religious mythology of the kind which the mass of mankind seems to require as the concrete embodiment of its faith. Julien is one of those who can 'comprendre la Divinité, l'immortalité de l'âme, la Vertu et la Beauté sans le secours grossier des Symboles'. The analogy with Vigny's own position is clear: his too is a spiritualism without a god, an ethic without a mythology. The Christians triumph over Julien, whose efforts have proved sterile and who acknowledges the victory of the 'Galilean' as he dies. And the reason is clear to Libanius: whilst the 'purer' faith of Julien and himself remains valid, it has compelling force only for the minority, for the 'âmes choisies', but not for the people as a whole. Libanius concludes with regret that the new religion of Christianity must now take over the protection and transmission of the moral treasure of the world and express it in 'symboles nouveaux et préservateurs'. For what supremely matters is the ethical truth symbolised by 'le Trésor de Daphné'. For the mass of men the ethic must be clothed in religious symbols, myths and dogmas, and though these will be transitory they may be necessary to safeguard and illuminate the truths they preserve.

How far do the conclusions of Libanius represent the views of Vigny himself? At times in later life he seems drawn in this direction. After the Revolution of 1848 he turned against socialism and regarded social Catholicism as a protection against it, and in this same period he stressed the value of a supernaturalist belief as a foundation for morality and attacked those who sought to undermine it – such writers as Comte and his disciples, 'les insensés positivistes qui ne voient pas que l'*idéal* est le charme, l'illusion, la seule *consolation* de la vie'. And earlier, in 1843, his *Journal* had developed a distinction that is central for him – between 'Croyance', the attempt to know the full truth about the Creation, and 'Religion', here understood as an attempt to establish a creed 'selon l'utilité qu'elle peut avoir comme point d'appui de la morale'.[15] On the

47

one hand he distrusted organised religion, but on the other hand he was too realistic and honest not to acknowledge that a pure, disembodied spiritualism or ethical idealism, without church or priesthood, could inspire only the most intellectual group within society.

Vigny highlights here a dilemma the relevance of which has become all the more evident in our own time, a century that has seen in the histories of Nazism and Communism the strength and irrationality of men's apparent need for an apocalyptic mystique. If he never resolved it, no succeeding thinker has done better. Meanwhile, he continued his private search for a faith, and, as his *Journal* bears witness, did so to the end of his life. Thus, for example, for a period he was attracted by Buddhism, particularly after reading Saint-Hilaire's *Le Bouddha et sa religion* (1858–60). It seemed purer to him than Christianity in various respects: it has no concern with our self-preservation in a future life; it has no belief in the resurrection of the body; it does not invoke fear of divine punishments. Yet these are negative reasons, and his praise of it significantly excludes any belief in the supernatural.[16]

His best-known affirmations in verse in these years – in 'La Bouteille à la mer' and 'L'Esprit pur' – have often been cited to illustrate his stoic rationalism, and fairly so. But even they, one may note, pay their linguistic respects to religion:

> Le vrai Dieu, le Dieu fort est le Dieu des idées!
>
> Ton règne est arrivé, PUR ESPRIT, roi du monde! . . .
> Colombe au bec d'airain! VISIBLE SAINT-ESPRIT!

And the celebrated last line of 'La Bouteille à la mer' is far from unambiguous:

> – Dieu la prendra du doigt pour la conduire au port.

In short, Vigny's thought about the religious crisis of his time seeks a compromise between the new scientific rationalism and the old religious faith. The rationalist in him leads him away from every form of supernatural faith, but conversely his sense of spiritual and religious values alienates him from the secular religious substitutes of his day and prevents him from ever dismissing the religious search – the search for a religion in the full sense – as ignoble or mistaken. He sums up his own final position as 'le scepticisme pieux';[17] he was too honest and spiritually perceptive to escape this dichotomy in either way.

Of Vigny's generation of Romantics the closest to him in religious inconclusiveness was probably Musset, whose views warrant at least brief mention even in a selective survey. Though Viatte may be right to

48

see Vigny as exemplifying a rational approach and Musset a greater emotionalism, both converge on a position of hesitant uncertainty. No less than Vigny, Musset was torn between religious yearning and intellectual doubt: we saw him suggest that this conflict is a major source of the *mal du siècle*. He, like Vigny, was alienated by the intolerance and dogmatism of the Catholic Church, but behind that lay deeper uncertainties. These stemmed above all from the difficulties of reconciling the existence of a perfect Creator with the existence of death, pain and evil in the Creation, as *L'Espoir en Dieu* especially stresses.

> Pourquoi, dans ton œuvre céleste,
> Tant d'éléments si peu d'accord?
> A quoi bon le crime et la peste?
> Ô Dieu juste! pourquoi la mort?

And yet he finds in himself a persistent desire for religious belief – wholly unsatisfied by the secular philosophies from Plato and Pythagoras to Locke, Spinoza and Kant which he surveys. Hence his interest in other world-religions and in the possibility of a syncretist creed, as summed up in a stanza in the same poem.

> De quelque façon qu'on t'appelle,
> Brahma, Jupiter ou Jésus,
> Vérité, Justice éternelle,
> Vers toi tous les bras sont tendus.

Hence, above all, the theme of anguished doubt in this poem and elsewhere, for it becomes an almost stultifying obsession for him, re-expressed in *La Coupe et les lèvres* in almost Baudelairian images:

> Le doute! il est partout, et le courant l'entraîne,
> Ce linceul transparent, que l'incrédulité
> Sur le bord de la tombe a laissé par pitié
> Au cadavre flétri de l'espérance humaine!

Yet this doubt, negative and over-effusively expressed though some may think it, illustrates all the same Musset's adherence to the notion of a reasonable religion, his aspiration to something he would never attain.

If Vigny and Musset ended with no more than 'pious scepticism', at least two of their fellow Romantics achieved a fuller, more positive faith: Hugo and George Sand. However, unlike Chateaubriand who remained within Catholicism, and Mme de Staël and Constant who drew from Protestantism, both found the main elements of their new creeds outside traditional Christianity.

Hugo remained loyal to his youthful Catholic commitment for longer than most of the Romantics, but gradually moved during the 1830s and

1840s to a looser, more unorthodox faith. Thus, for example, by 1834 he could write: 'Mon ancienne conviction royaliste-catholique de 1820 s'est écroulée pièce à pièce depuis dix ans devant l'âge et l'expérience. Il en reste pourtant quelque chose dans mon esprit, mais ce n'est qu'une religieuse et poétique ruine.'[18] But far from remaining in this state of regretful uncertainty he thereafter moved towards the virtually independent faith he would express in *Les Contemplations*, *Dieu* and *La Fin de Satan*. He derived it from occultist and illuminist sources above all and his own experiences of *spiritisme*, and the outcome was the most robustly affirmative creed attained by any of the Romantics. As one authority comments of his later thought: 'En fait, Hugo n'est pas un chrétien, mais sa vie religieuse reflète toute autre chose et beaucoup plus qu'un déisme voltairien.'[19] His new creed, described in chapter III below, leaves one question, however, from the standpoint here: how far is his a 'reasonable religion'; does he preserve the religious with the support of reason or at its sacrifice?

George Sand provides a parallel example, albeit her creed was quite different from Hugo's. Her progress from *Lélia* in its first version of 1833 to *Spiridion* in 1838–9 was a movement from doubt to conviction. Lélia, as the *Revue des deux mondes* noted, 's'efforce de raviver les flammes du spiritualisme chrétien' – but fails. Yet George Sand's reaction to religious scepticism was more positive than Musset's. As she wrote in the preface of 1839 to her revised edition of the novel, 'le doute et le désespoir sont de grandes maladies que la race humaine doit subir pour accomplir son progrès religieux'. Doubt furnishes a springboard for belief, she even implies: 'Mais, mon Dieu! ce désespoir est une grande chose! Il est le plus ardent appel de l'âme vers vous, il est le plus irrécusable témoignage de votre existence en nous et de votre amour pour nous . . .'[20] And under the influence of Pierre Leroux, she outlined in *Spiridion* and *Consuelo* a new 'Christianity' based on notions of social equality, progress, nature and love of humanity. One may think her creed to be in some ways utopian and at times dithyrambically vague – though a full study might reveal its intellectual merits also – but she, like her fellow Romantics, was clearly seeking to reconcile religion with the intellectual demands of the new age.

If Hugo and Sand moved markedly away from Christianity, Lamartine struggled for most of his career to preserve his links with it. His lifelong preoccupation with religion is thus of especial interest – between the final scepticism of Vigny and Musset and the positive but basically non-Christian beliefs of Hugo and Sand. His ideas thereby warrant a fuller description.

Lamartine's doubts about Christianity began in his youth when he encountered the philosophical agnosticism of the *philosophes*, but his most decisive difficulty seems to have concerned the problem of unmerited suffering; the deaths of Julie Charles in 1817 and of his daughter Julia in 1832 were both critical events in his religious development, provoking severe scepticism about the doctrine of a morally perfect Creator. This is already a major theme in his *Méditations poétiques* (1820). 'Le Désespoir' depicts God turning from His creation and abandoning it to evil and misery, and 'La Foi' expresses a similar revolt against divine cruelty. Yet the collection as a whole suggests that at this period he was able to transcend despair and doubt. 'La Providence à l'homme' opposes to 'Le Désespoir' a trust in God's purposes, a belief that evil will be transformed for good, and other poems in the volume reveal a movement from pessimism to at least a form of natural religion. 'La Prière' is, as he claimed, 'l'hymne de l'adoration rationnelle', centred on the virtues of faith, love and hope, and 'L'Homme', though symbolising rationalist doubt in the figure of Byron, moves on to laud the Divine Being:

> Gloire à toi, dans les temps et dans l'éternité!
> Éternelle raison, suprême volonté!

More generally, the grief brought by Julie's death has yielded to a faith in the Christian doctrines of the Creation and the Fall of Man, the reality of the human soul and its immortality, and in the existence of a deity who, if largely unknowable by man, is sufficiently revealed to us, especially through nature, to command our trust and worship.

His conversion to a more thoroughgoing Catholicism dates from his illness early in 1820, and for the next several years he was closer to the Roman faith than at any other period. Yet he remained critical of certain manifestations of clericalism – its 'missions politiques', its 'congrégations de police' – and of Catholic propaganda under the Restoration. Thus, in *Aux chrétiens dans les temps d'épreuves* (1826) he attacks ecclesiastical intolerance, and his 'Hymne au Christ' (1829) contrasts Christ's message with clerical oppression and hypocrisy. Even during these years, in fact, he seems to feel little need of organised Church and priesthood. In a letter of 1827 he defines his position as 'la tolérance chrétienne et philosophique', and this tolerance perhaps rests in part on a continuing scepticism, for he can write to a friend in the same year: 'La religion positive est en moi une chose de volonté et de raison plus que de sentiment.' 'Novissima Verba' (1829) illustrates the same doubts and suggests that Christianity may be only one imperfect reflection amongst others of the eternal truth, though he still retains in 1830 at least a pragmatic trust in Christ's teaching, as his *Harmonies poétiques et religieuses* attest.

By the early 1830s he was developing more strongly towards his later outlook. One finds him attacking 'cette foule d'abus de la foi' that has hidden 'l'éclatante splendeur de la religion chrétienne' beneath 'un nuage de superstition vulgaire',[21] and in his *Politique rationnelle* (1831) he develops the major idea of a continuing intellectual progress, through which the doctrines of the past are replaced by a developing understanding of truth. This is a process as applicable to religion as to secular affairs; he bluntly declares: 'Le règne futur et parfait du christianisme rationnel ne sera autre chose que . . . le règne de la raison, car la raison est divine aussi.'[22] Already too he is advocating the separation of Church and State and treating the doctrine of Hell as expendable. At bottom he is still a Christian, but of a distinctly liberal complexion – so much so that he can stigmatise even in Lamennais's otherwise sympathetic journal *L'Avenir* 'un vice, un principe de mort' – 'sa théocratie'.

It was at this stage that Lamartine embarked on his journey to the Near East, hopeful that to visit the Holy Land might dissipate his 'religious perplexities'. The reverse occurred: he largely abandoned his Catholicism under the impact of his daughter's death in Beirut in December 1832 and after an apparently disappointing visit to the Holy Sepulchre a few weeks earlier. Not – it should be stressed – that he lost all belief in God. Visiting Constantinople shortly afterwards he was greatly impressed by the Mohammedan faith as his *Voyage en Orient* recounts: by its 'théisme pratique et contemplatif', its absence of dogmas other than 'la croyance en un Dieu créateur et rémunérateur', its toleration and freedom from priestly control, and its simple, personal form of worship in which the mosque is 'une maison de prière et de contemplation où les hommes se rassemblent pour adorer le Dieu unique et universel'. Indeed, he thinks the Muslim creed is 'un christianisme purifié', a préfiguration of the religious outlook he now aspired to clarify.

Its main outlines are presented in his *Voyage en Orient* (1835), *Jocelyn* (1836) and *La Chute d'un ange* (1838). All three were to be placed on the Roman Index between 1836 and 1838: the writer who had earlier been eulogised as a leading Catholic poet was now seen – and with cause – as unfaithful to orthodox Christian belief. And whilst most of the ideas these works contain had been put forward in his writings prior to 1832, they now received a more forceful, coherent expression.

The basis of this newly formulated system was above all to be reason –

and the point deserves emphasis in view of those interpretations that over-stress his trust in feeling. Reason is, he asserts, 'l'infaillible et perpétuelle révélation des lois divines'; 'rien n'est impénétrable au jour progressif de la raison'. Making the distinction already popularised by Constant in *De la religion* and widely explored by such *philologues* as Creuzer, Lamartine affirms that all religions combine two elements, truth and mythology. But whereas most *philologues* saw the mythological as an entirely proper and perhaps inevitable means of expressing the true, he clearly adopts a more rationalist view. He regrets that religions possess 'une nature populaire, miracles, légendes, superstitions, alliage dont les siècles d'ignorance et de ténèbres mêlent et ternissent la pensée du ciel', and wishes to retain only the 'pure', rational kernel of religion; its other element is 'une nature rationnelle et philosophique que l'on découvre, éclatante et immuable, en effaçant de la main la rouille humaine'. Hence he can hopefully declare that Christianity, 'obscurci et mêlé d'erreurs . . . par les crédulités des siècles qu'il a traversés, paraît destiné à se transformer lui-même, à ressortir plus rationnel et plus pur . . .'[23] These assertions in the *Voyage en Orient* are reiterated in *Jocelyn* and *La Chute d'un ange*. The curé de Valneige has little use for sacred and patristic texts (though we see him meditating on the Bible), scorns miracles as 'ces vulgaires prestiges', elements of error and credulity that debase 'une foi céleste', and dismisses dogmatic theology as '[un] stérile savoir dont l'orgueil se nourrit'. His own teaching of his pupils follows reason working from observation of the natural world:

> La nature et leurs yeux, c'est toute ma science![24]

The 'fragment du Livre primitif' in *La Chute d'un ange* asserts a similar view:

> Le seul livre divin dans lequel il écrit
> Son nom toujours croissant, homme, c'est ton esprit! . . .
> L'intelligence en nous, hors de nous la nature,
> Voilà les voix de Dieu, le reste est imposture!

Or nearly so! Reason is limited and our understanding incomplete: hence the insights of our feelings, of our 'soul', may add faith to knowledge – and if so, that is welcome, for man, to Lamartine, is a fusion of reason, senses and soul, as *La Chute d'un ange* stresses:

> Et l'Éternel lui fit la voix pour le nommer,
> La raison pour le voir, et l'âme pour l'aimer:
> Pour être en harmonie avec son corps fragile,
> Il lui donna des sens de limon et d'argile . . .[25]

D.G. CHARLTON

But emotion remains subordinate and is never a primary source of his religion.

A second major feature of his system lies in his wish to separate his purer, more reasonable religion from control by an official Church, from the superstructure of dogmas, rites and rigid requirements which ecclesiastical organisations create and impose on the individual believer. Hence, in the *Voyage en Orient*, he criticises monastic institutions and the rule of priestly celibacy in the Catholic Church, and the very story of *Jocelyn* likewise condemns forced ordination as well as celibacy. We saw him praise the Muslim religion for its freedom from priestly intolerance and dogmatism, and by contrast he criticises strongly the 'temporal tyranny' of the Vatican in its secular role and its wealth and extravagance in a world of poverty, as well as its spiritual intolerance. He submits indeed that as Christianity develops it will come to dispense with organised Churches.

His own creed as given in the *Voyage en Orient* was extremely simple, a theology confined to basic essentials. 'Adoration d'un Dieu unique: charité et fraternité entre tous les hommes'; in another formulation: 'Dieu un et parfait pour dogme, la morale éternelle pour symbole et la charité pour culte'. This is indeed a 'practical and contemplative theism' of the kind he had praised in Mohammedanism and is very close also to eighteenth-century deism. And like the deists he wished his creed to be expressed in social as well as personal morality and aspired to see 'le christianisme législaté': 'en politique, l'humanité au-dessus des national-ités'; 'en législation, l'homme égal à l'homme, l'homme frère de l'homme'. Yet there is a salient difference between Lamartine and the deists. Where they offer a philosophy, he ardently believes that this system is a religion, and it is expounded as such in *Jocelyn* and *La Chute d'un ange*. He came to believe that its truths sum up the wisdom of earlier ages and of other religions, as well as embodying the kernel of Christ's teaching. Already in the *Voyage en Orient* he had described Socrates and Plato as precursors of 'la religion de la raison' which formed the basis for Christianity. In *Jocelyn* he broadened this view, and by 1837 he could proclaim in 'Utopie' a still more eclectic and even syncretist notion:

> Un seul culte enchaîne le monde,
> Que vivifie un seul amour:
> Son dogme où la lumière abonde,
> N'est qu'un évangile au grand jour . . .

Each of men's past creeds, he reiterated in *La Chute d'un ange*, has its share of truth and the various insights of all religions will eventually be

54

subsumed in a common mysticism. Undoubtedly Lamartine here glosses over certain differences – notably between deism and pantheism – but what is even more noteworthy is that far from wishing to erect a purely subjective creed his aim was eclectic and profoundly reconciling. He hoped to harmonise the religious experience of mankind throughout the ages, to appeal to a consensus of human conviction, to assert the truth of a universal, not a merely personal, apprehension.

A similar attitude is seen in other writers of the Romantic generation – from Ballanche's claim that all religious systems '[sont] émanés de l'éternelle vérité' to Nerval's attempt to 'rétablir l'harmonie universelle par l'art cabalistique et de chercher une solution en évoquant les forces occultes des diverses religions'. Vigny contemplates in *L'Almeh* the possibility of 'une sorte de moyenne proportionnelle trouvée entre la religion catholique et celle de Mahomet'; Michelet notes 'le parfait accord de l'Asie avec l'Europe'; and we saw a similar hope in Musset's *L'Espoir en Dieu*. Yet probably no Romantic author was more persistent than Lamartine, or more sincere, in expressing this syncretist conviction. He himself usually linked these perennial truths above all with Christ, whose divinity he never explicitly disavowed; in 'Utopie', for example, they are identified with 'le verbe pur du Calvaire'. But the fact, as he believed, that these same truths have been at the heart of all the great religions both strengthened his own commitment to them and also confirmed him in the view that they offer a truly religious, and not merely philosophical, system.

In his later years his religious preoccupations persisted. 'Le Désert', begun in 1832 during his journey in the Near East but only completed and published (in the *Cours familier de littérature*) in 1856, provides something approaching his final statement in verse of his religious ideas. He now seems more than ever persuaded of the limits of man's possible knowledge of God, of the great gulf between His reality and the confines of human understanding. God demands of the poet:

> Peux-tu voir l'invisible ou palper l'impalpable?
> Fouler aux pieds l'esprit comme l'herbe ou le sable?
> Saisir l'âme? embrasser l'idée avec les bras?
> Ou respirer Celui qui ne s'aspire pas?[26]

And in this mood his earlier trust in the insights embodied in men's religions appears weakened; they represent 'des *Babels* du doute', and God is portrayed as mocking the essentially anthropocentric doctrines found in the religions of Zoroaster, India, China and Ancient Greece.

Yet Lamartine's attitude here is less that of the agnostic or deistic rationalist than that of the mystic contemplating the ineffable – and the poem has as its alternative title 'L'Immatérialité de Dieu'. By an arresting transformation the poet re-states his doubts and uncertainties in the language of the religious contemplative. This is evident in the words attributed to God:

> Je ne suis pas un être, ô mon fils! je suis l'Être!
> Plonge dans ma hauteur et dans ma profondeur,
> Et conclus ma sagesse en pensant ma grandeur!
> Tu creuseras en vain le ciel, la mer, la terre,
> Pour m'y trouver un nom; je n'en ai qu'un . . . MYSTÈRE.

It is no less striking in the reaction of the poet. Words, creeds, intellectual discussion are all alike inadequate, and all that remains possible is, first, silent contemplation of the eternal mystery –

> Dans ce morne désert converser face à face
> Avec l'éternité, la puissance et l'espace:
> Trois prophètes muets, silences pleins de foi . . .

– and, secondly, a trusting faith:

> Ô Mystère! lui dis-je, eh bien! sois donc ma foi . . .
> Mystère, ô saint rapport du Créateur à moi! . . .
> Je renonce à chercher des yeux, des mains, des bras,
> Et je dis: C'est bien toi, car je ne te vois pas!

We need not and cannot decide whether agnosticism has truly been subsumed here in mysticism. What is hard to deny is that to the end Lamartine recognised that religion is more than an ethic of charity or fraternity of the kind that appealed to many of his contemporaries (and to him) in the forms of Saint-Simonism, Comtism and other socially directed religious substitutes, that he recognised also that religion is more than a metaphysical philosophy of the kind that appealed to others of his contemporaries (and to him) in the forms of Cousin's Eclecticism and other natural religions of the time. 'Derrière cette apparente dérision des choses humaines [he wrote in expounding his 'philosophie personnelle' in Entretien XII of the *Cours familier de littérature*], il y a donc un divin mystère; ce mystère, c'est la sagesse et la bonté de Dieu. L'adorer sans le comprendre encore, c'est notre devoir et notre vertu!' As has been succinctly remarked, he was 'fundamentally a rational and a religious man'[27] – fusing, along with his practical social concern, or at least seeking to fuse, both characteristics. The 'purified Christianity' for which he sought is not a merely theoretical theism nor is it a largely practical ethic. It must be, as he had said years before and continued to believe, 'un théisme pratique *et contemplatif*' [my italics]; it must involve, that is to say, and as 'Le Désert' bears witness, a recognition of the transcendental and numinous. The interest and significance of Lamartine's religious thought are that he, almost alone of his contemporaries, both separated himself from the Christian Churches and yet retained all three of these elements: rationality, as he believed; practical application; and mysticism, or something close to it.

The comparison with his fellow Romantics deserves emphasis. Vigny and Musset remained in a state of 'pious scepticism'. Hugo's later creed may be both practical and mystical but, arguably, is deficient in rationality. George Sand's system may be practical and rational but is surely lacking in any mystical dimension. Lamartine alone struggled to combine all these aspects of the religious outlook; those of us still concerned with these questions could well keep in mind the goals of the religious search that he so lucidly identified.

SOCIAL AND POLITICAL THOUGHT

'A history of French political thought which does not give some indication of the immense influence of men like Chateaubriand, Lamartine, Victor Hugo, and Michelet could hardly claim to be complete.'[28] The Romantics themselves, we saw, stressed the relation of literature and art to society and to the increasingly severe industrial, economic and political conflicts of their day and wished their work to be 'l'expression d'une société nouvelle'. A few adherents of 'art for art's sake' like Gautier might attack such commitments as amounting to cultural treachery, but most of his erstwhile allies aspired to the role of intellectual leader and wished (in Hugo's words) to 'marcher devant les peuples comme une lumière et leur montrer le chemin'.

Yet scholars have often linked them with vague, emotional progressivism, even with that 'political messianism' of 'the romantic phase' criticised most notably by Talmon.[29] From Lasserre attacking 'le messianisme romantique' and Maurras linking 'romantisme et révolution' to Shroder accusing them of 'messianic pretension', their critics have discerned in them a dangerously utopian impracticality, or at best 'a certain irrationalism', a 'sentimental liberalism', mere warm-hearted rhetoric.[30] Certainly they were deeply interested in such allegedly 'utopian' thinkers as the Saint-Simonians, Fourier, Leroux, Cabet, the Lamennais of *Paroles d'un croyant*, and others. Certainly too Hugo could define 'la fonction du poète' as to become 'l'homme des utopies'. But where in reality were they situated on the wide spectrum shading from pragmatic realism to perfectionist idealism, and can one discern any coherent attitudes within their social and political writings? There were marked differences between individual Romantics, needless to say – as wide as between Chateaubriand's support of Catholic monarchy and George Sand's republican socialism, or, indeed, between the younger Hugo or Lamartine and their later views. But behind the diversities it may be that constant themes and preoccupations can be found – or so this present survey will submit, albeit inevitably selectively and at risk of over-generalisation. It will contend that the more politically conscious Romantics were striving, in politics as in religion, for a middle way between the competing extremes of Catholic traditionalism and the new socialism, and especially between the authoritarian tendencies of both Right and Left. Though certain Romantics were undoubtedly linked at stages in their careers with one group or the other, these were passing phases in most cases within their persistent search for an empirical, undogmatic alternative to theoretical excess, for a union of new with old, of reform with stability. From the 1790s to the following mid-century the preoccupations naturally changed with events and situations, but not the concern with reconciling synthesis.

The first generation

The generation of Mme de Staël, Constant and Chateaubriand provides a first illustration of this essentially moderatist, non-utopian approach. Mme de Staël emphasised her opposition to extremism as early as 1791, in her essay entitled 'A quels signes peut-on connaître quelle est l'opinion de la majorité de la nation?' She is here attacking both the right wing of the Assemblée, the *aristocrats*, and also the left-wing Jacobins. Against the latter she argues for the preservation of monarchical legitimacy, but, against the former, without the notion of the divine right of kings and the illiberalism of the royalists. And that goes with an explicit attempt to compromise between the wish for equality and liberty and the need for order and legal authority, and she even advocates as a general principle the superiority of moderation over extremism, advocating the creation of 'un parti plus fort, plus prononcé, plus énergique que les deux extrêmes opposés'. She retained this attitude of 1791 to the end of her life, as her membership of the *doctrinaire* group from 1816 confirms.[31] It underlay her accusations in *Réflexions sur la paix intérieure* (1795) that the republicans wished to sacrifice the principle of monarchy to the certainty of liberty and the constitutionalists to betray democracy to secure public order. It prompted her well-known opposition later to Napoleon's despotism and would be constantly affirmed in her attacks on fanaticism, whether religious or political, and especially so in her *Considérations sur les principaux événements de la Révolution française*, in which she argues that the Revolutionary ideals were betrayed by the fanaticism common to both the Terror and Napoleonic tyranny. She also illustrates here the clear link to be seen in later Romantics between belief in moderation and belief in civil and individual liberty – a principle which has been described as 'le fil directeur de [sa] pensée politique'.[32] In the Ancient World, she notes, all citizens could share in decision-making and thereby enjoyed full political liberty. In the larger, far more complex societies of the modern age such popular participation is impossible and the citizen can only be represented, but this fact makes it all the more imperative to establish and safeguard personal freedom. She contemptuously dismisses the revolutionary notion that despotism can be a means of creating that freedom, and asserts that it must rest on the rule of law and legitimacy in alliance with balance and moderation. Fully aware of the inevitable tension between liberty and order, between excessive concern with politics (which may lead to extremism) and too little concern (which may open the way for a despot to seize control), she contends the mistake is to seek to evade the tension by embracing one principle to the exclusion of the other, and it is a natural step from this to her praise for the English governmental model of 'the balance of powers'.

Mme de Staël's great friend and liberal ally Benjamin Constant is so well-known a proponent of a similar attitude that it is perhaps sufficient merely to allude here to his role in opposing both Napoleon and the Restoration monarchy and to such works as *De l'esprit de conquête et de l'usurpation* (1813) and the writings collected in his *Cours de politique constitutionnelle*. One can note that even earlier, when he came to Paris in 1795, his support went to the moderate republican policies of Barras as against the competing extremes of left-wing Jacobinism and royalist reaction – as his two pamphlets of 1797, 'Des réactions politiques' and 'Des effets de la Terreur', make clear. Even his momentary alliance with Napoleon may be interpreted as an attempt to effect a practical compromise between the two sides, and his influence was constantly exerted against the violence of revolution and illegality and in defence of personal liberty. He even took the doctrine of the counterbalancing of political organs to the point of advocating not three but five in-dependent and mutually inhibiting powers in the central government – and also argued strongly for greater decentralisation in addition. And in campaigning for individual freedom he was as clear as Mme de Staël that it was menaced from every side, not least by popular democracy as well as the despotisms of Catholic clerics and revolutionaries alike.

If these attitudes are commonly associated with Constant, it is less often noted that a parallel approach is found in his great contemporary Chateaubriand – and the resemblance is all the more striking since in other respects he had very different political affiliations. Although he has been accused, perhaps not unfairly, of both ambition and vacillation in his own public career as a diplomat and minister, his writings from the *Essai sur les révolutions* of 1797 onwards show his preoccupation with political ideas. Prior to 1830 at least (whereafter he may have lapsed into a certain disillusioned nihilism), it is true to judge: 'témoin, il est aussi *écrivain engagé* dans une furieuse bataille des idées politiques'.[33] And what is here relevant is that his ideas not only remained faithful to his two major principles of monarchy and liberty but were continually concerned to fuse what, to others and in the historical context, seemed to be opposed. Already in the *Essai sur les révolutions* he had adopted a standpoint similar to that of Mme de Staël, declaring himself neither royalist nor republican but 'monarchien'. In his *Réflexions politiques* (1814) he proclaimed a related attitude that flees from both extremes: 'La Convention nous a guéris à jamais du penchant pour la République, Bonaparte nous a corrigés du penchant pour le pouvoir absolu.' His support for the Charte Constitutionnelle of 1814 stemmed from the same desire to combine order and stability with liberty, 'trouver un mode de gouvernement où la politique de nos pères puisse conserver ce qu'elle a de vénérable, sans contrarier le mouvement des siècles'.[34] This is achieved, he believes, in the system of constitutional monarchy provided for by the Charte. This he would significantly describe in *La Monarchie selon la Charte* (1816) as 'un traité de paix signé entre les deux partis qui ont divisé les Français', declaring with eclectic optimism: 'Elle réunit toutes les opinions, réalise toutes les espérances, satisfait tous les besoins.' His view is well known: order and liberty are reconciled by the king ensuring order whilst liberty is safeguarded by the separation of powers, the freedom of the press and, in his view, which he strongly defended against the socialists, the preservation of private property. What is sometimes less stressed is that underlying these ideas there was a profound sense, reminiscent of Burke, of the need for a middle way and for gradualism. 'Il y a deux moyens de produire des révolutions: c'est de trop abonder dans le sens d'une institution nouvelle, ou de trop y résister.' The Charte offers a compromise between these two routes to tyranny, albeit inevitably delicate and to be changed only with tactful discretion: 'la violence [le] briserait, l'inhabileté en arrêterait le mouvement'.[35] So characteristic of Chateaubriand is the attempt to find a middle alternative, indeed, that one interpreter can even write of his 'traditionalisme démocratique',[36] and a salient theme in his political thought is that Catholic religion and individual liberty – that liberty which he had earlier described as 'le plus grand des biens et le premier des besoins de l'homme' – far from being incompatible as both Liberals and left-wing reformers were contending, are in reality interdependent. He could even claim that 'il n'y a point de véritable religion sans liberté, ni de véritable liberté sans religion' – this latter assertion being based on the argument that without religion there can be no order in society and without order no liberty.

One may think that Chateaubriand had an unduly optimistic view of the Charte and of the Roman Church in the early nineteenth century, but what his ideas illustrate none the less is a deep commitment to a politics of moderation that might reconcile the concerns of Traditionalists and Liberals alike.

The second generation

Chateaubriand and even Mme de Staël and Constant were chiefly concerned to unite individual liberty with the values of the old order – and understandably so after the traumatic experiences of the Revolution and the era of Napoleon. Even their successors – Hugo, Lamartine, Vigny and others – were marked during the 1820s by a similar conservatism of attitude; in that decade all of them defended the monarchical system as well as asserting the rights of the individual. But by 1830 (the year in which Constant died and after which Chateaubriand withdrew increasingly from politics) the new Romantic generation was clearly aware of the new social, economic and political challenges of the time, conscious of the urgent demands for socialistic reform and even revolution. This development mirrors, obviously enough, the spreading effects of the industrial revolution in France: increasing urbanisation, the growth of a city proletariat living in conditions of severe poverty, a decline in real wages to a sub-starvation level, the exploitation of women and children as well as men, the savage suppression of such protests as the revolts of the Lyons silk-workers in 1831 and 1834. As the younger Romantics came to full maturity, the old régime represented by the Restoration monarchy was finally disappearing, and the voice of Catholic traditionalism seemed increasingly less relevant. The case of Lamennais was a particularly arresting symbol, not least for the Romantics, of the changing situation – the transformation of the leading exponent of orthodoxy into the prophet of the *Paroles d'un croyant*, condemned by Rome. The sense of social crisis seems to have provoked apprehension in the aging Chateaubriand. 'Nous marchons à une révolution générale' (he could declare in 1831); 'nous sommes arrivés à l'un de ces grands changements de l'espèce humaine'.[37] Lamartine was equally aware of the change but appears more hopeful – this is 'une de ces grandes époques de reconstruction, de rénovation sociale' – and Hugo had an equal sense of the political seriousness of the time. 'Le moment politique est grave: personne ne le conteste, et l'auteur de ce livre moins que personne', he declared in the Preface to *Les Feuilles d'automne*. And indeed the Romantics needed neither theories nor crisis to make them respond to the sufferings they observed around them: their compassion and social concern are obvious in their writings, and it was these above all that led them around 1830 into an alliance, even if short-lived, with the Saint-Simonians, with Christian socialists like Buchez and Lamennais or with other reformers like Pierre Leroux. It was, for example, Buchez who introduced Vigny to the Saint-Simonians, whose social programme Vigny would hymn in 1831 in the poem 'Paris'. There is no need to provide quotations to illustrate both their deep social sympathies and their interest in left-wing proposals for reform.

Yet even more than their predecessors they have been suspect to the Right for allegedly ill-considered progressivist sentiment and to the Left as typical of an upper-class liberalism that draws back when faced by the need for sweeping change. Lamartine in 1848 was typical in being accused either of incompetent vanity or of deliberate 'double-talk'.[38] Hunt notes a parallel attitude in Vigny's socialist critics, 'un mélange d'irritation et de sympathie'. They could approve the critique of capitalism in *Chatterton* – but also regret it being negative as to any positive alternative. Though Vigny might attack in *Stello* the right-wing absolutism of Joseph de Maistre, that did not preserve him from Buchez's strong attack on the book as fundamentally individualistic. And despite the Saint-Simonian undertones of 'Paris', the reviewer in *Le Globe* (by then left-wing) was sardonic: 'Pauvre poète malade! tu cherches ardemment le remède et tu le repousses quand il se présente à tes lèvres altérées.'[39] Such critical reactions as these no doubt stemmed in part from the reformers' impatience to progress to an instant utopia, but they were also related to a deep-seated ambivalence or tension within the political aspirations of the Romantics themselves. One could contend, as some critics have, that theirs was an idealism fearful of the full consequences of a liberation of the proletariat, that preferred progressivist declarations to the risks of action and revolution, at bottom an affair of emotional benevolence and not of practical political intelligence. But the ambivalence may have a more reputable source: it may reflect, in some instances at least, an attempt to find, like their predecessors but in a different context, a middle way between the claims of personal liberty, political order, and social justice.

Space allows only two representative examples, one negative and one more positive in outcome: Vigny and Lamartine. Vigny clearly saw the validity of the socialists' attack upon industrial capitalism. 'L'amélioration de la classe la plus nombreuse et l'accord entre la Capacité prolétaire et l'Hérédité propriétaire sont toute la question politique actuelle', his *Journal* declared in 1832. And humanitarian idealism was not far to seek in most of his works: his exaltation of freedom as early as *Héléna* (1822); the humane reforming outlook of De Thou in *Cinq-Mars* (1826); his sympathy already noted with the ideas of Saint-Simonism during the early 1830s; the critique in *Stello* (1832) of both Maistrian absolutism and the bourgeois establishment of the day; the democratic arguments expressed in *Servitude et grandeur militaires* (1835); *Chatterton*'s presentation of capitalism as a cruel, oppressive system to which the proletariat, no less than the poet, is sacrificed; the progressivism of such later poems as 'L'Esprit pur'. And yet he remained hesitant to the point of inconclusiveness; the liberal in him was as suspicious of the authoritarianism of the socialists (increasingly so from about 1840) as of the Catholics, the aristocrat was fearful that equality would mean levelling down, and he felt social order might be threatened by too much change. It is significant that his approval went to the American system of liberal rather than revolutionary or what Talmon terms 'totalitarian' democracy.

His view – and the conflict behind it – are well reflected in the celebrated 'Ordonnance du docteur Noir' in *Stello*, where he reacts against 'l'influence des Associations, même les plus belles': 'Toutes les Associations ont tous les défauts des couvents. Elles tendent à classer et diriger les intelligences, et fondent peu à peu une autorité tyrannique . . .' Clearly aware of the twin appeals of liberalism and socialism, Vigny seems to have found them finally incompatible, and though he sought for a reconciliation, its difficulties proved counter-productive, one may think. They served to reinforce a certain disillusionment with the world of politics – of the kind illustrated by his well-known remark in *Stello*: 'Tout ordre social est basé sur un mensonge plus ou moins ridicule . . .' This sceptical attitude, fed also by his long-standing regret at the aristocracy's loss of power and no doubt reinforced later, in the

1840s, by the failure of his own attempts to enter practical politics, was the final word even of the poem 'Paris'. It may laud Saint-Simonism, but its conclusion witnesses to his pessimism and stoic scepticism:

> Et songe qu'au-dessus de ceux dont j'ai parlé
> Il en fut de meilleurs et de plus purs encore . . .
> Des hommes pleins d'amour, de doute et de pitié
> Qui disaient: '*Je ne sais*' des choses de la vie . . .

Lamartine offers a less negative, politically more developed illustration of the attempt to fuse the best values of liberalism and socialism, and more than any other Romantic he was involved in practical politics. Yet his ideas have commonly been dismissed (as Guillemin notes) as 'un tissu d'incohérences, de contradictions, d'idées fausses et de généreuse folie',[40] and his brief exercise of political power has sometimes been interpreted as the result either of confusion of mind or of an attempt to defend by equivocation the privileges of his own social class. As to his role in 1848 there can be no doubt that he sought to appeal to both the conservatives and also Ledru-Rollin and his fellow Radicals, whom he wished to retain in the government; there is equally little doubt that, as is common with those who seek to please both sides, he finally pleased neither. Yet that perhaps stemmed less from incompetence or hypocrisy than from his consistent pursuit of a policy of the middle way, combining radicalism and moderation, that was central to his entire political thought and that helps to explain the impression of 'incohérences' and 'contradictions' of which his critics complain, whilst at the same time giving him a significance and comparative originality which have too rarely been acknowledged.

His political concern was evident well before he entered the Chambre des Députés in 1833. Already in his *Nouvelles Méditations* (1823) – in 'La Liberté, ou Une nuit à Rome' – and in his *Épître à Casimir Delavigne* (1824), *Le Dernier Chant du Pèlerinage d'Harold* (1825) and his *Chant du Sacré* (1825) his commitment to the idea of liberty had been clear:

> Liberté! nom sacré, profané par cet âge . . .
> LIBERTÉ! dont la Grèce a salué l'aurore
> Que d'un berceau de feu ce siècle vit éclore . . .

The freedom of the individual is a cardinal principle, as evident in the 1820s, when he still supported a Catholic monarchy, as in later years; it is characteristic that in a letter of 1829 he should see himself and Hugo as 'amis de la religion de conscience et non de la religion de police'.[41] This reflects a conviction he defended throughout his career – not merely as an abstract or emotional faith but by detailed proposals of the kind found in his declaration of 1831, *Sur la politique rationnelle*: liberty of the press; elective government with universal suffrage based on proportional representation; the suppression of hereditary aristocratic power in politics; free education; a reformed distribution of property.

But secondly – and increasingly as the 1830s and 1840s revealed the full consequences of industrialisation – Lamartine also embraced the principles of social justice and charity. Already in 1829, in his 'Hymne au Christ', he admires Christ as above all a social prophet and leader:

> Verbe incréé! source féconde
> De justice et de liberté!

In part his concern was with moral issues like the abolition of the death penalty and the reform of the criminal law – both items in his political programme of 1831 and the former the subject of his *ode politique* of 1830, *Contre la peine de mort*. But his overriding preoccupation was far wider than such individual reforms, however desirable. As Louis Blanc acknowledged in his *Histoire de dix ans*, Lamartine was one of the first to recognise that the plight of the urban proletariat presented the greatest problem of domestic policy facing the nineteenth century. 'Nous nous le dissimulons en vain [he wrote in 1835], nous l'écartons en vain de nos pensées, la question des prolétaires est celle qui fera l'explosion la plus terrible dans la société actuelle.' And in his *Résumé politique du Voyage en Orient* – another valuable document as to his political convictions – he likewise attacked the irresponsibility and harshness of *laissez-faire* economics: the proletarian class is 'dans une condition pire qu'elle n'a jamais été', to which he adds the prediction: '[elle] remuera la société jusqu'à ce que le *socialisme* ait succédé à l'odieux individualisme'. Repeatedly he showed his acute awareness that Europe – for his outlook was not limited to France – had entered 'une de ces grandes crises organiques dont l'histoire n'a conservé qu'une ou deux dates dans sa mémoire . . .'.[42] For Lamartine the Revolution was not yet finished, and though he has been accused of 'facile optimism', his *Résumé politique* in particular reflects his acute sense that France was in a period of painful and dangerous transition. This work may give some support to those who would see him as a timid progressive drawing back from the consequences of his own principles – seemingly appalled that liberty of discussion has led to '[un] esprit de dispute sans bonne foi', that popular education has produced 'une sorte d'éblouissement d'idées non encore comprises' and also 'une surabondance de capacités qui demandent un emploi social'. There is something too of patrician superiority as he notes the morally disturbing effects of urbanisation upon the people and regrets that equality before the law has led to a mood of jealousy, envy and instability, to '[une] égalité de prétentions et d'ambitions dans toutes les classes'. Yet his dominant concern, none the less, was to evolve a policy of social justice and welfare, a policy he did not hesitate to define as 'socialism'. 'La charité, c'est le socialisme; – l'égoïsme, c'est l'individualisme.' For Lamartine socialism equalled what we now term the welfare society. As to economics, he acknowledged 'le beau rêve de la communauté des biens, tenté en vain par le christianisme et par la philanthropie', and in 1848 he would argue for nationalising the railways and putting the unemployed on the state pay-roll, and oppose the abolition of the National Workshops. Yet at the same time he always defended private property, both in his writings and in 1848, maintaining that it is 'la condition *sine quâ non* de toute société; sans elle, ni famille, ni travail, ni civilisation'. His policy, in 1831, in 1835, and thereafter, was therefore based on a wider distribution of property and not its abolition. His support was (in the present-day term) for a 'mixed economy', albeit he invoked the notion of 'un droit au-dessus du droit de propriété, le droit d'humanité!' and urged that property must be held and used in trust, as it were – 'pour l'humanité tout entière' – possessed only 'à des conditions de justice, d'utilité, de répartition, d'accession pour tous'. One may certainly accuse him here of a failure to think through to the consequences of his position; he has nothing to propose but exhortation against a property-owner who neglects these conditions. And for those without property he holds out little more than the prospect of emigration to the underpopulated and undeveloped countries of the East. He envisaged colonial 'protectorates', run by Europeans but guaranteeing the native inhabitants against dominance by their tribe or prince and ensuring their right to property, and foresaw the growth within them of 'free European cities' to serve as 'principaux centres de liberté, de propriété et de civilisation'. Here too, though this policy *was* in historical fact to be followed in the succeeding decades by the imperialist countries, his solution can only seem inadequate for the larger issue.

Yet to attribute these deficiencies to lack of good faith or of thought is, once again, to undervalue the difficulties of the political balance Lamartine was seeking, of what he described in *Sur la politique rationnelle* as his central political aim, 'une organisation progressive et complète de l'ordre social sur le principe de la liberté d'action et d'égalité de droits'. Furthermore, he was keenly sensitive to the dangers of violent revolution, of the anarchy and suppression of freedom which – as a child of the French Revolution – he believed such a catastrophe would bring in its wake. 'Tout plutôt que l'anarchie!' – that was his basic conviction, and it called for a still more delicate compromise between (as he described it to Cazalès in 1830, after the revolutionary events of that year) 'l'excès du pouvoir' and 'l'excès bien plus périleux de liberté'. To reconcile liberty with order, equality and a wider distribution of wealth, to usher in revolutionary change without a revolution: these were the problems he tried to resolve, however inadequately. Guillemin succinctly states his goal: 'Double effort, parallèle: l'un de conservation, l'autre de progrès. Toute la politique de Lamartine tient dans cette détermination virile.'[43] To walk such a tightrope – and in the first decades of modern industrial society, moreover – was a task of perhaps insoluble complexity (as may perhaps be thought demonstrated in our own day by the twin failures of the Communist countries to ensure personal liberty and of the capitalist system to ensure social justice and equality). Lamartine's achievement was partly to propose concrete reforms, to anticipate, for example, the major elements of what is now termed 'welfare socialism', but above all to perceive the complex political demands of his time and to avoid the simplistic solutions being proposed by other writers of his day.

Lamartine approached his task with two preconceptions that are worthy of note. The first was a belief in gradualism – no doubt partly the product of the timidity of a wealthy bourgeois but no less, one may think, of a conviction as to the dangers of over-rapid, over-radical change; this itself lends him a certain originality in an age given to proposing dramatic solutions to difficult problems. And the second (which has unjustly helped to feed criticisms of his lack of principle) was a suspicion of all political dogmas and systems – an attitude already apparent in a letter to Virieu in 1831 in which he castigated all allegedly definitive theories, monarchical or republican, traditionalist or Saint-Simonian, as 'risibles'. His approach, by contrast, was one of pragmatic practicality, not only when in power and under the pressure of events but much earlier and in theory, as when he writes to Hugo in 1829: 'Nous voulons l'ordre et nous estimons la liberté . . . Nous savons que toute politique est une science expérimentale où les principes ne se jugent bien qu'aux conséquences.' In an age divided in its political theories between dogmatic Catholics and monarchists and equally dogmatic left-wing reformers Lamartine retained a refreshing sense of reforming realism – as one observer justly notes, a 'mixture of idealism and practical common sense'.[44]

Only brief mention of Lamartine's other fellow Romantics is possible here, nor were any of them involved in practical political decisions in the way he was. This is true even of Hugo, albeit he became by the end of his life the very symbol, to the public who flocked to his funeral procession, of republican socialism – for, as Jacques Seebacher wryly comments of him: 'Il a passé sa vie à manquer toutes les révolutions.'[45] *Pair de France, député*, influential exile during the rule of Louis-Napoléon, and finally *sénateur*, Hugo's ideas remained imprecise, and he has been accused even more than Lamartine of inconsistency and changeability, of taking flight into the rhetorical to avoid the challenges of hard choice.

Nevertheless, the central themes of his political outlook over the years resembled those of Lamartine. He was, first, a liberal and (despite reservations about universal suffrage if it meant votes for the un-educated) a democrat, and in well-known words in the preface to *Hernani* he declared: 'Le romantisme, tant de fois mal défini, n'est à tout prendre, et c'est là sa définition réelle, . . . que le *libéralisme* en littérature.' And just as that play stood in his mind for 'la liberté dans l'art, la liberté dans la société', so too *Les Orientales* at the same date – though usually connected with *l'art pour l'art* – contained poems on liberty and the heroes of the Greek struggle for independence. There and in later works he often stressed the view behind his celebrated assertion in *Les Feuilles d'automne* in 1831:

Je hais l'oppression d'une haine profonde . . .

Improbable though it may seem, even his admiration of Napoleon was apparently linked with the same commitment. As Descotes's study concludes, one finds in him 'l'utilisation du mythe de l'ex-Tyran pour le service de la cause de la liberté'. There seems, indeed, no reason to doubt his own claim in 1875, in the preface, 'Le Droit et la loi', for *Actes et Paroles*, that the 'unity' of his life had lain in his dedication to freedom: 'jamais on ne trouvera une ligne contre la liberté'. '[L'auteur] cherche à faire en tout prévaloir la liberté. La liberté, c'est, dans la Philosophie, la Raison, dans l'art, l'Inspiration, dans la politique, le droit.'[46]

Yet this liberal also claimed that he had been a socialist since 1828 – and would arrestingly contend: 'Romantisme et socialisme, c'est, on l'a dit avec hostilité, mais avec justesse, le même fait.'[47] The explanation of this apparent contradiction is that for him, as for Lamartine, socialism is primarily concerned with concrete abuses and injustices. His plea against the death penalty in *Dernier Jour d'un condamné* (1829), his wider attack on the social and prison systems alike in *Claude Gueux* (1834), his depictions of the poor, oppressed and exploited in poems like 'Dans une mansarde', 'Les Pauvres Gens', and 'Melancolia', all these and other writings well before *Les Misérables* show his commitment to major practical reforms, and his ends are movingly clear even though he is often vaguer as to the means to achieve them. He distrusted political doctrines and sought 'la substitution des questions sociales aux questions politiques' – after, at least, his youthful support for a Catholic monarchy. He feared inflexible theories and the authoritarianism they led to in his view, and above all he dreaded violent change and revolutions:

> Les Révolutions, monstrueuses marées,
> Océans faits des pleurs de tout le genre humain.

Revolution, he reaffirms in *Les Misérables*, cannot ultimately be beneficial: 'La misère amène les peuples aux révolutions, et les révolutions ramènent les peuples à la misère.' Hence he opposed both the extremer radicals of 1848 and the dogmatism of their socialist theories: 'Je suis contre les monastères et pour la famille . . . J'ai lu les écrits de quelques socialistes célèbres, et j'ai été surpris de voir que nous avions . . . tant de fondateurs de couvent!' He himself was a committed gradualist – as he declared, '[un] socialiste à tâtons'.[48]

Comparable analyses could be developed as regards the positions of Sainte-Beuve, Musset and George Sand. Sainte-Beuve wished literature to express 'le sentiment de l'humanité progressive', he declared in his notable article on 'Espoirs et vœux du mouvement littéraire', and for a short period around 1830 he was closely involved with the Saint-Simonians before turning to Lamennais's Christian socialism. *Volupté* and his criticism alike attest to his continuing political involvement – but his attitude moved steadily away from any theoretical commitment. Musset was perhaps less concerned with politics – and yet *Lorenzaccio* could be thought the outstanding political drama of the whole Romantic movement. As with Vigny, so with Musset the conflict between idealism (as in Lorenzo) and harsh realities is explored but leads to a negative response of withdrawal. Insurrection and the murder of the tyrannical Alexandre are presented as counter-productive, and in one respect at least Musset may have gone further than any of his fellow Romantics: the Strozzis illustrate the ineffectiveness also of benevolent liberal humanism on the model of Lamartine and Hugo. George Sand has been interpreted as 'révolutionnaire', as fighter for the rights of both women and the proletariat – and justly so, despite her imprecision as to concrete measures. Yet she too remained, finally, in a middle position. The firmer socialism of her explicitly social novels yielded, in 1848 and in her pastoral novels, to the charming but unrealistic idyll of the mistress of Nohant. Nor need this surprise us; her political 'sauveur', Pierre

Leroux, before whom she felt herself 'un disciple muet et ravi', had himself clearly identified the crucial issue. Whatever his 'messianic' tendencies, he was an individualist democrat. An article in the *Revue sociale* in 1845 reasserts his approach: for the socialists there is no liberty, for the individualists no equality and thus no complete social justice; the dilemma lies in their reconciliation.

It may be just that the Romantics are rarely discussed in histories of political thought, for their reactions to the age were less at the level of theory than of practicalities. To offer a speculative synthesis or a dramatic solution to its problems was outside their interest or even, it may be, their intellectual range, but perhaps their achievement was none the less more valuable and original than usually acknowledged: to ask the *right questions*. To reconcile order, liberty and social justice has remained the goal of much political debate since their day; they were amongst the first in Europe to appreciate and confront its difficulties.

NOTES

1. Cf. S. Mellon, *The Political Uses of History* (Stanford UP, 1958).
2. Cf. V.E. Starzinger, *Middlingness: 'Juste Milieu' Political Theory in France and England, 1815–48* (Charlottesville, UP of Virginia, 1965) and, on links with the Eclectics, cf. bibliography below (and, for the following references, my own essay cited there).
3. A. Viatte, *Le Catholicisme chez les romantiques* (Boccard, 1922), p. 375.
4. Senancour, *Rêveries sur la nature primitive de l'homme* (2 vols., Geneva, Droz, 1940), II, 79.
5. For discussion of these charges, cf. P. Moreau, 'L'Auteur du *Génie* et le christianisme', in *Chateaubriand: Le Livre du Centenaire* (Flammarion, 1949), pp. 77–111, and R.M. Chadbourne, 'The *Génie du christianisme* revisited', *Romanic Review*, 48 (1957), 3–16.
6. Cf. S. Balayé, *Mme de Staël: Lumières et Liberté* (Klincksieck, 1979), and especially pp. 182–190. The major primary source is *De l'Allemagne*, Part 4: 'La Religion et l'enthousiasme', vol. v. in the 'nouvelle édition' (5 vols., Hachette, 1958–60).
7. The opening part of *De la religion* is conveniently included in Constant, *Œuvres* (Bibliothèque de la Pléiade, Gallimard, 1957).
8. 'Christianisme', in *Encyclopédie moderne* (vol. 7, ed. M. Courtin, Mongie Aîné, 1825), pp. 30–52.
9. This final version is the edition by B. Le Gall (Didier) (Geneva, Droz, and Paris, Minard, 1970).
10. Cf. especially on this tension M. Larroutis, 'Monde primitif et monde idéal dans l'œuvre de Senancour', *Revue d'histoire littéraire de la France*, 62 (1962), 41–58.
11. *Libres Méditations d'un solitaire inconnu*, 2nd edn (Vieilh de Boisjoslin, 1830) (1831 on title page), pp. 9, 179, and 168.
12. *Ibid.*, pp. 34 (and cf. 11–12), and 129.
13. *Ibid.*, pp. lx, 37, 63–4, and 26–7.
14. H. Girard, 'La Pensée religieuse des romantiques', *Revue de l'histoire des religions*, 89 (1924), 157.

15. *Journal*, Vigny, *Œuvres complètes* (2 vols., Bibliothèque de la Pléiade, Gallimard, 1948–50), II, 1280 and 1205.

16. Cf, for example, *Journal* (1862), *ibid.*, II, 1368 and 1377.

17. *Journal*, 14 August 1857, *ibid.*, II, 1332.

18. Hugo, *Littérature et philosophie mêlées* (Albin Michel, 1934), p. 133.

19. J.-B. Barrère, *Victor Hugo: Les Écrivains devant Dieu* (Desclée de Brouwer, 1965), p. 85.

20. G. Sand, *Lélia* (Garnier, 1960), p. 353.

21. Ms. of *Devoirs civils du curé*, cited by H. Guillemin, *Le 'Jocelyn' de Lamartine* (Geneva, Slatkine Reprints, 1967), p. 177.

22. *Sur la politique rationnelle*, in *Œuvres complètes de Lamartine* (41 vols., by the author, 1860–6), vol. XXXVII, p. 384.

23. These last two quotations from the 1842 edition were to be modified or deleted in the 1860 edition.

24. *Jocelyn*, IX, in Lamartine, *Œuvres poétiques complètes* (Bibliothèque de la Pléiade, Gallimard, 1963), pp. 756–7.

25. *La Chute d'un ange*, *ibid.*, pp. 942–3 and 954.

26. For this and succeeding quotations from 'Le Désert', cf. *ibid.*, pp. 1473–84.

27. J.C. Ireson, *Lamartine: A Revaluation* (University of Hull, 1969), p. 13.

28. J.P. Mayer, *Political Thought in France from the Revolution to the Fifth Republic*, 3rd edn (London, Routledge, 1961), p. 25.

29. J.L. Talmon, *Political Messianism: The Romantic Phase* (London, Secker and Warburg, 1960).

30. P. Lasserre, *Le Romantisme français*, new edn (Garnier, 1919), p. 324; C. Maurras, *Romantisme et révolution* (Nouvelle librairie nationale, 1922), collecting earlier works; M.Z. Shroder, *Icarus: The Image of the Artist in French Romanticism* (Cambridge, Mass., Harvard UP, 1961), p. 48.

31. Mme de Staël, *Vie privée de M. Necker*; *Mélanges* (Brussels, Wahlen, 1820–1), pp. 277–9. On her links with the *doctrinaires*, cf. especially G.E. Gwynne, *Mme de Staël et la Révolution française* (Nizet, 1969), pp. 294ff. I have developed the argument summarised in the following pages in 'Utopia and the politics of balance: a theme in French Romantic thought', *Australian Journal of French Studies*, 11 (1974), 193–209.

32. Gwynne, p. 52.

33. *Politique de Chateaubriand*: textes choisis et présentés par G. Dupuis, J. Georgel et J. Moreau (Colin, 1967), p. 8.

34. Chateaubriand, *Œuvres complètes* (36 vols., Pourrat, 1836–9), XXVI, 137.

35. *Ibid.*, XXX, 197 and XXVI, 269.

36. M. Prélot, cited in *Politique de Chateaubriand*, p. 15.

37. In his brochure *De la Restauration de la monarchie légitime* and in the preface to his *Études historiques*.

38. Cf. G. Wright, 'A poet in politics: Lamartine and the Revolution of 1848', *History Today*, 8 (1958), 616–27.

39. Cf. H.J. Hunt, *Le Socialisme et le romantisme en France* (Oxford, Clarendon Press, 1935), pp. 238–40.

40. H. Guillemin, *Lamartine, l'homme et l'œuvre* (Boivin, 1940), p. 54.

41. Cited by H. Guillemin, *Lamartine et la question sociale* (Geneva, La Palatine, 1946), p. 51.

42. For this and following quotations, cf. Lamartine, *Résumé politique du Voyage en Orient*, in *Œuvres complètes*, new edn (vol. VIII, Gosselin, 1847), pp. 240ff.

43. Guillemin, *Lamartine, l'homme et l'oeuvre*, p. 56. A related interpretation is found in H. Michel, *L'Idée de l'État* (Hachette, 1896), pp. 327–35. By contrast, Talmon, *Political*

Messianism, recognises his 'democratic liberalism' but understates his socialistic commitment (pp. 331ff.).

44. R.H. Soltau, *French Political Thought in the Nineteenth Century* (New York, Russell, 1959), p. 106.
45. J. Seebacher, 'Poétique et politique de la paternité chez Victor Hugo', in *Romantisme et politique, 1815–1851* (Colin, 1969), p. 111.
46. M. Descotes, *La Légende de Napoléon et les écrivains français du XIXe siècle* (Minard, 1967), p. 206; Hugo, *Actes et Paroles* (3 vols., Albin Michel, 1937–8), I, 21. Cf. also K. Wren, 'Victor Hugo and the Napoleonic myth', *European Studies Review*, 10 (1980), 429–58.
47. Hugo, *William Shakespeare* (Albin Michel, 1937), p. 165.
48. Hugo, *Actes et Paroles*, I, 127–8 and I, 21.

BIBLIOGRAPHY

A. The Romantics are given little attention, perhaps understandably, by the principal histories of nineteenth-century philosophy. Useful for the background to their ideas, however, are the following works in English: F. Copleston, *A History of Philosophy*, vol. IX, *Maine de Biran to Sartre* (London, Burns and Oates, 1975), a particularly comprehensive survey; and, especially relevant to their religious thought, D.G. Charlton *Secular Religions in France (1815–1870)* (London, Oxford UP, 1963). Two older studies are G. Boas, *French Philosophies of the Romantic Period* (Baltimore, Johns Hopkins UP, 1925), and A.L. Guérard, *French Prophets of Yesterday* (London, Fisher Unwin, 1913). On French Catholic thought in the period general works include G. Weill, *Histoire du catholicisme libéral en France (1828–1908)* (Alcan, 1909); L. Foucher, *La Philosophie catholique en France au dix-neuvième siècle* (Vrin, 1955); and H. Guillemin, *Histoire des catholiques français (1815–1901)* (Geneva, Paris, Montreal, Éditions du Milieu du Monde, 1947). For non- and usually anti-Catholic thought in the period, general studies in English are: D.G. Charlton, *Positivist Thought in France (1852–1870)* (Oxford, Clarendon Press, 1959), and, on selected thinkers, F.E. Manuel, *The Prophets of Paris* (Cambridge, Mass., Harvard UP, 1962); a long-standing major study is S. Charléty, *Histoire du saint-simonisme*, 2nd edn (Hartmann, 1931). There are numerous works on individuals, for which the reader should consult the bibliographies in the works above. On Eclectic thought there is no general study and only a few works on individuals, on which cf. bibliographies in Copleston and in D.G. Charlton (ed.), *France: A Companion to French Studies*, 2nd edn (London, Methuen, 1979), ch. VI, which also gives a short general survey of 'French thought in the nineteenth and twentieth centuries'. Two articles which discuss the relation of Cousin and Eclecticism with the Romantics are A. Hoog, 'Un intercesseur du romantisme: Cousin vu par Stendhal', *Revue des sciences humaines*, 62–63 (1951), 184–200, and D.G. Charlton, 'Cousin and the French Romantics', *French Studies*, 17 (1963), 311–23. On political and social thought in general, cf. section C below.

B. On the Romantics' ideas on religion there are numerous discussions in literary–historical works noted in the bibliographies to other chapters, but the studies that follow are more directly concerned with them, in addition to some of the general studies mentioned in section A above. P.-M. Masson, *La Religion de Rousseau*, 2nd edn (3 vols., Hachette, 1916), vol. III, is an old but still interesting study, albeit arguably overstressing the Romantics' debt to Rousseau. A. Viatte, *Le Catholicisme chez les romantiques* (Boccard, 1922) is the best of the critical studies of their thought, far surpassing the more emotive attacks of Lasserre, Seillière, Babbitt and others noted in chapter I and its bibliography. Good and more sympathetic studies are: H. Girard, 'La

Pensée religieuse des romantiques', *Revue de l'histoire des religions*, 89 (1924), 138–62; P. Moreau, 'Romantisme français et syncrétisme religieux', *Symposium*, 8 (1954), 1–17; H. Tronchon, 'Une Crise d'âmes: 1830', *Revue des cours et conférences*, 27 (1926), 385–99, reprinted in *Romantisme et préromantisme* (Les Belles Lettres, 1930), and a recent colloquium volume, with several interesting detailed studies, *Romantisme et religion* (PUF, 1980). In addition, H.G. Schenk, *The Mind of the European Romantics* (London, Constable, 1966), gives limited attention to the French Romantics, from a mainly critical standpoint. On the Catholic elements in their thought, as well as Viatte's book, there are V. Giraud, *De Chateaubriand à Brunetière* (Spes, 1938) and H. Guillemin, *Histoire des catholiques français*. On their affinities with occultist, illuminist and related thinkers, cf. chapter III below and its bibliography. A still valuable study on an aspect of their ethical ideas is given by R. Canat, *Du sentiment de la solitude morale chez les romantiques et les parnassiens* (Hachette, 1906).

Numerous books on individual Romantics discuss their religious thought; only a brief selection can be given here. The series on 'Les Écrivains devant Dieu' (Desclée de Brouwer) has especially useful studies on Chateaubriand (by P. Moreau, 1965), Constant (by H. Gouhier, 1967), and Hugo (by J.-B. Barrère, 1965). On Chateaubriand also, V. Giraud, *Le Christianisme de Chateaubriand* (2 vols., Hachette, 1925 and 1928), vol. II, and P. Moreau, *La Conversion de Chateaubriand* (Alcan, 1933) remain major. On Constant, short studies in English are W.W. Holdheim, *Constant* (London, Bowes and Bowes, 1961) and J. Cruickshank, *Constant* (New York, Twayne, 1974); major works in French include D. Bastid, *Constant et sa doctrine* (2 vols., Colin, 1966); P. Deguise, *Constant méconnu: Le Livre 'De la Religion'* (Geneva, Droz, 1966); and P. Thompson, *La Religion de Constant* (Pisa, Pacini, 1978). On Mme de Staël, S. Balayé, *Mme de S: Lumières et Liberté* (Klincksieck, 1979) is a valuable recent examination and makes redundant earlier books by E. Ollion, M. Souriau and others; this can be supplemented by various essays at successive *Colloques de Coppet* as listed in Balayé's bibliography. Senancour has been too often interpreted as a religious nihilist; the major authority who helps to give a wider view is B. Le Gall (Didier), notably in *L'Imaginaire chez Senancour* (2 vols., Corti, 1966).

Amongst the major Romantics of the second generation, Hugo has attracted a variety of studies. Some concentrate on his links with the occultist tradition: A Viatte, *Hugo et les illuminés de son temps*, 2nd edn (Montreal, Éditions de l'Arbre, 1943); D. Saurat, *Hugo et les dieux du peuple* (La Colombe, 1948); and (within a wider context) P. Albouy, *La Création mythologique chez Hugo* (Corti, 1963). Others give equal attention to his more 'reasoned' ideas: notably, the long-neglected study by the Criticist philosopher Charles Renouvier, *Hugo le philosophe* (Colin, 1900), and also C. Lecœur, *La Pensée religieuse de Hugo* (Bordas, 1951); M. Levaillant, *La Crise mystique de Hugo (1843–1856)* (Corti, 1954); and J. Roos, *Les Idées philosophiques de Hugo* (Nizet, 1958). A special aspect is treated in G. Venzac, *Les Origines religieuses de Hugo* (2 vols., Bloud et Gay, 1955). On Lamartine, M. Citoleux, *La Poésie philosophique au XIXe siècle: Lamartine* (Plon–Nourrit, 1905) remains very useful. More recent works include H. Guillemin, *Connaissance de Lamartine* (Fribourg, Librairie de l'Université, 1942) and *Le 'Jocelyn' de Lamartine* (Boivin, 1936). A persuasive article by R. Trousson, 'Lamartine et Rousseau', *Revue d'histoire littéraire de la France*, 76 (1976), 744–67, argues that Lamartine is indebted to Rousseau in his religious thought but opposed to his political ideas. On George Sand, her debt to Pierre Leroux is explored by D.O. Evans, *Le Socialisme romantique: Pierre Leroux et ses contemporains* (Marcel Rivière, 1948), but the attention given to her social ideas has not been matched as regards religion, other than in chapters in P. Salomon, *Sand* (Hatier, 1953) and M.-L. Pailleron, *Sand* (3 vols., Grasset, 1938–53), and incidentally in W. Karénine, *George Sand, sa vie et ses œuvres* (4 vols., Plon, 1926). Vigny is especially well served by the major study by G. Bonnefoy, *La Pensée religieuse et morale de Vigny* (Hachette, 1944), as well as by more general works on him such as E. Estève, *Vigny, sa pensée et son art* (Garnier, 1923), P. Flottes, *Vigny* (Perrin, 1925), and F. Germain, *L'Imagination de Vigny* (Corti, 1963). On Sainte-Beuve there is a rather unspecific study in M. Leroy, *La Pensée de Sainte-Beuve* (Gallimard, 1940). Théophile Gautier's thought other than in aesthetics has been almost wholly neglected, except in a somewhat unsatisfactory study by H. Van der Tuin, *L'Évolution de Théophile Gautier* (Amsterdam, Holdert, and Paris, Nizet et Bastard, 1933). Whilst many may think the neglect justified, further research might modify that judgment, as even more in the case of Musset – on whom, however, cf. Philippe Van Tieghem, *Musset* (Hatier, 1944), and P. Gastinel, *Le Romantisme de Musset* (Rouen, Imprimerie du Journal de Rouen, 1933).

C. Political and social thought in the earlier nineteenth century is treated in numerous books, of which several are in English: notably, J.P. Mayer, *Political Thought in France from the Revolution to the Fifth Republic*, 3rd edn (London, Routledge, 1961), R.H. Soltau, *French Political Thought in the Nineteenth Century* (London, Benn, 1931 and New York, Russell, 1959), and, on specific aspects, A. Gray, *The Socialist Tradition* (London, Longmans, 1946) and J.B. Bury, *The Idea of Progress*, 2nd edn (New York, Dover, 1955). J.L. Talmon, *Political Messianism: The Romantic Phase* (London, Secker and Warburg, 1960) is an important but sometimes tendentious interpretation. In French major works include D. Bagge, *Les Idées politiques en France sous la Restauration* (PUF, 1952); C.C.A. Bouglé, *Socialismes français*, 2nd edn (Colin, 1933); R. Aron, *Les Étapes de la pensée sociologique* (Gallimard, 1967); M. Leroy, *Histoire des idées sociales en France* (3 vols., Gallimard, 1947–54), vols. II and III; and (more discursive) P. Bénichou, *Le Temps des prophètes* (Gallimard, 1977). On one important political group a work in English is V.E. Starzinger, *Middlingness: 'Juste Milieu' Political Theory in France and England, 1815–1848* (Charlottesville, UP of Virginia, 1965). On Catholic socio-political ideas a major work is J.-B. Duroselle, *Les Débuts du catholicisme social en France (1822–1870)* (PUF, 1951) and a helpful English book is B. Menczer, *Catholic Political Thought, 1789–1848* (London, Burns Oates and Washbourne, 1953). On history and historical thought, see chapter VIII below and its bibliography.

On the Romantics themselves only a few of the above make more than passing comment, but 'social romanticism' has been thoroughly treated in several works: D.O. Evans, *Social Romanticism* (Oxford, Clarendon Press, 1951), an excellent short survey with full bibliographies, and the same author's more detailed but restricted study of *Le Socialisme romantique*; R. Picard, *Le Romantisme social* (New York, Brentano's, 1944); and, another major work, H.J. Hunt, *Le Socialisme et le romantisme en France* (Oxford, Clarendon Press, 1935), which examines the 'socialism' of the Romantics and the 'romanticism' of the socialists. There are several very useful studies in a colloquium volume on *Romantisme et politique, 1815–1851* (Colin, 1969). J. Pommier, *Les Écrivains devant la Révolution de 1848* (PUF, 1948) gives short studies of the reactions of several of the Romantics, and A. Cuvillier, *Hommes et idéologies de 1840* (Marcel Rivière, 1956) likewise studies individuals at a particular historical moment. P. Flottes, *Histoire de la poésie politique et sociale en France de 1815 à 1939* (La Pensée universelle, 1976) has much that is relevant, even though the title indicates its primary focus.

On individual Romantics, for Chateaubriand E. Beau de Loménie, *La Carrière politique de Chateaubriand de 1814 à 1830* (2 vols., Plon, 1929) remains important; a shorter, more recent survey, with a selection of texts, is G. Dupuis, J. Georgel et J. Moreau, *Politique de Chateaubriand* (Colin, 1967). On Constant, cf. the works in section B above and also F. Bartholoni, *Introduction à la politique de Constant* (Évreux, 1964). On Mme de Staël, S. Balayé, *Mme de Staël*, is again major, as are G.E. Gwynne, *Mme de Staël et la Révolution française* (Nizet, 1969) and for her early ideas B. Munteano, *Les Idées politiques de Mme de*

Staël et la Constitution de l'an III (Les Belles Lettres, 1931). An Anglo-Saxon perspective is given by R. J. Forsberg and H.C. Nixon, *Mme de Staël and Freedom Today* (London, Vision Press, 1963).

As regards their successors, Lamartine has received fullest attention, notably in E. Harris, *Lamartine et le peuple* (Gamber, 1932), H. Guillemin, *Lamartine et la question sociale* (Geneva, La Palatine, 1946), and, in part, A.J. George, *Lamartine and Romantic Unanimism* (New York, Columbia UP, 1940). For Hugo a still useful starting point is P. de Lacretelle, *La Vie politique de Hugo* (Hachette, 1928); a short discussion is by A.R.W. James in his edition of Hugo, *Littérature et philosophie mêlées* (2 vols., Klincksieck, 1976), vol. I, 'Etude'. On a major preoccupation cf. P. Savey-Casard, *Le Crime et la peine dans l'œuvre de Hugo* (PUF, 1956). Vigny is still best studied by P. Flottes, *La Pensée politique et sociale de Vigny* (Les Belles Lettres, 1927). On Sainte-Beuve a short survey is M. Leroy, *La Politique de Sainte-Beuve* (Gallimard, 1941); cf. also essays by R. Molho and R. Fayolle in *Romantisme et politique*, pp. 244–54 and 255–64. On Musset there are only isolated articles, of which one may note C. Duchet, 'Musset et la politique', *Revue des sciences humaines*, 108 (1962), 514–50, and B. Masson, 'L'approche des problèmes politiques dans *Lorenzaccio* de Musset', in *Romantisme et politique*, pp. 303–15. George Sand has been more fully treated, and especially in J. Larnac, *George Sand révolutionnaire* (Éditions Hier et Aujourd'hui, 1947), E. Dolléans, *Féminisme et mouvement ouvrier: George Sand* (Éditions ouvrières, 1951), as well as in such general studies as P. Salomon, *George Sand* (Hatier, 1953). D.O. Evans, *Le Socialisme romantique*, is especially relevant since she was strongly influenced by Leroux. Cf. also essays in special numbers devoted to her in *Revue d'histoire littéraire de la France*, 76 (1976) and *Romantisme*, 16 (1977) and G. Lubin, 'George Sand et la révolte des femmes contre les institutions', in *Roman et Société* (Colin, 1973), pp. 42–51.

III · *Illuminism, utopia, mythology*

FRANK PAUL BOWMAN

IN MEMORIAM ANN VAN ZANTEN*

Alfred de Musset, in his *Confession d'un enfant du siècle* (1836), depicts his age as one without faith or hope. The past is irretrievably gone, the future nowhere near. The sexes are at war. The poor, bereft of the consolations of religion, are moving toward violent revolt. The Revolution's goals and hopes had turned sour, the glories of the Napoleonic era were over, the Restoration's pretence of a return to the institutions and beliefs of the *ancien régime* received little real adherence. Indeed, Romantics such as Musset, Vigny, Hugo wrote with a background of crises in political institutions and also in systems of belief – in Catholicism, in Lockean sensationalism or a Condorcet's confidence in a progress produced by reason and science. Faced with these crises, many sought new kinds of religion, of philosophy, of politics, in part by re-examining the intellectual and cultural tradition. I am here concerned with three aspects of this quest: the re-formulation of the illuminist tradition and the religious revival; the efforts to give new significance and forms to mythology; finally – and this is perhaps where the age made its major mark – the proposal of new models of political and social organisation, 'utopian socialism'. However, the picture is complex. The socialist projects are informed by illuminism, the new religions are not easily distinguished from efforts to renew Catholicism. It is simpler to describe first the critiques of the traditional systems; then the efforts to create new systems of belief; then formulations of these efforts, first in utopian projects, secondly in a sampling of myths; finally, to discuss the contradictions of these efforts, the ways they failed.

---

*Secondary sources are identified in the bibliographic note at the end of the chapter. The dates given for primary sources are those of first publication, except for certain works published posthumously, where the date (preceded by a 'c.') is that of composition.

This essay is dedicated to the memory of my late friend Ann Van Zanten, a brilliant young art historian working on nineteenth-century French socialist theories of architecture and city planning, who was killed in the massacre of the rue des Rosiers, Paris, August 1982.

76

THE CRITIQUE OF SENSUALISM AND OF ENLIGHTENED SELF-INTEREST

Already under the Consulate it was clear that something was wrong in the Heavenly City of the eighteenth-century *philosophes*, as the excitement with which Mme de Staël and her *groupe de Coppet* examined Kant's transcendentalism indicates. The Revolution had shown that enlightened self-interest could not justify going to the guillotine with courage, whence the need to posit an innate sense of moral right and wrong. The political situation only precipitated an awareness of something the *Sturm und Drang* of the eighteenth century had already made apparent: one cannot create faith, hope, or the sublime while measuring responses to pleasure and pain. Germaine de Staël set out to combat egotism and ended up substituting for it enthusiasm, defined as 'God in us', the presence of the divine transcendent spark which could lead to moral conduct when faced with adversity. Enthusiasm, she also proposed, was an essential element in the creation of true works of art. She thus moved from Rousseau's sensibility, via Kant, to an appreciation of Fénelon's *pur amour*. She did not abandon a liberal political stance; freedom for the individual, and for history, to work out their problems remained her essential concern. Her friend Benjamin Constant was also tempted by the inner voice of quietist mysticism, but this did not keep him from leading the liberal opposition during the Restoration. His quietism does reflect introspective tendencies which led to an interesting journal and some remarkable autobiographical novels. Perhaps more symptomatic is the evolution of a Bonstetten, who abandoned a neo-classical sensation-based aesthetics for one governed by the superior faculty or pneuma within us. The Coppet group never broke radically with the past, never rejected reason in favour of irrationalism. Rather, they sought to enrich the mind and the creative capacities by recourse to idealist philosophy and to the spiritual tradition.

Stendhal presents a different picture. Faithful to the tradition of the *idéologues*, he cultivated 'la lo-gique' to the point where some would refuse to call him a Romantic. Yet Julien Sorel and Fabrice del Dongo also know the joys of contemplation. More important, Stendhal insists on energy as an essential component of man. If he still defines happiness in terms of enlightened self-interest, its pursuit involves recourse to irrational or inspired action; the 'naturel' which can lead to happiness tends to be the contrary of 'la logique' which forces the hero to don a mask and do what he wants not to do. For even the *idéologues* evolved, studying the problem of sympathy, of energy and movement, of insanity, enlarging their definition of man who becomes more varied, individualised, complex. If their psychology remains essentially biological, it becomes markedly less mechanistic. The concern with insanity is shared by many – not because the Romantics themselves were insane; indeed, few were. Rather, it was a matter of reintegrating madness into culture, proposing that any adequate definition of the mind had to include the phenomena of insanity, that madness had metaphysical meaning.

TRADITIONALISM AND THE CRISIS OF CATHOLICISM

French philosophy of the first half of the century is usually divided into four schools: the *idéologues*, the Traditionalists, the Spiritualists, and the Eclectics. Romantic writers often owed something to all four. Traditionalism first appeared in a Catholic context. The Church faced many problems. Thomism had been replaced by a neo-Cartesianism which even Rome was soon to condemn; moral theology reflected a rigorous Jansenism which tended to make daily life impossible. The Revolution and the Napoleonic wars had emptied the seminaries; theologians were few in number, and badly trained. Indeed, the major ones were laymen. The situation did have the virtue of encouraging renewal within a freedom the Church had not known since the Council of Trent. The age's theological and apologetic innovations seem in retrospect intellectually weak and doomed to fail, but at the time created considerable excitement. Chateaubriand, by proposing in his *Génie du christianisme* (1802) that Christianity was true because it was good and beautiful, may have turned things upside down but did put the Church back into the world and insist on its contributions to creating at least an image of the Kingdom here below. His aesthetic apologetics called for a renewed presence of the spiritual in literature and the arts; many would heed the call, enriching poetry, painting and music. Chateaubriand's sincerity is too complex to be examined here, but he was typical in asserting that the road to faith went via suffering and despair: 'j'ai pleuré, j'ai prié, j'ai cru'. If the theology and spirituality of the period were disproportionately centred on the Crucifixion, this is because of the conviction that religion was a response to the tragic sentiment of life.

The Traditionalist apologetics of Bonald and Maistre at first seem more coherent and conservative, but they, too, provided several openings for renewal. Maistre's emphasis in his *Soirées de Saint-Pétersbourg* (1821) on sacrifice as the keystone of society and on the reversibility of the sacrifice of the innocent, providing grace for the guilty, is less a sadistic authoritarian theory than another effort to justify a transcendent moral order, and introduced a dialectic according to which, out of seeming evil, good will come. The notion that there are negative moments in life and history, and that they are meaningful, is widespread in France long before Hegel became known. Bonald's application, in his *Législation primitive* (1802), of the Trinity to grammar, to the family, to all social structure, and his emphasis on sacrifice as the mechanism of ternary mediation, prefigures what at times seems a mania for trinitarian and Joachimist three-age thinking among socialists such as Saint-Simon and Leroux and poets such as Hugo. Both Bonald and Maistre were preoccupied with the problems of language and myth. They – and many Romantics after them – propounded a theory of language as given by God, prior to thought, corrupted by sin or history and so susceptible of restoration. Language thereby becomes reinvested with mystical qualities, is something which forms us, not just something we form. Maistre, a Freemason as well as a Catholic, was more open to illuminism than Bonald. His defence of ultramontanism did not keep him from believing in inhabited planets, the transmigration of souls, and the sacrificial regeneration of nature as well as of humanity. His major contribution was surely his traditionalism. The word does not mean today what it meant then. Traditionalism proposed that a universal revelation of religious truth had been given to man by God at the beginning of history, and transmitted – or corrupted – by man ever since, but vestiges of it remained in the traditions of humanity. That revelation included not only the truths of natural theology, but also the mysteries of the virgin birth, the redemptive sacrifice, the Trinity. Indeed, natural theology was usually held in disdain, perhaps because of doubts about reason. Traditionalism led to a renewed interest in mythology, conceived not as an exaggeration of historical events and persons (Euhemerism), nor as a poetic means of explaining natural phenomena primitive science could not cope with, but as the corrupted embodiment of divine revelation. Whence a quest for Chinese legends of the virgin birth and Aztec symbols of the crucifix. Traditionalism could easily become syncretism – one thinks of Nerval. Above all, it revalidated mythology as the vehicle of a profound truth, collective to all mankind, paving the way for Jung. It also reinvigorated figural thinking. If the myths of the past were figures of Christian truth, the events and people of the present could also be seen as meaningful figures of that truth, or of some other. Napoleon as Christ, the worker as Christ, are not just factitious parallels, but propose an essential relationship

79

among the phenomena of history which provide in diverse guises the one, transcendent truth.

Lamennais adopts and revises Traditionalism; in the *Essai sur l'indifférence*, 1817–23, he also sloughs off various old apologetic arguments, including that of religion as good for the people (which did not prevent Cousin from reiterating it, but then Cousin was not a Catholic), and rejects any tergiversation in matters of religion. From the beginning, Lamennais was a radical. He extends Traditionalism by asserting that the common sense of humanity is the repository of universal revelation. That which is true is that which has always been believed, everywhere, by everyone; *vox populi* then becomes *vox dei*, which prepares his later 'leftist' stance in the *Paroles d'un croyant* (1834) and also valorises folk-lore and popular tradition as well as myth.

The most symptomatic of these theologians was Cousin's pupil Louis Bautain, a priest who accumulated numerous doctorates in law, medicine, and so on, like Lamennais was condemned by Rome but did not let it bother him unduly. A neo-fideist, Bautain asserted that the leap to and acceptance of faith was the prerequisite to any true understanding of philosophy, the sciences, art, history. The assertion is really a hypothesis, and so difficult to refute, but, if the foundations of Bautain and his disciples were shaky, they were better at understanding and refuting pantheism or German idealism than were other Catholics. Like Pascal, he believed in the metaphysical leap, and justified it ontologically.

These were not the only figures who attempted a religious renewal. Gerbet was a more brilliant theologian than his friend Lamennais, and there were many others. Including Protestants, for francophone Protestantism also knew a revival in the first third of the century, with the Réveil, a movement somewhat parallel to English Methodism, bringing with it a renewed belief in dogma as well as a renewal of piety, an awareness of the immediacy of the divine and a heightened sense of moral responsibility toward the poor. The movement eventually split French Protestantism; it reflected the age in its emphasis on the essentially subjective, emotional nature of the religious experience.

THE AMBIGUITIES OF THE RELIGIOUS REVIVAL

Musset's *Confession* suggests that the problem with the much-touted return to religion was that no one believed; the *lycéens* used the host to seal their letters. Much evidence supports him, including some statistics and even more the mediocre quality of religious poetry and the transient nature of the conversion experience among the leading Romantics. For them, the return to dogma and faith was not sufficient to inspire; it was the subsequent loss of faith that generated literature. Lamartine comes to mind as exemplary. The childhood faith lost, then refound (thanks to the Restoration? to the tragic death of Julie Charles?), produced texts of rather dubious orthodoxy, such as 'Le Crucifix' where the two loves become quite confused. Then he again lost that faith, perhaps because of another tragic death, his daughter's. His most religious texts, such as 'Novissima verba' or *La Chute d'un ange* (1838) come afterwards; only then is his imagination, enriched by heterodoxy, unleashed. Practically all the Romantics move in and then out of Catholicism, or maintain a tenuous relation with it, express a desire to believe, rather than belief itself. Religious doubt is the force which leads to religious poetry and the creation of myths and a new symbolism. Even Maurice de Guérin, who remained ostensibly orthodox, achieved poetic greatness only when he expressed his pantheistic vision of man and nature in *Le Centaure* (c. 1835). Lamennais is another instance; only with *Paroles d'un croyant* does his writing acquire real force and move as well as convince. Rather than any return to religion, a re-examination of the loss of faith characterises the age. The eighteenth century shed the faith easily, happily, and wittily; Hugo, Lamartine, Vigny lost faith in order to know a sense of the holy, of the aweful, of the need for symbols which they then try to recreate, without perhaps ever fully believing in them. Vigny's *Daphné* (c. 1837) expresses through Julian the Apostate this perturbation in front of the change in beliefs, of a new religious hypostasis.

Indeed, the theme of the death of God produced some of their most impressive texts. That Mme de Staël in *De l'Allemagne* (1810) should have discussed Jean-Paul Richter's dream of Christ announcing that the skies were empty, that in his cosmic voyage he had found not God but the infinitely empty eyesocket, is proper; she was presenting German literature to her contemporaries. That, to Richter's annoyance, she should have truncated his text, making of it, not a statement of the necessity of belief, but a cry of despair, may be explained by the death of her idolised father. But it was her version of the dream, the image of the eye of God as an empty, infinite pit, of the sun as black, which was to dominate, horrify and delight the next generation, inspire works by Balzac, Gautier, Nerval, above all Victor Hugo. Quinet turned the symbol into a theory of history as a cycle of endless sacrifice. Vigny demanded the Stoic response, a 'no' to the God who said 'I am not' to man. Nerval maintained the ironic distance of ambiguity; secrets, and significance, remain unknown. Only Hugo managed to transform despair into light and convert Goethe's death-bed 'mehr Licht' into his own 'je vois de la lumière noire'.

One should not, however, dismiss the religious 'revival' as a superficial affectation. Like Mme de Staël, the philosopher Maine de Biran spent his last days annotating Fénelon. Beginning as a disciple of the *idéologues*, he moved to a consideration of the significance of energy as certifying the self, rather evocative of Stendhal, and from there, in a philosophy increasingly introspective and expressed in an autobiographical journal, went on to a conviction of the three lives in us, physical, intellectual, spiritual, the last (in a very Platonised Christianity) inspired by the presence of the Holy Ghost. He comes at the beginning of the era; its other great philosopher (one should perhaps add Jouffroy, deeply tormented by his lack of faith), Jules Lequier, at the end, could be described in much the same way. Lequier centred his meditations on the problem of liberty, especially in his contemplation (dear to the Surrealists) of the *feuille de charmille*, opting for the leap into freedom and concluding that man is he who does. Lequier's spirituality is centred not on the Holy Ghost but on the incarnate Jesus whom he considered his brother; the Gospel was an experience he relived until his final ordalium when he swam out into the ocean never to return. Both he and Maine de Biran are closer to Bautain than to the Positivist apologetics of Chateaubriand or Lamennais; faith is the product of an introspection which leads to a new reading of man and the universe.

INTROSPECTION, INITIATION, ILLUMINISM

Introspection often led to something other than Christianity. Few periods of modern history have been more marked by new religious formulations, though these often are recastings of an old tradition, and, particularly, re-formulations of the illuminist current, which, going back to Gnosticism and the cabbala, flourished in the eighteenth century as an underground, esoteric movement. With Romanticism, it surfaced, entered into the domain of spirituality and also of politics and poetry. The illuminist tradition saw Creation (and man, *imago dei*) as emanating from the divine Principle and thus to some extent, in each of its members, possessing a divine presence. It also proposed an emblematic reading of not only nature but man's mind and its creations, including myth and literature, in order to detect that divine presence. In history it saw a return of emanated being to divine unity. It valued introspection, organicism, and progress. The marriage with Romanticism is hardly astonishing, even if that marriage took some refurbishing of the old bride.

The marriage took place in part through Swedenborgianism, influential in two waves, the first in the late eighteenth century, the second in the 1820s and 1830s. The second shed the occultist trappings of the first and proposed a new metaphysics as much as a new religion. Less important than Swedenborg's definition of God as the Divine Man was his double emanation of the divine into spiritual and material worlds, intimately related by analogous forms and substances, both marked by the three degrees of being: love, wisdom, and use, with the divine goal of life (and history) being the reunion of the worlds of nature, spirit and God. Angels and androgynism were poetic images which enhanced this reading of Creation as a harmonious analogy of the divine.

The word 'harmony' appears often in Romantic texts, in key positions, possessing a variety of meanings, some of small import, others associated with analogy and 'correspondance', Baudelaire's term for what was by mid-century a widespread, even trite mode of asserting the union of Creator and Creation. Harmonious analogy expresses and reveals the links between the divine, the self, and the world. Romantic nature-poetry differs from that of the eighteenth century because of these theories of harmony. At times, it is a matter of reinvigorating the old theme, 'The Heavens declare the glory of God', by recourse to an emanationist panentheism – God is present, to a varying extent, in the whole chain of being (as opposed to pantheism which would identify God with all or part of nature). At times, the venerable *figura* theory is extended to assert the harmony among all religious and mythic structures, explained by traditionalism and leading to syncretism. Finally, often via Malebranche, later Hegel, a harmony is proposed between the reason of man and the divine Logos; the Word is within us, contained in our mental constructs. This leads to the ontological proposition that ideas are in God, but can be perceived by man's loving intelligence. In all instances, harmony is now veiled, imperfect; initiation, poetic vision, the study of comparative religion and mythology, arithmosophia, the restructuring of society, are all means of knowing, creating, or restoring harmony.

Initiation is another eighteenth-century occultist theme which, with the Romantics, moved into the general realm of literature, in a pure, explicit form in Sand's *Consuelo* (1842–3), but Hugo's *Les Misérables* (1862) is also a novel of initiation, as are many Romantic philosophical epics. Here again, the realist novel integrates the epic tradition, while changing its modes. In *Consuelo*, a heroine, not a hero, is initiated, and in Hugo the initiation is transferred from the fanciful world of the *Magic Flute* into the base reality encountered by a former convict; the descent into hell is transformed into a struggle with the adversity society offers man. In Nodier's *La Fée aux miettes* (1832) and Nerval's *Aurélia* (1855) madness constitutes the descent into hell which leads to illumination. Initiation may also lead to the discovery of a truth which has political implications. *Aurélia* ends with both a gesture of fraternal love and a vision of cosmic reconciliation where evil disappears – the same conclusion reached in Hugo's epico-lyric autobiography of his own initiation, *Les Contemplations* (1856). In *Les Misérables* as in *Consuelo*, the lesson learned is more explicitly a call to social action. Initiation involves acquiring new knowledge by undergoing suffering and pain. If Musset asserts that 'rien ne rend plus grand qu'une grande douleur', it was not out of masochism but because suffering was a means of validating the poet's message. The structure of initiation lent itself well to the theme, out of evil, via suffering, good will come.

The major figure in this integration of the illuminist tradition into literature was the 'unknown philosopher', Louis-Claude de Saint-Martin, appreciated by Mme de Staël, the Schlegels, Lamartine, popularised by Sainte-Beuve, Guttinguer, Balzac. His pervasive influence is explained by his skill as a writer, and by the fact that, 'the Luther of occultism', he condemned the superstitious practices of other illuminists and thus helped make illuminism respectable. His writings, especially *Le Ministère de l'homme-esprit* (1802), offered a justification of many basic tenets of Romanticism. He synthesised panentheism and initiation and thereby provided a programme for poetry, explicitly, and implicitly for politics. Convinced that Creation was a divine emanation, he saw in all phenomena an emblem of the divine, providing symbolic knowledge. The acuity of the symbolic vision depends on the spiritual progress of the perceiver; the poet–seer then might be, as Sainte-Beuve put it, he who possesses the key to the symbols and the knowledge of the figures, for whom what to others seems incoherent and contradictory is only a harmonic contrast, a chord on the universal lyre. The analogical view of the universe thus becomes enriched with a dialectic moving toward the restoration of harmony. Saint-Martin defined the motive force as 'desire'; the holy man was the 'man of desire', yearning for the good and the absolute, and charged by God with the task of creating that good and seeking that absolute – for man alone is free. The progress of the man of desire must follow that of Christ, incarnate the consciousness of the Word and then by being and doing good and by knowing suffering create the Kingdom – a task not completed by Christ, and in that sense man, and the history of humanity, can go beyond Christ. Saint-Martin envisages a continuing progress toward spiritualisation, where by integrating and expiating fallen nature in sacrificial suffering the man of desire can fulfil his mission. From which he derives an aesthetic which announces the assertions of Romantic manifestos. Content, not form, determines what is poetry, and Saint-Martin calls for the prose poem; measured verse is for him as much a *cache-sottise* as is the alexandrine for Stendhal. That content must include both honey and gall, *miel* and *fiel*; the spiritual function of literature requires that the ugly be present in its highest forms. He put the *bonnet rouge* on the dictionary as did Hugo, and for much the same reasons. Except that he was not that much concerned with politics; if he clearly perceived a goal for history, he was not very explicit about the social (as opposed to individual) means of achieving it.

There, it is rather Pierre-Henri-Simon Ballanche who wedded the illuminist tradition to the philosophy of history and political action – and to Catholicism. He proposed the theses of the *Génie du christianisme* before Chateaubriand, read Vico before Michelet. He shared many of Saint-Martin's ideas, indulged in arithmosophia (numbers are the accessible forms of eternal thought, and so on). Erudite, he counted among his friends Lamennais and Hugo. If his ideas aimed at synthesis, his writings tended toward dispersion, but in *La Vision d'Hébal* (1831), he offered a prose epic of the history of humanity which contains in condensed form his theory of history as palingenesic process and progress. The Fall was an emancipation, but man misused the gift of freedom, so God has imprisoned him in matter, in time, in society, in language, in order that he may expiate his fault, and thus be rehabilitated. Expiation is identical with initiation; it is a suffering descent into hell whereby the will is redirected, the good is known and can be accomplished. Society is divided into initiators and initiables, but this inequality gradually disappears as man progresses through the ages. Abel and Cain will be reunited, as will Orient (initiator) and Occident (initiable), patrician and plebeian. Societies are marked by inequality so that conflict may lead to progress, and the plebeian, who wishes to hasten that progress, is the motive force for change. Ballanche justifies 1789 as such a hastening of change, the Restoration as a necessary prolonging of initiation. The process of history spirals ever upward toward equality and the reintegration of man in perfect unity. The process is exemplified and actualised by Jesus, who replaced class solidarity with the notion of charity, extended initiation to plebeian as well as patrician. The religious emancipation he began must now become civil.

Ballanche is a historical syncretist in religion and mythology. Myths contain a truth which each century must rediscover, interpreting and translating them; this is one of the functions of the poet–seer. He opened the illuminist heritage to a progressive conception of history in which the *vox populi* becomes a *vox dei*. He never moved as far left as did Lamennais but, more than anyone else, he made possible the socialist readings of the Gospel so common in the 1840s.

Saint-Martin and Ballanche were very much concerned with history as process, with the organic relations between spirit and matter. The kind of thinking they represent reflects some fundamental changes in man's way of conceiving the universe between 1750 and 1850. A.O. Lovejoy in *The Great Chain of Being* outlined the main developments. The world was no longer conceived of as static, but as dynamic, undergoing constant change not only in institutions and cultures but also in the realm of matter, a change described by various theories of evolution. In a like way, existence was conceived of, not as mechanistic, but as organic. Judith Schlanger, in *Les Métaphores de l'organisme*, shows how prevalent such metaphors – and the organic way of viewing things – were in a variety of domains, in historical, linguistic (languages began having roots, manuscripts stems), political, scientific thought, as well as in poetry and fiction. Such metaphors reflect the desire to integrate the human with the biological as well as the social, creating correspondences among the multiple domains. This organic reasoning often has recourse to the integration of differences and oppositions in an equilibrium, a meaningful whole. Polarity thereby becomes the matrix of unity, producing a cult of the antithesis (Hugo is exemplary) where opposites are integrated, dualism destroyed.

Gabriel Madinier traces a parallel evolution in his *Conscience et Mouvement*. The period conceived of consciousness not as something static, perceived by reflection, but as movement. Starting with Maine de Biran's assertion that the reality of the self consists in the perception of that self thanks to the sense of effort, psychology evolved toward the vitalist Bergsonian position. Particularly, in Jouffroy, Madinier traces the move from a philosophy of substance to one of force, via the notion of a *pouvoir personnel* which directs the capacities of consciousness, and which informs the conception of the hero in both Stendhal and Balzac. This move toward a dynamic conception of the self is paralleled in the development of an organic sense of time, which Georges Poulet has analysed. The past was no longer conceived of as dead and fixed, but as alive in present man. The cult of paramnesia and of the sense of 'existences antérieures' are extreme forms of this fusion of the past with eternity. In the same way, the dream revealed the unity between the individual and the universe; the unconsciousness represented a collective reality. The notion of history as break or rupture was replaced by the conception of history as organic change. This organic sense of time gives myth a dwelling place; myth is a seme of the past which continues to possess significance today, though that significance can, indeed must, change.

THE NEW BOUNDARIES OF POETRY, MYTH, LANGUAGE

In his sonnet 'Vers dorés' (1845) Nerval proclaims:

> Souvent dans l'être obscur habite un Dieu caché;
> Et comme un œil naissant couvert par ses paupières,
> Un pur esprit s'accroît sous l'écorce des pierres!

The tercet synthesises this whole complex of ideas: panentheism throughout a whole united chain of being (from animal to vegetable to mineral) possessed with consciousness and movement. To say this, Nerval substitutes metamorphosis for metaphor. The eyelids change into bark and then into the rugged surface of stones. His readers were accustomed to such visual metamorphoses in Grandville and other artists. Imagery no longer served to decorate, or to elucidate by comparison; rather, because of the dynamic unity of all creation, the image itself conveys the meaning.

In its second quatrain, Nerval's sonnet asks the reader to fear the eye of the divine – within us, within nature, within the teleology of history which presented the individual's free consciousness with an ambivalent situation, particularly when accompanied by the conviction that the harmonious unity had been lost and that it was man's task to restore it. How to perceive and restore that harmony becomes a complex question which involves a variety of attitudes toward the nature of myth, toward religious syncretism, and toward the question of language. I have noted how religious syncretism was a two-edged sword, an argument either in favour of Christianity, as with Lamennais, or against. Many tried to view Olympus in the light of Tabor, as Laprade requested in his *Psyché* (1841), but the light often obscured the two. Nerval asserted that he had at least seventeen religions, but his doubt about their relations, unity or conflict, is at the root of the haunting ambiguity of his *Chimères* (1854). The quest for unity was no more successful here than elsewhere, but did lead to some very important consequences: the valorisation of the *vox populi* as expressing religious truths, of myths themselves, and of language as the vehicle of truth.

Traditionalism reinvigorated the belief in the primitive mind as near to original innocence, in the value of the truths primitive man expressed in his myths and religions. This easily led to the notion that the *peuple* was gifted with the same religious perceptions today. Vico had already propounded the significance of myth as an expression of universal truth and of the *vox populi* as the voice of truth, and Ballanche propagated Vico in France, emphasising the permanent meaning of myths and the function of the *plebs*. Michelet instead turned to discerning new myths which, for him also, had to be validated by popular credence: the myths of France, of the Revolution, of the sorceress. Myth, religion, superstition then got confused if not fused, and superstition (which Maistre considered a high religious form and Nodier defined as the science of highest matters) was considered a popular expression of profound, valid perceptions. Mérimée's *Vénus d'Ille* (1837) is exemplary; the myth of Venus the man-slayer is placed in a contemporary setting linking pagan past and Christian present, and popular superstitions about the statue are largely, if ironically, validated. The superstitious and the fantastic acquire psychological and metaphysical meaning.

The domain of mythology was geographically extended by the 'oriental renaissance' – the term is Quinet's (1841). The renaissance began earlier; much of the scholarship was done in the eighteenth century and Cousin taught Hindu doctrine in his *Cours* of 1829. Discoveries of the riches of Sanskrit literature brought new proofs of the universality of myths and religion. The supremacy of the Graeco-Roman tradition was questioned, and the mythological heritage included more than the world of Olympus. Egypt and the Near East became not the cradle of civilisation, language and religion, but the place of an eclectic synthesis between Orient and Occident. The oriental renaissance also proposed a new spirituality, subordinating the human to a divine conceived as both the universe and the negation of the universe, and where the act of meditation became the act of faith, the 'inconscient' rather than consciousness the goal of asceticism; it blended quietism and Spinozism. Yet the reading given the Hindu texts varied considerably, pantheist for some, unitarian for others, even Christian. For poetry, the renaissance provided new sources of 'local colour' and new proof that figurative language, primitive and poetic, expressed the substantive relation between man and transcendent reality. And the oriental primitive was not a noble savage, but superior to Europeans in philosophy and literature.

That renaissance, primarily a philological venture, provided new material for Romanticism's favourite subject of study and meditation, the nature of language. Language theories generally fell into three contradictory schools: the neo-Lockean explanation of language as the product of sensation and convention, the neo-Cratylist schools for whom language by onomatopoeia, and so on, imitates (or should imitate) the essence of things, and the divine origin theories of the word as Logos, revealed to man, corrupted by the Fall, which it was the poet's task to restore. Many combined several of these theories, and all sought a renewed language, both richer and more transparent than the literary discourse of the neo-classicists. Even the neo-Lockean analysis insisted on the organic links between language and thought. Destutt de Tracy proposed to create a highly logical utopian language, linked language and progress, and called on poets to improve language rather than imitating earlier writers. But the *idéologue*'s stance, propitious as it was for Stendhal's precise, ironic prose, was on the whole spurned by poets. The new Cratylist theories were more fruitful for literature and even permeated official teaching. Nodier provided a humorous collection of examples, attributing great importance to metaphor as the means by which onomatopoeia had produced the complex languages of civilisation. Hugo followed suit, enriching poetry with puns and a renewal of assonance and rhyme as conveyors of meaning and not just decorative or mnemonic aids. The divine origin theories flourished, whether in the adaptations of Jacob Boehme proposed by Saint-Martin and Lamennais, or in Bonald's theory that God created society which then produced a language whose structures reflect the divine-willed organisation of society (and so bad grammar and bad politics go hand in hand; 'j'avions' betrays popular misconceptions about the structure of power). Ballanche and Saint-Martin insisted on the distinction between poetry and verse and demanded that the poet seek not the beautiful but the sublime. From this stance came the Saint-Simonian definition of the poet who, in the critical age, indicates what is wrong and laments chaos – Byron was cited as exemplary – and then in the organic age provides the new religion, the bond of faith which will allow a synthesis of science and enthusiastic adherence to society. Since society was now in transition between critical and organic epochs, the poet was to play both roles. Finally, so far as the divine origin theory postulated that God was manifest in both language and nature, it invited poetry to offer not a description but a contemplation of nature. 'A la matière même un verbe est attaché', Nerval proclaimed, and trees, flowers, lakes served as something more than emotion-creating scenery, acquired symbolic meaning.

Nerval was marked by many of these ideas. His significance lies as much in his representativity as in his exploration of the worlds of dream and madness. He is representative in both the way he presents the multiple beliefs of the period and the ambivalent attitude he takes toward them, which expresses itself by the ambiguous stance of his poetry. In a reading of his 'El Desdichado' (1853) Vadé suggests that the inheritance that poem's narrator has lost is the treasure of a cultural heritage collectively assumed which could have offered a sure reference, figures of identity. Nerval's sonnets about the relations between the self and the mythical – religious heritage are appropriately called *Les Chimères*, not 'les mythes'. Romanticism has a cult of *ressourcement* in history and myth but also presents them as crumbled, destroyed, trivialised. Nerval at times proposes the syncretism of all religious systems in one mythic structure of the malevolent Father God who kills his son, who is then resurrected by the Earth Mother goddess; at others, he opposes the gods of the North and those of the Orient, or Christianity and paganism, the latter kept dormant by the former's strength, or suggests that the skies are empty, God is dead. Even more central is his ambivalence about his 'figures of Beatrice'; sometimes the woman condemns, sometimes she is the pardoning Redemptrix. His beliefs are all *bifrons*, and his most positive statement of them, the 'Mémorables' of *Aurélia*, is extremely lyric, allusive, paratactic.

Nerval's mythological and religious syncretism resembles the philosophical Eclecticism of Victor Cousin, who also sought to combine systems previously considered contradictory: sensualism, sentimentalism, spiritualism, idealism, but whose quest for unity led to an archaeological study of the history of philosophy and finally to a lack of belief in anything except his own importance. It is possible to speak of Romantic mythologies, but not of a Romantic mythological system. Rather, the period saw a proliferation of varied mythic structures, some re-formulating old constructs, others inventing new ones from the material of recent science, history or politics, each structure having its proponents, its revisionists, its opponents.

UTOPIAN SOCIALISM

Nowhere are these contradictions more manifest than in the expressions of political hope on the part of those 'prophets of Paris' who abound under the Restoration and the July monarchy, often indebted to illuminism and much concerned with problems of religion. Socialist writing reflects many currents of Romantic thought, particularly the desire to encourage a full development of the individual by rendering society less oppressive (these socialists are quite anti-egalitarian), and many Romantic writers found their theories attractive.

Saint-Simon turned the triad of human faculties he found in Bichat (thought, action, feeling) into a triple categorisation of men: scientists, workers–industrialists, artists–priests. Economics came first; the administration of things should replace the governing of persons, and men will move from antagonism to association, the organic society. At first, faithful to Condorcet, he gave the scientists pre-eminence and suggested that the clergy should start studying science. Later, he made the scientists subservient to the class of action, hierarchically organised according to capacities and whose leaders would control the new industrial society. Aggression could then be directed toward conquering nature and increasing productivity. Artists at first play a largely decorative role, but Saint-Simon became increasingly concerned with the historical pattern of organic and critical periods, convinced that the time had come for a new synthesis, and aware that social conflict impeded the development of his industrial society. So in his last years he attributed ever greater importance to the sentient faculty. The artist–priests were to prepare the new organic world and cement it by evangelising the *nouveau christianisme* which in 1825 he proposed as essential to the unity of the new society.

His disciples, at least those who remained faithful to père Enfantin and participated in the picturesque community life at Ménilmontant, went much further, attempting to create the religious structures needed by the New Society, including paraliturgical banquets of social communion. The artist–priests were given an essential role in propaganda and in the educative process, seeking new sacraments where the Golden Rule could be transmitted to people of varying capacities. The association of the imaginative–sentient with women blossomed into demands for sexual equality, the liberation of women politically, socially, and from the bonds of marriage, the rehabilitation of the flesh, and finally the quest for the Female Messiah whose coming was to inaugurate the Kingdom. The Saint-Simonians thus rejoined the Faustian and Marian theme of woman as Co-Redemptrix. At the same time, in part by meditation on Lessing's *Education of the Human Race*, the history of humanity was seen as one of growth in and through religion. Saint-Simon's industrial vision was transformed into an organic one where the poet became priest, prophet and law-giver.

Charles Fourier stands in another tradition, that of the theory of harmonies. He cleverly wrote in the Land-of-Cockaygne utopian mode, promising satisfaction of desire in all its varieties, taking many of his examples from the appealing domains of gastronomy and sex. The father of vocational testing, he proclaimed that men are happier and more productive when doing what they want to do and are gifted for, and that those desires or attractions vary according to a dosage of psychological traits or passions where his system of thirteen categories and a scale of eight is at least more complex than that of Saint-Simon. His dream of a better world depends rather on the proposal that attractions are proportionate to destinies, that there are as many young who want to play with filth as there are refuse-bins to be cleaned; if matters were properly ordered, all would operate in a harmonious manner. He claimed to derive this insight from Newton's discoveries, but the hypothesis is also an application of the illuminist tenet of the essential albeit presently lost harmony of all Creation. Vertical correspondences were also dear to Fourier who provides a rich emblematic reading of nature. He offers a scathing criticism of the institutions of contemporary society along with a utopian model, not in fictive form but in appealing bits and pieces of vision. The illuminist gradual spiritualisation of man and matter by initiation and expiation is replaced by the establishment of satellite phalansteries which would leap into perfection. With that change in man would come the change of matter, the ocean not so much spiritualised as becoming a very pleasant-tasting lemonade. Fourier was sarcastic, comic, impatient, and it is hard to know how to read him; did Nero's misdoings really stem from the fact that he would not become the useful hunter–butcher whose attraction to blood could have been proportionate to the destinies of animals waiting to be slaughtered and gourmets eager to eat them? In any case, he made the illuminist transcendent very immanent and material.

His disciples never went to the lengths of the Saint-Simonians in creating a religion, but they did 'christianise' Fourier's message, in part to propagandise but also because of a quest for the charismatic and for syncretism. They established that Fourier's message completed that of Jesus, and also, by a process of translation where correspondences played a major role, synthesised Fourier with Catholicism, with Saint-Martin, with Hahnemann. Homeopathic medicine was surely one of the most beautiful statements of the Romantic theme that out of evil, properly administered and dealt with, good will come, and Fourier had said as much in talking about Nero – as Balzac did with Véronique, in *Le Curé de village* (1838), the adulteress accomplice in murder who transforms her village into a model community. She did so in expiation, which is absent from Fourier's world, except in the joyous satire of the Counter-Crusaders who bomb Constantinople with champagne corks and then clean its sewers.

Minor authors present similar evolutions. Alphonse-Louis Constant, like Lamennais, began as a good Catholic. If he later became famous as

Éliphas Lévi, the expositor of esotericism, it was only after a socialist phase centred on the cult of the woman as Redemptrix, as a figure of the Virgin. His *Mère de Dieu* (1844) is a prose epic about the history of mankind and the healing and progress-making function of women therein, combined with violent attacks against the rich. The epic ends with a beatific vision of universal peace. He also published a *Bible de la liberté* (1840) where, like his friend Esquiros and his enemy Cabet, he proved that Jesus was a communist, and a poem 'Les Correspondances' (1845) in which some have seen a source for Baudelaire.

Alphonse Esquiros is perhaps the most extreme of these socialist 'petits romantiques'. His political ideas touch on the problems of religion and madness both. The masses are the Messiah incarnate and the saving force of history which will bring about the Kingdom – but only by suffering as Jesus did on Golgotha and as the messianic people–France had done at Waterloo, its Golgotha. More suffering lies ahead, and Esquiros derives from his christological referent a justification for revolutionary violence. To this he adds the theme of 'Christus insanit'; if Jesus were to return today, he would be treated as mad, and the insane are messianic figures in their revolt against things as they are. Esquiros was also a feminist, and saw in Mary's role in the Incarnation and in her Assumption figures of the instrumental function woman must play in the revolutionary process and of her eventual glorification. His predilection, however, was for the Madeleines, the prostitutes whose love and suffering are active agents of redemption–revolution.

Many other socialist utopians merit attention: Joseph Buchez, the most avowedly Catholic; Pierre Leroux, perhaps the most metaphysical, who greatly influenced George Sand and whose aesthetic theories are discussed below; Théodore Dézamy, the most radical; Flora Tristan with her dream of a workers' union and her plural 'dieux', the most picturesque of the many women socialist writers of the period. Their debt to illuminism and concern with religion reflect a quest for the charismatic but also the traits of the tradition here studied. Others, such as Cabet or Proudhon, owed little to that tradition or indeed rejected it.

If one compares the utopianism of Balzac's *Curé de village* with Clarens in Rousseau's *Nouvelle Héloïse*, several differences are apparent. The utopian drive in Balzac stems from a desire to overcome an evil which is sensed as personal disruption and figured as crime or disorder. That drive is justified in religious terms, the redemption of man and of matter, of all Creation, and even takes religious forms. Yet, this utopian activity is embedded in technological projects: road building, irrigation. Utopian socialism was of course not the only school of political thought of the time, but more than the *doctrinaires* or the liberals, the utopians reflect this triple concern with practical matters, with the moral problem of putting an end to strife and creating harmony, and with the transcendent. That they should have veered toward religious language and forms is less to be explained by Marxist analysis (they lacked the conceptual instruments necessary to appreciate the realities of the industrial revolution) than by this quest for fraternal unity among men, and harmony between man and creation. Their theories stem from the utopian tradition as it was re-shaped, on the one hand by the Enlightenment, the 'Condorcet' concept of progress, on the other by illuminism, the 'Restif de la Bretonne' utopianism. In the 1830s and 1840s, the industrial revolution created an audience for socialist thought, but enriched rather than contradicted their vision. Class was also perceived in a rather different way. Siéyès had declared that the Third Estate was the whole of the nation, and bourgeois (and poets) thought of themselves as embracing that whole. The bourgeoisie dreamed of being the *totum* of humanity including the *peuple* who supposedly shared its aspirations and values; any sign that this was not so was dismissed as a symptom of criminality. The poet (or socialist prophet) could both speak for and teach the people so far as they were potential bourgeois, and the two fought side by side in 1830. Stendhal's Julien Sorel suggested, in his speech to the jury which condemned him, that things were not that simple; but even Stendhal had to 'criminalise' his revolt, make Julien shoot Mme de Rênal. The dream of a bourgeoisie allied with and speaking for the working class only disappears in June 1848. Thus these utopian projects are for 'humanity', not for the *peuple*, and Balzac's *Curé* starts with a love-affair between a bourgeois and a worker. The dream of unity – cosmic and political – still seemed possible.

THE PHILOSOPHICAL EPIC

This dream was not only expressed in political writings; its major literary home was the epic. Romanticism's contribution to the literary heritage was undoubtedly made in prose fiction, the lyric, and the theatre, but many continued to consider the epic the highest literary form, devoted their major energies to it. At least one such epic, Lamartine's *Jocelyn* (1836), knew considerable popularity. The Romantic epic differs rather markedly from the Homer–Virgil tradition. It owes something to the long religious or scientific poems of the Renaissance and the late eighteenth century, something to Milton,

Goethe, and Klopstock, a great deal to the cult of history, even more to
the redefinition of the poet as seer. It is highly didactic and philosophical, and often describes the whole course of history (Hugo's *La
Légende des siècles*, 1859–83), or the events of the antediluvian age, of the
end of time (Grainville's remarkable *Dernier homme* (1805) initiated the
fashion), or even of the post-apocalyptic age. Alexandrine couplets
predominate, but the form is often varied to indicate moments of
rhapsody or intensity, and the epic may be written in prose or even
assume the form of drama. It is not always easy to distinguish between
these epics and such works as Michelet's *La Sorcière* (1862), except in
terms of authorial voice which in the epic is usually non-existent or
relegated to the role of witness. *Jocelyn* is an exception; it has a narrative,
placed in contemporary France, a story of thwarted love and imposed
religious vocation, but which serves to express a neo-Mennaisian
version of Catholicism and a progressive theory of history. The final
vision of the poem is androgynous, the hero is united with his beloved in
a quite Swedenborgian heaven. Lamartine's other epic, *La Chute d'une ange*
(1838) is more remarkable in its tale of the tragic tribulations of Cédar, a
fallen angel who is also a Tarzan type, and his beloved Daïdha. They
encounter an old prophet who recites to them a 'fragment du Livre
primitif', a Bible-within-an-epic full of theosophic wisdom. The
prophet's message later inspires the people to revolt against their
tyrannical, sadistic masters. This revolution is among the epic's most
remarkable passages. If Lamartine is guilty of a predilection for scenes of
concupiscence and cruelty, he also, like Hugo, has a sense of what
constitutes a popular myth. *La Chute* would make an excellent Cecil B.
De Mille pornographic film with a leftist message.

Vigny called his epic 'Eloa' (1824) a *mystère*; an angel born of Christ's
tear tries to save Lucifer but instead, because of concupiscent love, joins
him in hell. Other philosophical epics merit resurrection: Ludovic de
Cailleux's *Monde antédiluvien* (1845); Laprade's syncretist *Psyché* (1841);
Ménard's *Prométhée délivré* (1844); Reboul's *Le Dernier Jour* (1839). 'The
epic is a synthesis', declared A.-L. Constant, a synthesis of narrative,
history and religion aiming at a total statement. Quinet was the most
ambitious with *Merlin l'enchanteur* (1860), a noble effort to combine all
legends into one. That statement is always heterodox; Soumet thought
he was a good Catholic, but his *Divine Épopée* (1841) is universalist. The
philosophy and religion offered is syncretist, often owes much to gnostic
emanationism. Sometimes the epic renews pre-existing myths; at others,
it gives history, including biblical history, mythical status. In a sense
Michelet's *Histoire de France* and Balzac's *Comédie humaine* are spill-overs

from the epic endeavour. The Romantics were perhaps less good at reinterpreting the symbols of the past than at creating new symbols from history, but they did both, and managed to do so because they quested for meaning, rather than possessing it. That these epics seem illegible today is perhaps to be explained by the fact that we no longer seek that totality of meaning.

THE MEANING AND DEFINITION OF MYTH

What was the Romantic concept of myth? The period on the whole remained within the Platonic tradition of seeing myth both as a means of apprehending a truth that reason alone could not grasp and as a presentation of that truth which supplements logical discourse, either because a story is more pleasant and effective than an argument, or because the truth in question is somewhat an object of faith rather than of rigorous demonstration. After that, they offer a considerable variety of theories about myth which often becomes confused with fable or symbol. Vico's interpretation of myths as figures of the primitive age, the profound symbols of a society, is widely accepted; Euhemerism survives in some quarters; Court de Gébelin popularised an agricultural interpretation. Dupuis and Volney insisted myths were allegories of nature and particularly of the solar cycle. For Saint-Martin and the illuminists, myths embody those truths which are most important to man, express the hidden doxa. Traditionalism imports this illuminist view into religious orthodoxy; myth becomes the vehicle of the universal revelation and embodies an absolute truth, but a hermeneutics is necessary in order to uncover that truth in myth's disfigurations. Pierre Leroux, in his theory that poetry, including myth, is an emblematic representation, a symbol of the universal transcendent analogy, rejoins that tradition, as does the Creuzer–Guigniaut school. Creuzer posited a unity between the soul of man and nature, where nature was articulated by man through the symbol, defined as the primitive form of human intelligence, the idea rendered both personal and palpable. The myth, by a tale or *récit*, explains and illustrates the symbol. Egypt is the motherland of symbols, Greece of myths, leading to the creation of the mysteries with their initiations and symbolic rites. Myths and legends are the products of the collective soul of humanity, and express a collective truth. Creuzer however insisted on the variety and multiplicity of mythic systems, as opposed to the syncretism of the naturalists and the traditionalists; part of Nerval's problem was his inability to opt between Creuzer and traditionalism. More influential was Victor

Cousin's neo-Hegelian distinction between the non-symbolic truths of philosophy and the symbolic truths of religious (including mythic) systems, with the proposition that man progresses from mythic to philosophical language. Cousin's position again demanded a hermeneutics of mythic and religious traditions. These theories prevailed until the 1840s, when Ottfried Müller, Max Muller and Alfred Maury deprived myth of its transcendental meaning and broke with the Platonic tradition.

A mythic statement in the strict sense then requires some reference to a narrative code (*récit*) which may be historical (Napoleon) or traditional (Orpheus) which the text re-presents, both keeping parts of that code and offering new significances. Simple paraphrases of the Gospel, as poets such as Alletz and Turquéty practised, are not mythical; rephrasings which pose a new significance, such as Vigny's 'Le Mont des oliviers' (1843) are. Myth requires a hermeneutic analysis because it proposes a polyvalence of significance. Finally, because myth so defined is a narrative code it has a syntax as well as a semantics; indeed, the Romantics specialised in playing with the syntactic endings of myths (the wandering Jew stops wandering, Christ gets re-crucified, Satan saved) as much as with their semantics (Christ as a member of the working class, Satan as the giver of light). Perhaps for this reason Romantic versions of myth tend to centre on the crisis events, the crucial moment in the syntax.

Myth should be distinguished from certain figurations, however important they may be, which are thematic and do not have a traditional *récit* to embody them nor, then, a syntax: the city of Paris, the 'new city', the prison, the masses, women, though each of these themes was important. Perhaps the most peculiar of them was that of cosmogony and the transmigration of souls. Jean Reynaud gave this notion its most thorough treatment, but it is widespread from Maistre and Fourier (with his copulating planets) to Hugo. Fourier's literally insane disciple, Victor Hennequin, colonised the copulating planets with metaphysically significant individuals. The theories of transmigration allowed progress to be spatially located in an unknowable elsewhere and thus reconciled with the incomprehensible nature of God and history. Transmigration was a consoling source of hope, and became even more widespread after the failure of 1848.

In discussing Romantic myths, certain absences should be noted. The clown–pierrot, so important at the end of the century, rarely appears, probably because the divorce between writer and public, despite the desire to 'épater le bourgeois', had not yet been effected. Oedipus' incestuous relations with Jocasta are of little concern; the Romantics are instead interested in Oedipus and the Sphinx – incest was widespread in literature if not in life, and metaphysical questions mattered more than perturbations within the nuclear family. The Æneid is largely absent; Virgil is primarily the author of a passage from the *Fourth Eclogue*. The appeal to Rome of the Revolution of 1789 became muted, replaced with appeals to the Orient, to Greece, to 'nos ancêtres les Gaulois'.

SOME REPRESENTATIVE MYTHS

All the Romantic myths, for want of space, cannot be examined here; an evocation of Orpheus, the androgyne, Prometheus and his figures Cain and Job, of Napoleon, Ahasverus, Satan and Jesus will have to suffice to suggest the major themes and the mechanisms of mythic recreation.

Evocations of Orpheus were widespread, yet only one major work was specifically devoted to him, Ballanche's *Orphée* (1827), and it presents a rather original, truncated version of the myth. Elsewhere – the fact is perhaps to be explained by the myth's diffuse nature – Orpheus serves as a cautionary allusion, or as a structuring principle. Creuzer proposed that there were two Orpheus, the one Apollonian, the other Dionysiac, and Juden has shown the rich and complex heritage the Romantics faced, from antiquity and the Renaissance. Orpheus had come to stand for almost anything connected with the arts, the occult, initiation and the descent into hell, and the transcendent powers of literature and music. All these are reinvigorated, and H. Riffaterre, noting how widespread they were, defines Orphism not as a body of theories and doctrines but as a poetic effort and effect which seeks to perceive the invisible in the visible, or at least to suggest that such perception is possible. The myth of Orpheus is the link between esoteric philosophy and the poetic mimesis of that philosophy. But, before examining that function where the idea of the symbol is central, several emphases should be noted. Orpheus becomes a symbol of the agents (and means) by which humanity progresses. For Ballanche, he is a civiliser who offers not an individual but a social initiation, the successor of Prometheus and Job who also demonstrated the links between wisdom and suffering, and the precursor of Jesus in that Orpheus showed how the initiated kill the initiator and how progress can only be known through suffering which alone can reconcile man's fallen state with his hope of redemption. Ballanche suppresses the visit to hell as a means of knowing life beyond the tomb; that other life becomes located in the future of history. In his epic Eurydice is the saving woman who leads man to the way of redemption by uniting human will or Destiny with divine will or Providence. Following Ballanche's lead, Fourier, Leroux, the Saint-Simonians evoke Orpheus in their schemes for creating progress. Orpheus symbolises how that can be done by a reunion of love, art, suffering–initiation, and a perception of the transcendent. Finally, Orpheus is he who descended into hell, knew the initiation, had crossed the Acheron and returned; *figura christi*, he validated the initiation theme.

However, perceptions of the transcendent are always problematic. Surely part of Ballanche's art – and that of many expositors of the esoteric – lies in leading the reader to feel that he is about to make some great discovery, even if he never does. The Romantics were aware of the inevitable inadequacy of any representation of the transcendent, and explained it by their definition of the symbol. Orpheus, as the archetype of the poet, casts that poet in the role of seer, possessing an esoteric knowledge which he communicates to humanity; this he does by recourse to the symbol which expresses a rich, emblematic meaning as opposed to two-dimensional allegory. The symbol is first the sensible form which gives an idea an exterior manifestation, created by the imaginative faculty – thus Lamennais. Jouffroy proposed that 'everything we perceive is symbolic because everything we perceive excites in us the idea of some other thing we do not perceive'. Leroux thought the privilege of art resided in its capacity to express the harmonious vibrations hidden in the unity of life stemming from the domains of sound, movement, colour; when their 'accord' is expressed, the result is the symbol. Music and painting can create the symbol, just as well as poetry, and all symbols are imperfect expressions of the hidden relations. These definitions presuppose a belief in the system of harmonies and a microcosm/macrocosm relation between idea and expression. Writers are creators of symbols of a transcendent which, like God, cannot be beheld face to face but only by the symbols of art. The most successful works in the Orphic tradition tend to emphasise music rather than poetry as the effective symbolic language. This is true of Sand's *Consuelo*, rich in themes of initiation, esoteric societies, utopian socialism, the woman as intercessor, as it is of her other major Orphic effort, *Les Sept Cordes de la lyre* (1838), the closest thing to Goethe's *Faust* that French Romanticism produced. That philosophical drama presents a compendium of the themes of Romantic mysticism, and a telling portrait of contemporary society, but the lyre is terribly allegorical – each of its seven strings has its meaning. As Mephistopheles says, 'tout est symbole' in the intellectual as well as the material order, the two obey analogous laws and produce analogous phenomena, but the eventual product is rather trite.

A myth could be defined as a treatment of the symbol, as the Romantics understood it, in which that symbol is first personified or concretised, and then set in dramatic conflict with other symbols. It is probably by doing this, while at the same time accepting Cratylist notions of language and paying heed to the value of deriving symbols from concrete reality as well as using previously elaborated ones, that Hugo succeeded where others did not. The failure to give the cult of Orpheus concrete content is disquieting, and H. Riffaterre appositely quotes, at the end of her study, Lamartine's 'Ô Mystère . . . sois donc ma foi . . . / Plus l'objet est divin, plus l'image est obscure'. Orpheus then returns from hell not only without Eurydice, but with an empty bag of tricks. Orpheus (as opposed to Orphism) was perhaps neglected also for another reason; Orpheus gave the poet a very demanding role to play, and most of the Romantics (but not Hugo) had the humility to shed off part of that role on the *peuple*, or history, or religion, or music.

The myth of the androgyne in nineteenth-century France has been analysed by A.J.L. Busst. A long mystical tradition insists on the hermaphroditic nature of God and of the first man, Adam Kadmus. Blended with the Platonic theme of erotic and particularly pederastic love as a means of attaining the ideal, with speculations on the wound of Christ's side as parallel to that of Adam (producing not Eve but his Spouse the Church), the heritage of the androgyne myth presents a peculiar mixture of teratology and aspiration for unity. In nineteenth-century France, it changes significance. In the first half of the century, it served theories of progress; in the second, it became a decadent myth, associated with homosexuality, onanism, and sado-masochism. The turning points are Gautier's *Mademoiselle de Maupin* (1835), where transvestism is lubricious *marivaudage*, and Balzac's *Comédie humaine*. The androgynous Seraphitus–Seraphita (1834) represents the achievement of transcendent unity via love. Balzac's other works, such as *La Fille aux yeux d'or* (1833), turn the androgynous myth toward themes of sexual perversion. The grand advocates of positive androgynism are, once again, the socialists for whom the androgynous nature of God and of future humanity symbolises the restoration of lost unity. Busst gives due attention to the Saint-Simonian quest of the female Messiah, to the Evadism of the Mapah Ganneau and to Tourreil's fusionist definition of God as the 'MerAmourPère', but properly emphasises Ballanche's use of the hermaphrodite as a social symbol. Since the sexual division of man, according to Ballanche, two principles have been at work in history, the volitive or passive and the initiatory or active. The distinction is sexual, cultural and social, and progress will reunite active and passive, male and female, Will and Destiny in an androgynous being. With A.-L. Constant, Flora Tristan, the Saint-Simonians, the myth of the androgyne proposes the possibility of rehabilitating matter, of reuniting spiritual and material, self and non-self; for Leroux, charity will create androgyny, and eventually the union of subject and object, man and God. The cult of the female Messiah, the hope that in the Kingdom there will be *neque vir neque femina sed vir ut femina*, reflect a belief in human solidarity and in a progress seen as a return to edenic origins. When these beliefs disappeared, the hermaphrodite became a symbol of decadence and left Chenavard's sketches for the Panthéon to head toward the pornography shops of Soho.

Prometheus tended to be a subsidiary figure to Jesus and Satan; Prometheus is the bringer of light to humanity (Lucifer) who suffered for having done so (Jesus). That light was a symbol of more than fire for cooking meat. Quinet devoted an epic to him in which, as the prophet of the Logos in Ancient Greece, he is freed not by Hercules but by the archangels Michael and Raphael. For Ballanche, he is the figure of man constantly called on to conquer the laws of necessity, to seek perfection in spite of destiny. Michelet in the same vein asserts that each man is his own Prometheus. In his *Bible de l'humanité* (1864), Prometheus is identified as liberty, the child of justice, as opposed to the injustice of Heaven. Hugo associated Prometheus and Eve, the bearers of gifts of fire and knowledge to man. He is also associated with Job and Cain, the victims of divine injustice who complain about God defined as the symbol of evil fate; Černy has analysed the importance of these figures of titanism in Romanticism. Cain also serves, particularly for Nerval, as the image of the double, the brother–enemy, though Nerval's sympathies, and those of most Romantics, were with Cain rather than Abel; Cain's race are those who struggle to transform matter and man, the alchemist–masons who build a better world. Job often serves as a figure of the Christ who doubts, develops the 'My God, why hast thou forsaken me?' theme.

The myth of Napoleon transposed, in a way which could justify Euhemerus, the events of Bonaparte's career into the domain of the legendary and the universally significant, but its meaning again varies – according to dates or political viewpoint. Balzac always remained an admirer, and a propagator of the legend; Stendhal, however much his heroes worshipped Napoleon, was ambivalent, criticising the Emperor who restored Church and nobility while admiring the general who brought revolution to Italy. Hugo changed, anti Napoleon, then pro, then only pro so far as he could use the myth to attack Napoléon-le-Petit. Napoleon himself had a major hand in creating the myth, a political rags-to-riches story explained by intelligence, energy and will, and the painter David, along with others, propagated it. Géricault was perhaps closer to the heart of its meaning in emphasising the energy of the Napoleonic epic. For the major thrust of the myth was the cult of wilful energy; that is what Julien Sorel admired in Napoleon, and Maine de Biran shared with him. That cult involved two secondary components, one the solitude and suffering of the energetic man of destiny, poignantly evoked by Vigny in his *Servitude et grandeur militaires* (1835), and in his 'Moïse' (1823), a thinly disguised portrait of the sufferings of both Napoleon and Vigny. The other was the sense of being born too late for the epic of energy, expressed by Musset in his *Confession d'un enfant du siècle*. The Napoleonic myth thus becomes tragic; the imprisonment on Saint Helena (Prometheus on his rock), the death in 1821, imposed that reading as one of a rise and fall of the mighty, a cult of energy and heroism but also a comment on their vanity. The political variations follow expected lines. Napoleon is viewed as an ogre both on the right (Chateaubriand) and the left (Proudhon), as a hero by those who favour order (Balzac) and those who place their hopes in a messianic liberation (Mickiewicz, Esquiros). Less expected is the extremism of this last group who turn Napoleon into a Christ figure, crucified at Waterloo/Golgotha; what began as a refutation of Dupuis's interpretation of Jesus as a solar myth (Napoleon too rose in the east and set in the west, the twelve apostle-marshals are the twelve signs of the zodiac, etc.) was given serious expression. The myth of Napoleon as liberator was encouraged by Las Cases's *Mémorial de Sainte-Hélène* (1822), but the alacrity with which certain extremists of the left embroidered the theme might seem to justify the association between socialism and fascist messianism, were it not that their emphasis was on the suffering Napoleon had known, and not, for instance, on Napoleon as he who institutionalised Jacobin centralism. If the propagation of the myth is the work of painters, poets, novelists, even historians (Quinet's epic *Napoléon* (1836) is perhaps its most complex expression), they often placed the myth in various *voces populi*. Géricault painted not Napoleon, but his soldiers. The poet Béranger's peasant grandmother sang of his exploits, his simplicity, his immortality, and Balzac's Goguelat in *Le Médecin de campagne* (1833) rehearsed the same themes. With the Napoleonic myth the cult of the hero and his will to power becomes the cult of the people and the drive to democracy; Emerson synthesised the two. Barbéris has suggested that the myth gave those whom the Restoration had deprived of power a grasp on history, but also betrayed the fact that the masses were not yet capable of being the agents of history; the myth was popular because it was a substitute for an impossible revolutionary praxis. It was indeed often the vehicle by which to express exacerbated desire and despair, but Barbéris perhaps neglects its function of offering hope for realising the Revolution despite perversion and defeat.

To speak of a French Romantic myth of the Wandering Jew (as opposed to England, where Shelley assured its success) may seem presumptuous for, aside from numerous adaptations of Schubert's rhapsody, only two major works treat the theme; the Ahasverus corpus is nowhere as rich as that on Orpheus or Napoleon. Yet no other myth better helped surmount the polarities of hope and despair by proposing a politically-oriented *immer streben*. First presented in France by Nerval in 1831, Schubert's is a violent text of despair and yet of pietistic faith, which stresses the eternity of the Jew's wanderings as a sign of the meaninglessness of history. Ahasverus, in a titanic revolt, tries, but in vain, to commit suicide. Ahasverus will remain the victim of the injustice of God as known in history. Quinet's epic (1833) substitutes, for the eternal damnation because of sin the legend proposed, a progressive theory of history. The poem begins with the Creation and the Flood, then the universal desire for the unity of God, then the birth of Jesus who rejects the Kings of Orient in favour of the gifts of the humble shepherds. Then comes the Crucifixion, Ahasverus's refusal to aid Christ, and his punishment. He lives through the various stages of history; in the Middle Ages he encounters the two female forces, Mob, the symbol of death, and Rachel, the symbol of pity who is also condemned to live through all history because during the Passion she chose to pity Ahasverus rather than Jesus. She falls in love with Ahasverus. Their marriage is a kind of *Walpurgisnacht* with a dance of the dead who deny Christ, who then appears. Rachel joins Ahasverus in his wanderings. At the Last Judgment, where the elect are chosen largely in terms of their promise of democracy, Christ tells Ahasverus that he need no longer 'marche, marche' but is to 'monte, monte', becoming a symbol and agent of progress. Harmony reigns, he and Rachel become the androgynously united symbol of the marriage of heaven and earth. The apotheosis is followed by an epilogue; God and Mary are dead, Christ too would like to die, but Eternity informs him he must imitate the fate of the Wandering Jew and history begins anew. Quinet's *Ahasvérus* might be termed the greatest failure of French

Romanticism. Hardly readable, it presents a synthesis of history, of moral philosophy, of doubt and hope, of suffering and redemption.

Quinet thus turned Ahasverus into a leftist myth, which Sue vulgarised in his *Juif errant* (1844), set in the world of crime of contemporary Paris. Ahasverus, who strives to do good but brings cholera wherever he goes, is consoled by Hérodiade, the figure of the ever-suffering woman. Most of the novel describes the sufferings of the working class and propagandises for socialism; such combinations of realism and supernaturalism are common at the time. Ahasverus reappears in several texts by A.-L. Constant; he is the symbol of the poor worker in whom the Christians continue to crucify Christ, but thanks to the intercession of Mary in his favour, the Kingdom of liberty and love will come. Other authors continue to see in him the figure of the punishment of the Jews, etc., but Quinet and Sue, each on his own level, turn him into a symbol of humanity's progress, and both use the myth to that end because Ahasverus demonstrates that progress is not easy.

Perhaps the Romantics speak little of the Resurrection of Jesus because they substituted for it meditations on apocatastasis, that is, the universal redemption not only of humanity but of the fallen angels as well, especially Satan, restored to his position as Lucifer, the bearer of light. Satan's significances are multiple and varied, even contradictory, as he moves between the poles, sublime and grotesque, oppressor of humanity or symbol of oppressed humanity. The variations are in part historical; the century opens with a rather superficial use of the diabolic fantastic, often comic, but already with Nodier that fantastic is preoccupied with evil, destruction, imperfection. Byron gave Satan metaphysical status as the absolute of negation, accusing the inequities of existence and creation, adding seriousness to the irony of Goethe's Mephistopheles. As Romanticism moved from optimism toward a sense of despair and the awareness of the power of evil, the figure of Satan – and figures of Satan – acquired new power, but even that power is tempered by the wry comedy of the *roman noir*, by the voluptuousness associated with Satan, by the conviction that Satan, the outlaw hero – the 'maudits' – proffer just complaints about the social order or man's fate. Satan then rejoins Cain; the criminal is admired without justifying the crime, the causes of revolt without much concern about its consequences. After 1830, matters change, and for a time at least Satan, if he is admired, must also be saved; the Satanic Byron had died for the noble and Christian cause of Greece, and Satan becomes Lucifer, associated with Prometheus, punished – unjustly, but necessarily – for having brought light to humanity, whose revolt and the evil it produced can be integrated in the economy of humanity's salvation. Only revolt could give birth to liberty and matter, without darkness light could never be manifested, and so in the logic of history Lucifer should be rewarded; when finally love prevails, Satan too, as an instrument of progress, should be saved. Prior to Hugo's *Fin de Satan* the major expression of this theme, rehearsed by Vigny and satirised by Gautier, came from the Catholic Alexandre Soumet, whose *Divine Épopée* (1841) takes place after the end of earthly time. Soumet replaces Lucifer, who becomes an advocate of the love of God, with Idaméel, a human who tried to keep the race going on earth and, subsequently, the revolt going in hell. In the epic's double ending, Christ undergoes a second Passion which Idaméel tries to reject, but Semida, the loving and pardoning female, prevails and all ends with universal salvation. Milner suggests that the fixed, caricatural iconography of the devil kept the imagination in check; no one took the long-eared, tailed figure too seriously despite the efforts to rehabilitate him by these analogies with Byron, Cain, Prometheus. The following generation of poets – particularly Baudelaire – had to give him another meaning.

It is more difficult to speak of a Romantic myth of Jesus. The literature – theological, devotional, historical, political – is immense; Jesus also appears in poems, novels, even plays. Every possible position is expressed – even some that had not been recently heard, thanks to a renewed familiarity with the Church Fathers and early heresies, especially Gnostic. However, the figure of Jesus changed between 1789 and 1848. In the literature of 1789 references to him are sporadic, and mostly limited to anticlerical evocations of the 'sans-culotte' of Nazareth who chased the money-changers from the temple. In 1848, Jesus is frequently cited, as the friend of the poor, an advocate of communism who, by his example, justified the use of revolutionary violence; and the clergy sprinkled holy water on the newly planted trees of liberty. In short, Romanticism saw the rise of the socialist Gospel. How, when and why is complicated, but several trends are clear. The period neglects the *didache* of the Gospels to concentrate on the Passion. Certain texts are endlessly debated ('Render unto Caesar', 'My Kingdom is not of this world') or reinterpreted in a socialist vein ('Sell all you have and give it to the poor'). There is a predilection for Mary Magdalene and for Lazarus, but on the whole, among believers and non-believers, it is the drama of the Passion which counts. Even the Virgin is primarily the *mater dolorosa*. The suffering Jesus is seen as a figure and validation of the prophet–poet who proclaims the truth, is despised and rejected for having done so, but whose sufferings constitute the seal which guarantees that his message will prevail. The same mechanism is extended to the masses who become *figurae christi* as both sufferers and *voces dei*. Then, the myth is enriched by the emanationist notion that the Logos Jesus incarnates is present in man, indeed throughout the chain of being. This panentheism coupled with mystical versions of the doctrine of progress, leads to the theory that the Logos is contained in history which is seen as essentially a spiritualisation of all Creation and restoration of the lost unity. Here Hegelian thought joins forces with the old illuminist tradition. However, once the Logos is contained within history, God himself becomes historical – which indeed the study of the history of religions had already made the case. For some, God was already dead – the Richter theme; for others, he was dying or at least changing, but the dying of God gave new life to the Jesus of history as the exemplary myth of man's conduct and destiny. The Trinity is endlessly redefined, by Lamennais, Leroux, the Saint-Simonians, and such Catholics as Blanc Saint-Bonnet. These redefinitions move toward a dialectic; indeed, the fundamental significance of Christ for the Romantics is that out of suffering will come redemption – but the redemption is located in history. Socialist appeals to the Gospel at times quote to propagandise, at others centre on the theme of suffering in fraternal love as a utopia-creating mechanism. French reactions to Strauss's life of Jesus are symptomatic. Some try to refute him with the old apologetic arsenal, but others, Quinet in the lead, insist that Strauss's thesis is beside the point, that Jesus's being lies in his present significance for mankind's struggle for salvation here below.

THE SYNTHESIS OF VICTOR HUGO

The author most fully representative of this congeries of suppositions, myths and convictions (though he did not agree with all of them) was surely Hugo, who also, more than anyone else, developed a new writing appropriate to them. He is the Dickens and the Blake of French Romanticism, and its Goethe as well. It would take a lengthy book to do him justice, but it has been written, Albouy's *La Création mythologique chez Victor Hugo*; I can here only suggest its riches. Nor can I deal with the 'chronological' problem Hugo presents. He was indeed the 'écho sonore', who kept or perhaps found the Romantic faith in exile, after 1848, and only then explicitly expounded it. But recent criticism emphasises the early development of many of his themes and images; his main evolution consists in turning the psychological into the mythical.

Hugo justifies his theory of progress by a theory of creation in which evil is not autonomous. Creation, which emanates from the divine, is already an imperfection which gives rise to the imperfection of action, defined as evil; evil creates ponderable matter. From there, Hugo accepts the 'chain of being' theory, associating heaviness, immobility, lack of soul with evil. Evil is a necessary component of created being, not the result of a guilty free choice, and out of that evil good will come as Creation strives toward its future, moving from fatalism and immobility toward liberty and charity, ending with a victorious universal salvation prefigured by the redemption of the criminal, etc. Good germinates in the thorns of evil, and the germination is often violent; Calvary required Judas.

The theory achieved poetic expression thanks to a complex mythic structure. Man is the microcosm, both beast and angel, of the dialectic drama of Creation, and Hugo himself the 'representative man'. The Titans, Cain, Prometheus, Job are paralleled by creations of his own (Quasimodo, Gwynplaine) who embody the coinherence of good and evil, sublime and grotesque. Jesus and Satan figure the drama of redemption by suffering, as does Jean Valjean. The whole of nature is involved in a process of universal manducation, where roots are emblems of devouring terror, mountains of genius and liberty. The hydra-ocean, constantly attacking the earth, is the symbol of aggressive violence, eventually to be harnessed by Fulton, by the 'machine maréemotrice', by its own desire for reconciliation with God. Astronomical poetry, before Hugo, was widespread but dully descriptive; thanks in part to Fourier and Jean Reynaud as well as Flammarion, in part to his own anthropomorphising imagination, Hugo created a new genre, charged with energy and meaning, where the struggles of history are worked out in transmigrating solidarity throughout the cosmos. His imagination blends the gigantic and the concrete.

His mythology varies in certain ways from the major Romantic mode, in part because he never abandons the ambiguities of his thought, never suppresses his complexities. He often treats Greek mythology in a comic vein. Nature is less a forest of symbols than one of apparitions with which man struggles. It is the object of contemplation, not, as with Lamartine, of meditation. Hugo's at times guiltful priapism produces the monstrous earth-mother Geo. He refuses Maistre's executioner, while accepting expiation. His mythology is more marked by tension, less by idealisation, than the systems of his contemporaries, which helps explain his attitude toward the *peuple*, a dangerous, destructive force in which hopes for the future are invested. God is both the inaccessible numinous, incomprehensible and yet near, and He whose Eye is powerful and terrible. God intervenes in, indeed espouses history, to punish and reward, and usually acts the way Hugo would want him to act, but Titan man may also try to pierce the veils which hide God, to shatter his Eye, to kill God in the quest for freedom. This God is perhaps Hugo's greatest antithetic concept, and yet his antitheses only reflect the paradoxical complexities of the Romantic attitude toward religion. A sonorous echo of Fourier, of Saint-Simon as well as of illuminism, of Lamartine and Soumet, Hugo offers a highly original amalgamation and expression of ideas, theories and images proposed and discussed by his contemporaries. The expression is characterised by a combination of realism and fantasy where the mythic imagination governs not only narration but also the stylistic figures of personification and comparison. The metaphor expresses the mythic potential of reality and history; indeed, with the metaphor maxima and the recourse to metamorphosis, the two become identified. Hugo not only created a mythology, he believed in it, and symbols and metaphors express his intuitive comprehension of man's fate; a new way of thinking is also a new way of writing. He went furthest, of the Romantics, along the path of mythopoesis.

DOUBT AND HOPE

The venerable image of the poet as bird would seem quite appropriate to the Romantic venture; both sing, fly into the ether, console and inspire. But the image, when it occurs, is duplicitous. From Musset's pelican, spilling his bloody words, who may or may not be Christ, to Baudelaire's self-righteous albatross who cannot make it here below, the references are laden with ambivalent implications. The French are an ironic nation, given to self-mockery, and the student is struck by the absence of a Peacock or a Mesonero y Romanos, a satirical author devoted to spoofing and destroying the myths of the age. Of course, parodies of *Hernani* (1830), and of Fourier abound, and indeed, in Gautier's *Une larme du diable* (1839), in Reybaud's *Jérôme Paturot* series (1842 sq.), in Alphonse Karr, found gifted writers. But the parody of Romanticism in France is probably a minor literary enterprise because the Romantics built the parody into their own works, proffered hope and failure simultaneously, and thus took the rug out from under the parodist's feet – which makes them a happy hunting-ground for deconstructionist criticism, and has led some English and German readers to conclude that French Romanticism was superficial. Sophisticated is surely a better term. Nerval is a clear instance; in his *Nuits d'octobre* (1852), in his journalism, he writes in a comic vein of matters to which elsewhere he gives a treatment which is serious but always ambivalent. Nodier well deserved his title of 'le dériseur sensé' and blends the comic, the serious and the fantastic to a rare degree. Musset made a speciality of attacking not only the bourgeoisie but also his fellow Romantics, and Stendhal was a master of irony about his heroes and himself as much as of sarcasm about the oppressive world in which they dwelt. This self-critical parody even crops up in socialist literature; Enfantin made fun of the quest for the female Messiah and Fourier excelled at mixing the comic with the serious. This comic is often a sugar-coating for the pill, but these authors want us to laugh both with and at them. The myths of the new religion were offered with hope and doubt, and the prophets of the new age did not take themselves too seriously.

A loss of hope in all these ideas was brought by the failure of the Revolution of 1848. Between February and June, they reached their fullest diapason, and Flaubert's *Éducation sentimentale* (1869) gives a correct, if satirical, even dyspeptic representation of how the myths of the female Messiah, of Christ the revolutionary, etc., were popularised and sought to move to action. Proudhon later observed that France was then in a dream; the dream turned into a nightmare, with a rude awakening. So far as Romantic mythology was bent on inflecting the course of history, it had to be abandoned. Many went to exile in Belgium, England, Switzerland. The intellectual exiles were more revealing. Some, like Sand, turned to the pastoral; some turned to art for art's sake, or to esoteric occultism. Nerval became increasingly ambivalent, Lamartine went in for hack-writing and literary history. Pius IX in Rome had the gas-lights removed; he extinguished the lights of Christian socialism for a much longer time. So far as the Romantics had tried to make myth historically significant and part of a doctrine of progress, the failure of 1848 provoked a severe questioning of that mythology and its presuppositions. Indeed, 1848 may have been profoundly symbolic of things to come. In our Freudian age, these myths are read psychoanalytically, no longer in the political or metaphysical vein. Cratylist language theories now reveal, not the divine essence, but the eruptions of the unconscious; oneirism now opens not the Gates of Horn or even of Ivory, but the cesspool of incest. Utopian communites have moved from Fourier's passionate attraction to Skinner's behaviourist lollipops. In a similar way, the notion that material and spiritual existed in synthesis, already warped by Hegel into the unity of the Absolute, with Marxism became anchored in the world of economics. The divorce between poet and public was surely less devastating than that between Freud and Marx, between psyche and materialism; Fourier would be aghast.

Not everything can be explained by the failure of 1848; indeed, the tendency toward parody reveals a sense that the quest for unity and total meaning was impossible. Balzac's Frenhofer and Gambara are representative failures; the absolute could not be found and transmitted through art. The reinvestment of myth, of art, of the poet, the creation of new faiths, the dreams and hypotheses of utopian socialism in many ways were efforts to patch up the intellectual constructs of the preceding century so that they could continue moving forward. But the doubts concerning myth's metaphysical validity were reflected in literary creation. What J. Seebacher has observed about Michelet is true of many; he incessantly fabricated myths, but admitted they were myths and even disavowed them as such, in order to make the contradictory more manifest and more intolerable, to show that history still remained to be made. Ballanche, Michelet, Cousin, Vigny tried to get beyond the mythic and envisaged a process of de-symbolisation which would free the truth from its mythic modes of expression. They decided it was impossible to do so because the masses still needed myths – a rather patronising attitude. At the same time Bréal, Maury, Muller were depriving myth of its metaphysical content, which would only be restored several generations later by Jung, Bespaloff, T.S. Eliot. The literary destruction of myth was accomplished by later writers, by Flaubert in *La Tentation de saint Antoine* (1874), and Rimbaud in *Une Saison en enfer* (1873); but the Romantics already maintained together in exacerbated tension hope, doubt, and despair. For these texts contribute, each in its own way, to a relocation of hope from space into time, of the transcendent from the above to the future. This is the history of German thought as it moves from Kant through Hegel to Marx; the movement is more convoluted in France, in part because it was lived through historically, and the times of hope (1789, 1793, Napoleon, the July days of 1830, February and then June 1848) turned out to be moments of bitterness and defeat. So hopes still had to be certified by measures of transcendence, kept up there as well as out there. This Victor Hugo could manage, confounding ocean and sky; others failed. French Romanticism's greatness and uniqueness lies in its awareness that there was a 'réalité rugueuse à étreindre', its focusing not on myth and philosophy (as in Germany), nor on history and psychology (as in England), but on the interplay between the two. The texts then become necessarily more hesitant, and may seem superficial because of that, but, perhaps thanks to its Romantic heritage, France has continued to hew to the strait and narrow path between the failures of praxis and the delusions of grandeur.

BIBLIOGRAPHY

The critique of sensualism and of enlightened self-interest: B. Munteano, 'Episodes kantiens sous le Directoire', *Revue de littérature comparée*, 15 (1935), 387–454; *Le Groupe de Coppet: Quatrième Colloque de Coppet* (Geneva, Slatkine, 1977); Simone Balayé, *Mme de Staël. Lumières et Liberté* (Klincksieck, 1979); Patrice Thompson, *La Religion de Benjamin Constant* (Pisa, Pacini, 1978); *Benjamin Constant. Actes du congrès de Lausanne* (Geneva, Droz, 1978); Francine Marill-Albérès, *Le Naturel chez Stendhal* (Nizet, 1956); 'Écriture et Folie', *Romantisme*, 24 (1979).

Traditionalism and the crisis of Catholicism: *Histoire spirituelle de la France* (Beauchesne, 1964), pp. 287–348; Edgar Hocédez, *Histoire de la théologie au dix-neuvième siècle* (Brussels, Edition universelle, 1949), vol. I; Alexander Vidler, *Prophecy and Papacy; A Study of Lamennais, the Church and the Revolution* (London, SCM. Press, 1954); Louis Le Guillou, *L'Évolution de la pensée religieuse de Félicité de Lamennais* (A. Colin, 1966); Paul Poupard, *Un essai de philosophie chrétienne au dix-neuvième siècle, l'abbé Louis Bautain* (Desclée et Cie, 1961).

The ambiguities of the religious revival: Claude Pichois, *L'Image de Jean-Paul Richter dans les lettres françaises* (Corti, 1963); Henri Gouhier, *Les Conversions de Maine de Biran* (Vrin, 1948); Jean Grenier, *La Philosophie de Jules Lequier* (Les Belles Lettres, 1936).

Introspection, initiation, illuminism: Auguste Viatte, *Les Sources occultes du romantisme* (Champion, 1928); Annie Becq, 'Les traditions ésotériques en France de la Révolution à la Restauration' in *Manuel d'histoire littéraire de la France* (Éditions sociales, 1972), vol. IV:I, pp. 274–301; 'Théorie des harmonies', *Romantisme*, 5 (1973); Léon Cellier, *Parcours initiatiques* (Neuchâtel, La Baconnière, 1977); Robert Amadou, *Louis-Claude de Saint-Martin et le Martinisme* (Éditions du Griffon d'or, 1946); A.J. George, *Pierre-Simon Ballanche* (Syracuse University Press, 1945); Ballanche, *La Vision d'Hébal*, ed. A.J.L. Busst (Geneva, Droz, 1969).

Organism and dynamism: Arthur O. Lovejoy, *The Great Chain of Being* (Cambridge, Mass., Harvard UP, 1936); Judith Schlanger, *Les Métaphores de l'organisme* (Vrin, 1971); Gabriel Madinier, *Conscience et Mouvement* (Louvain, Nauwelaerts, 1967); Georges Poulet, *Études sur le temps humain* (Plon, vol. I, 1950; vol. II, 1952; vol. IV, 1968).

The new boundaries of poetry, myth, language: Albert Béguin, *L'Âme romantique et le Rêve* (Corti, 1939); Pierre Moreau, *Âmes et Thèmes romantiques* (Corti, 1969); Raymond Schwab, *La Renaissance orientale* (Payot, 1950); 'Conscience de la langue', *Romantisme*, 25–26 (1979); Gérard Genette, *Mimologiques, voyage en Cratylie* (Seuil, 1976); F.P. Bowman, 'Occultism and the language of poetry', *New York Literary Forum*, 4 (1980), 51–64; Yves Vadé, 'Le Sphinx et la Chimère', *Romantisme*, 15 (1977), 2–18.

Utopian socialism: F.E. Manuel, *The prophets of Paris* (Cambridge, Mass., Harvard UP, 1962); Maxime Leroy, *Histoire des idées sociales en France*, vol. II, *De Babeuf à Tocqueville* (Gallimard, 1962); Sébastien Charléty, *Histoire du saint-simonisme*, 2nd edn (Hartmann, 1931); Michael Spencer, *Charles Fourier* (Boston, Twayne, 1981); F.P. Bowman, *Éliphas Lévi visionnaire romantique* (PUF, 1969); J.P. van der Linden, *Alphonse Esquiros. De la bohème romantique à la république sociale* (Nizet, 1948).

The philosophical epic: H.J. Hunt, *The Epic in Nineteenth-Century France* (Oxford, Blackwell, 1941); Léon Cellier, *L'Épopée romantique* (PUF, 1954); Anny Detalle, *Mythes, merveilleux et légendes dans la poésie française de 1840 à 1860* (Klincksieck, 1976).

The meaning and definition of myth: Pierre Albouy, *Mythes et mythologies dans la littérature française* (A. Colin, 1969); Harald Weinrich, 'Structures narratives du mythe', *Poétique*, 1 (1970), 25–34; Michel Nathan, *Le Ciel des Fouriéristes* (Lyons, Presses universitaires de Lyon, 1981).

Some representative myths: H.B. Riffaterre, *L'Orphisme dans la poésie romantique* (Nizet, 1970); B. Juden, *Traditions orphiques et tendances mystiques dans le romantisme français* (Klincksieck, 1971); A.J.L. Busst, 'The image of the androgyne in the nineteenth century', in Ian Fletcher (ed.), *Romantic Mythologies* (London, Routledge and Kegan Paul, 1967); Raymond Trousson, *Le Thème de Prométhée dans la littérature européenne* (Geneva, Droz, 1964); Václav Černy, *Essai sur le titanisme dans la poésie romantique occidentale* (Prague. Éditions Orbis, 1935); Jean Tulard, *Le Mythe de Napoléon* (Colin, 1971); Pierre Barbéris, 'Napoléon; structure et signification d'un mythe littéraire', *Revue d'histoire littéraire de la France*, 70 (1970), 1031–58; Eugène Knecht, *Le Mythe du Juif errant. Essai de mythologie littéraire et de sociologie religieuse* (Grenoble, Presses universitaires de Grenoble, 1977); Max Milner, *Le Diable dans la littérature française de Cazotte à Baudelaire* (Corti, 1960); F.P. Bowman, *Le Christ romantique* (Geneva, Droz, 1973).

The synthesis of Victor Hugo: Pierre Albouy, *La Création mythologique chez Victor Hugo* (Corti, 1963).

Doubt and hope: J. Seebacher, 'Michelet' in *Manuel d'histoire littéraire de la France* (Éditions sociales, 1973), vol. IV:2, pp. 459–66.

IV · *Poetry*

J.C. IRESON

IDENTIFICATION

Two dates effectively mark the period of the Romantic movement in French poetry. These are 1820, which saw the publication of Lamartine's *Méditations poétiques*, and 1840, which marks a point of termination and a clear divide in the poetry of the nineteenth century. Within these two decades, the values and procedures of French poetry were revolutionised. The whole of Lamartine's poetry, with the exception of a few isolated pieces such as 'La Vigne et la maison' and 'Le Désert, ou l'Immatérialité de Dieu',[1] was written by 1839. Musset's significant contribution had been made by 1840,[2] and Gautier's Romantic phase came to an end with the publication of *España* in the same year. The poetry of Vigny likewise completed its Romantic phase about the same time, the definitive edition of *Poèmes antiques et modernes* appearing in 1837. The verse of his second period, written mainly during the 1840s, shows a move away from Romantic forms and values. In Hugo's case, the year 1840, marked by the publication of *Les Rayons et les ombres*, closed two brilliant decades which saw his triumph as the leader of the Romantic school, in poetry as in the theatre. A gap of ten years intervened between this and the poetry of his years of exile. His mature verse, like that of Vigny, was overlapped by the work of new generations subscribing to a view of poetry which was no longer that of the Romantics.

This chapter attempts to show the individual and collective contribution made to French Romanticism by these five poets. Reference is also made to Sainte-Beuve, whose poetry, though slight in volume, was influential. The order is mainly chronological. After tracing the formation of Romantic poetry in France, and its triumph in the years around 1830, the chapter follows the divergent trends which ensued. It is not possible, in such a short span, to give full details of the work of Vigny and Hugo beyond the Romantic period itself, but a brief evaluation of their work up to the early 1860s is attempted in the closing pages.

FORMATION

Poetry appears to have enjoyed a favoured status in the Napoleonic and Restoration societies. The officer classes in the later years of the Empire seem to have viewed the writing of verse as a fashionable accomplishment; Joseph-Léopold Sigisbert Hugo, a general in Napoleon's army and latterly governor of a province in Spain, gave his son advice on prosody when Victor was serving his apprenticeship in the art. Vigny appears to have had little difficulty in combining, in the Parisian salons around 1820, the appeal of a fashionable officer with the prestige of a promising young poet. More importantly, the society of the returned *émigrés*, however reactionary in politics, had expectations of a revived artistic and literary culture, and although these expectations were circumscribed by monarchist and Catholic values, enforced contact with other European cultures had produced a general awareness of the limits of the former traditions and a desire to see the forms of art adapted to the new period.

In her work *De l'Allemagne* (1810), Mme de Staël had underlined the main factor inhibiting the progress of French poetry in a period of changing political and religious conditions: the failure of its form and language to evolve with the mental universe of the writer, and above all to give adequate expression to the lyrical genius of the race, so that for her the great lyricists of France are not to be found among the poets, but among the great prose writers such as Bossuet, Fénelon, Buffon and Rousseau. Yet, in the years following 1815, the poets most in vogue were, for lack of new models, the masters of verse of the eighteenth century: Delille and Parny, both recently dead, Voltaire, Fontanes, Lebrun, Lemercier, Viennet, Baour-Lormian and J.-B. Rousseau. Little in the ideas and attitudes expressed in this poetry had direct relevance for the reading public of 1820. A restored monarchy, a restored aristocracy, automatically brought with them values which seemed new after the upheavals of the Revolution and the Empire; and legitimism and Catholic orthodoxy were the values to which the new writers subscribed. In poetry, three newcomers appeared whose impact determined the course of French poetry for several decades. These were Lamartine, Hugo and Vigny.

It is noteworthy that each initially chose poetry as his preferred form, and each appears to have considered throughout his life, despite achieving fame in other genres, that poetry was first among the literary arts, potentially the most powerful and the most universal. That potential remained, however, at the beginning of the 1820s, largely to be realised, or rediscovered.

Lamartine was the first poet to break through into the new period. The twenty-four poems of the original edition of his *Méditations poétiques* mark a departure from previous poetry, not in the form or language, for both of these clearly follow the models presented by the eighteenth century, but in the range and treatment of themes and in the sensibility which they express. With two exceptions ('Chants lyriques de Saül' and 'La Poésie sacrée'), which are adaptations into French verse of lyrical passages from the Old Testament, the themes are contemporary and are brought into a sharp focus by being apparently related to the direct experience of the poet himself, experience which is, however, held within an ambivalent perspective, so that it is not clear whether imagination or memory is at work. Revelations by Lamartine himself, in the form of commentaries published with the 1849 edition (which includes the subsequent volume, *Nouvelles Méditations poétiques*), throw a discreet light on the circumstances which gave rise to individual poems, but are subject to caution in many cases over precise questions of fact. Popular imagination has fastened on a few poems where elevated passion and grief at separation or bereavement are expressed lyrically against allusions to events personally experienced ('Invocation', 'L'Isolement', 'Le Lac', etc.), and biographical details have been made to obtrude upon the text. The main facts concerned refer to the liaison between Lamartine and Julie Charles, the wife of the President of the Académie des Sciences. Meeting at Aix-les-Bains in Savoy, a little more than a year before her death, the two lived out an idyll which passed rapidly from sensual love to a deep, spiritualised passion, thwarted by convention and separation. 'Ma vie est liée à celle d'une femme que je crois mourante!' wrote Lamartine to his friend de Virieu on 16 December 1816, and Mme Charles was indeed moving into the terminal stages of tuberculosis. News of her death in Paris, following a year of frequent meetings while the illness visibly grew upon her, reached Lamartine at his family's house in Mâcon in late December 1817. This event, the first major crisis in his life, marked a rapid change in his poetry, deepening and widening the range, linked, as it immediately became, with the problem of religious faith and doubt.

It also intensified the special quality of his verse, the sense of immediacy with which he appeared able to communicate with his reader through the formality of the verse instrument which he used. Looking back in 1849, in the first detailed preface which he added to his *Méditations*, he wrote: 'Je suis le premier qui ait fait descendre la poésie du Parnasse et qui ait donné à ce qu'on nommait la muse, au lieu d'une lyre à sept cordes de convention, les fibres mêmes du cœur de l'homme, touchées et émues par les innombrables frissons de l'âme et de la nature.'

This quest for a new power of directness in poetic language will be at the centre of most developments in French poetry in the nineteenth century. Lamartine's formulation is significant. It shows the extent to which he himself is constrained to work within the limits of the old conventions and style; and it also shows his personal sense of the transposition achieved through poetry: a resonance set up by inward and outward events and seeking its equivalents in language. He notes, in the same preface, the two main ways in which poetic language makes its impact: through images and through verbal harmony, leaving aside the ratiocinative function, perhaps as an unwanted legacy from the previous century. The image he sees as deriving from imagination, and imagination as inseparable from memory ('l'*imagination*, c'est-à-dire la mémoire qui revoit et qui repeint en nous'). The recalled image arouses associated feelings, and the play of such images enlivens the field of ideas set up by the poem. The primary quality of poetry appears, however, to have been, for Lamartine, its verbal harmony, a pre-cognitive feature which he himself exploits with great facility.

This facility, which becomes a fault in the later poetry, is not too readily apparent in the *Méditations poétiques* of 1820. Lamartine claims (also in his preface of 1849) that these first published poems were the result of several years of preparation. The earliest go back to about 1814 ('A Elvire', 'Le Golfe de Baya'). The lyrical extracts from *Saül* recall the relative success, through readings in the salons, of a tragedy turned down by Talma in 1817. In his search for a form and style adapted to his needs (what he calls 'la voix'), he was particularly affected by the writings attributed to Ossian (read, presumably in Letourneur's translation of 1777, or Baour-Lormian's of 1801), and ascribed some of the melancholy of his descriptions of natural scenes to the example of the Gaelic bard. But, in the first instance, he turned his hand to the composition of elegies in the manner of Bertin (*Les Amours*, 1780) and Parny (*Poésies érotiques*, n.d.; in *Œuvres complètes*, 1808), who wrote short, amatory pieces, without the necessary inclusion of the theme of grief or melancholy. Millevoye (*Élégies*, 1814) had recently provided examples of the latter kind. Out of these exercises Lamartine developed his own form of lyrical poem. He acquired, probably from Parny, the technique of increasing the impact of a poem by bringing together two opposed themes within a single piece in order to produce a heightened emotional intensity and, by an original handling of the internal structure of the poem, created the characteristic tone and movement of the *méditation poétique*, which was virtually a new form of the lyric in France. The external forms of the poem have not changed. Lamartine uses short sequences of quatrains to form what are recognisably elegies ('L'Automne', 'Le Vallon', 'L'Isolement'). He constructs odes in the ten-line and six-line stanzas used by J.-B. Rousseau ('Le Génie', 'L'Enthousiasme', 'Le Désespoir'), an epistle to Byron ('L'Homme') and a *discours en vers* ('Dieu') in the traditional alexandrine. 'Le Lac' was originally titled 'Ode au lac du Bourget', and is in fact an ode to time, apostrophising the lake and the landscape around it, while other formal devices, such as the rhetorical recall of an episode, antiphone, syntactical repetition, are used to provide a clear structure, without inhibiting a freer movement suggesting intuitions about time and the personal experience which has induced them.

This capacity to combine reflections on universal themes with notations of personal feeling, without departing from accepted conventions of form and expression, is an essential part of the formula developed by Lamartine. The *méditation* is thus a personal construction, and could hardly exist independently of the poet who conceived it. Isolated yet confidential, deeply involved with the life of his time, as well as with the universal questions, the spirit of Lamartine engaged the feelings of his readers as no poet had done for a century or more. Something aloof and intangible in his personality kept his poetry from becoming a confession, while the sense of vulnerability and world-weariness impinged larger than life on the sensibility of his contemporaries. Episodes and figures from his private life, where they occur in his poems, are transposed to a level of imagination which enables him, for example, to bring together references to mistresses other than Julie and to use the faintly surprising designation of 'Elvire'.[3]

But the personal *méditations* are relatively few in number in the original volume. Lamartine is at pains to extend the range of his poetry to include public themes and fundamental questions of religion. In 'L'Homme', he is able to combine familiar references to the fashionable poet of the English Satanic School (he was unknown to Byron at this time) with references to his own life, which he uses as an exemplar of the human condition, and with a passionate plea for faith and confidence in the unseen divine purpose. Public themes become more numerous after his appointment to the Embassy at Naples in 1820 ('Ode sur la naissance du duc de Bordeaux' and the 'Ode' written to the French people were included in later editions of the *Méditations poétiques*, while 'Bonaparte' and 'La Liberté, ou Une Nuit à Rome', showing an evolved technique, were written for the *Nouvelles Méditations* of 1823). But the strongest theme, whether considered in the original collection or in the collected editions, is the theme of conflict between doubt and faith.

Concerned as he was to present himself as the new poet of a royalist and Catholic period, Lamartine hardly comes across in his religious poetry as orthodox in the matter of religion. 'Le Désespoir' and 'La Providence à l'homme', placed together in all editions, form a diptych, in which sentiments of revolt against a fallen and suffering world are countered and, supposedly, overwhelmed by the certitude that can be derived from the order of the universe and the magnificence of the earth and the heavens, symbols of a higher glory. The poem of revolt, originally called 'Ode au Malheur', is spoken according to a human perspective on creation. The reply is, supposedly, given by the Creator and is spoken in the first person, in the manner of the words of Jehovah in the Old Testament. These two pieces, the first of which gives a powerful, lyrical tone to an attitude of scepticism, were probably brought together in order to maintain, or perhaps to summarise in more dramatic form, the theme of conflicting forces in the poet's mind. In the poem to Byron, Lamartine concludes with what he calls 'l'hymne de la raison', in which reason is used to look beyond the discouraging realities of individual life towards the universal order in which existence has its context. The limitations of this same reason are asserted in 'L'Immortalité', where an idealism based on a symbolistic view of the world, attributed to Elvire, reverses the poet's pessimism and counters the view of materialist philosophers, the 'troupeau d'Épicure' This view of nature as a symbolic temple forms much of the substance of 'La Prière', human intelligence being presented as the means whereby intuitions of a divine presence may be sought in the solitude of remote places. In 'La Foi', developing this theme of quest, he sets beyond death the stage of full revelation:

> Cette raison superbe, insuffisant flambeau,
> S'éteint comme la vie aux portes du tombeau,

and beyond death, too, the idealised presence of the lost mistress remains, still sensually apprehended. Flight into the 'pures régions' is evoked, in 'Dieu', as a natural movement of the poet's mind, bringing him, at privileged moments, 'face à face avec la réalité'. This 'reality' Lamartine attempts to convey by a description of God, represented in what appears to be a generally pantheistic view,[4] as coextensive with the universe, sustaining and controlling it with His material being. In some respects, the passage anticipates the notion of the Brahmanistic God described by Leconte de Lisle in 'Bhagavat', though Lamartine's aim is to give a universalised vision of a God perceptible to human reason and freed from credulity and superstition, capable of intervening in the history of the world.

Successive and expanded editions of the *Méditations poétiques*, and the publication of the *Nouvelles Méditations poétiques*, added variations to the themes of the initial volume: 'Ischia' and 'Chant d'Amour', both from the 1823 collection, parallel the sublimated love poetry of 1816–20 with lyrical stanzas on shared happiness and amorous pleasure, prudently controlled by the conventions of decorum of the time; 'Les Étoiles', again from the second volume, adds a range of cosmic imagery to the lyrical, highly personalised treatment of the theme of individual consciousness; 'Bonaparte', begun at some point after the death of the Emperor in 1821 and completed in 1823, is a solidly constructed ode in which each stanza is marked by a dominant image accompanying the argument of the poem. But the vital contribution of Lamartine to the development of French poetry was made in 1820. Though in some respects the *Nouvelles Méditations* show a maturing of his talent, they are more uneven in quality, and the pressure of demand from his publishers to produce a second volume following the great success of the first, at a time when the style and condition of his life had changed considerably with his marriage and the beginnings of his diplomatic career in Italy, meant that he was obliged to return to earlier material, passed over for the first volume, in order to fill out the second.

La Mort de Socrate, also published in 1823, is an experimental poem of another type: longer than the *méditation*, which rarely extends to 200 lines, it develops, over approximately 800 lines, the themes of idealism and religious syncretism already seen in 'Dieu', but uses an episodic framework, based on Plato's *Phaedo*, in which Lamartine invests the final message of Socrates with his own lyrical view of death and immortality. Perhaps the return to classical sources and the narrative and descriptive form of the poem account for the relative lack of enthusiasm with which it was greeted on publication. It should nevertheless be said that in the main lines of its technique, the projection of ideas through a figure engaged in heroic or tragic action, it offers interesting points of comparison with some of Vigny's early pieces; and that some of the descriptive effects already anticipate the manner of the Parnassians. A fourth work, *Dernier Chant du Pèlerinage d'Harold* (1825), was written after the death of Byron as an additional episode to those recounted in Byron's four cantos. Lamartine divides his 'Chant' into forty-nine sections, all but one composed as a short sequence of alexandrine couplets, in place of the Spenserian stanzas used by Byron. The manner is grandiloquent and, in its superficial mannerisms, classical, with a more modern technique used in some of the descriptive and narrative passages. The soliloquies are used to present thinly disguised aspects of Lamartine's opinions and attitudes at a restless and perplexed period of his development.

Throughout the 1820s Lamartine had intuitions of a great poetic work to be accomplished, and ideas for a form of lyricism which would express, and possibly resolve, the religious problem which dominated his private thoughts at a time when his reputation and career were beginning to take him towards public life. These plans were to form the second half of his work as a poet and, historically, form part of the second decade of Romantic poetry. Lamartine's major contribution was already made, however, with the *Méditations poétiques*.

The other two poets making their appearance at this time, with strong views on the importance of the art and on the methods by which it could be regenerated, found it necessary to proceed in a rather different fashion, publishing at an earlier stage of their development and using early publications as part of a careful sequence of work. The progress of each during the decade presents some interesting parallels. Common interests brought them together in Paris, where Hugo lived and where Vigny returned when permitted by his duties as an officer in the royalist army. Both contracted early marriages, Hugo, at twenty, to Adèle Foucher, Vigny, at twenty-three, to Lydia Bunbury, the daughter of an English colonial family. Both started their literary careers by publishing poetry, Hugo with *Odes et poésies diverses* in 1822, Vigny, anonymously, with *Poèmes*, in the same year. Both made experiments in the novel and both began to write for the theatre. Towards 1830, Vigny's achievement, with *Cinq-Mars* (1826) and verse pieces such as 'Éloa', seemed the more impressive and mature, until the bravura of Hugo's poetry in *Les Orientales* (1829) and the extraordinary success of *Hernani* at the Comédie-Française established his brilliant ascendancy. Differences of temperament and, probably, the effects of rivalry in the theatre, led Vigny away from Hugo's circle in the 1830s and towards an independent, and ultimately solitary, road as a historical poet.

The titles of the first published collections of the two poets are already significant. Each appears to have followed the example of Lamartine in giving a new impetus to forms which had become ritualised or had fallen into disuse. Hugo turned to the ode; Vigny, after one or two experiments with classical forms, probably under the influence of André Chénier whose *Poésies* had appeared in 1819 (Vigny wrote an idyll, 'La Dryade' and an elegy 'Symetha'), began to develop his own form of the *poème*. Hugo, who had started his literary career by winning prizes at the *jeux floraux* of Toulouse, was given a pension by Louis XVIII on the publication of the first *Odes*, and further prepared his way by founding a literary review, *Le Conservateur littéraire*, jointly with his two brothers (1819–21). He and Vigny were among those collaborating with Guiraud in *La Muse française* (1823–4). Both frequented the circles in which the new artistic values were promoted. Hugo was prominent among the writers meeting at the Arsenal, where Nodier was librarian, the group becoming known as the *Cénacle*; later, in 1826, he himself was the centre of a group of artists and writers who formed the second *Cénacle*.

The apprentice work of Hugo forms a volume in itself. A *cahier de vers français*, started when he was fourteen, a three-canto *Déluge* written at the same age, a series of *poésies diverses* written over the next year, a group of poetical *essais* composed in his sixteenth year, in addition to the pieces presented to the Académie des Jeux Floraux and the Académie Française in 1819 and 1820, lead up to the *Odes* published in 1822 and developed in four more volumes up to 1828. This definitive edition omitted the three *poésies diverses* originally included. Each successive edition is accompanied by a preface, and these five essays cover both the scope of the poems presented and the situation of poetry as Hugo saw it.

The preface of 1822 is the most succinct, and in some ways the most clearly indicative, both of Hugo's appreciation of his immediate interests and of his longer view of the nature of poetry. In each case, he draws upon current opinions. On the one hand, contemporary political events were seen as an important subject of literature, provided that they were viewed through royalist and Catholic sentiments; on the other, an idealist view of literature in its treatment of inward experience had been fostered by various influences tending to restore poetical quality to writing (in this respect, Hugo was particularly influenced by Chateaubriand). In his preface, Hugo states the militant *ultra* position quite clearly: 'l'histoire des hommes ne présente de poésie que jugée du haut des idées monarchiques et des croyances religieuses'. At the same time, he states his own view that the inner world of the writer is as important as the public world of political events. The double preoccupation that will control his poetry throughout his whole career is therefore present from the outset. In 1822, the idea which he appears most eager to express is that which concerns the dichotomy of poetry into form and idea: 'la poésie n'est pas dans la forme des idées, mais dans les idées elles-mêmes'. Although the connection is not made completely clear, the nexus of ideas grasped by the individual would appear, in Hugo's view, to reflect an ideal dimension, luminous if not distinguishable, to the eye of the meditative artist. Later on, much of his poetry will be the record of attempts to penetrate, by an act of vision, the mystery in which the world exists: 'un monde idéal, qui se montre resplendissant à l'œil de ceux que des méditations graves ont accoutumés à voir dans les choses plus que les choses'.

The prefaces of 1824 and 1826 are more directly polemical, taking up the two contentious issues of the moment, the defence of the new literature and the relevance of the debate over the terms *classique* and *romantique*. His contribution to the first of these is to argue the superiority of the role of contemporary poets, who attempt to draw literature away from the representation of pagan subjects and guide the nation towards the future in line with its Christian and monarchist traditions. His attitude towards the second is to adopt a pose of guarded neutrality, going as far as to attack the limited classifications imposed by the proponents of the terms, but falling back upon a position that permits both admiration of the past and the ambition to create a better literature: 'Admirons les grands maîtres, ne les imitons pas.'

The *Odes* themselves, to which Hugo added, in the 1826 edition, fifteen *ballades*, are the record both of their time and of the constraints which he accepted in order to make his mark. The first three books are mainly taken up with the celebration of contemporary events, or with reverberations of the preceding periods. Three pieces from the first book are devoted to the assassination of the duc de Berry and to the subsequent birth and baptism of his son, the duc de Bordeaux ('rejeton qui deviendra la tige!'). The funeral of Louis XVIII and the coronation of Charles X form the centre of Book III. 'Les Vierges de Verdun' and 'Quiberon' commemorate Revolutionary episodes of particular poignancy to the returned *émigrés*, as do the sentimental and religious reflections on the death of the Dauphin in 1795 ('Louis XVII'). The stern tone of the verses to 'Buonaparte' is contrived to satisfy prevailing opinion and, at the same time, to present a historical perspective in which Napoleon is seen as the victim, rather than the agent, of providence. As the composition of the *Odes* continued, Hugo began to free himself from political subjects. As the first book shows, only one piece ('Vision') was written before 1822 on a theme that was religious rather than political, and even here it is the technique (the judgment of the eighteenth century before God, presented as a dialogue) which imposes a religious perspective on history. But in Books IV and V a more varied line of inspiration is apparent, though it is not to any marked extent religious. There are two exercises on biblical subjects, an adaptation ('Moïse sur le Nil') and an imitation ('Jehovah'). The most interesting development is in the combination of a personal lyricism with biblical style and images, as in 'Actions de grâces', which anticipates Baudelaire's 'Bénédiction' in its themes and Verlaine's *Sagesse* in certain qualities of style. For the rest, there are exercises in historical fancy, such as in the three poems of the fourth book evoking sport and combat in the Greek arena, the Roman circus and the medieval tournament, and a number of pieces reflecting events of the poet's life and some of his preoccupations, such as the conservation of the national heritage in its buildings and monuments, which had suffered in the Revolutionary period: 'La Bande noire' is the beginning of a campaign against vandalism which Hugo will continue both in his writings (*Notre-Dame de Paris* (1831); 'Guerre aux dé-molisseurs', *Revue des deux mondes*, 1832) and in his support of the Comité des Arts et Monuments. Stanzas to his fiancée, written in 1821 and 1823, already show a tendency to slip away from the ode in poems of intimate inspiration, and this is clearly the direction in which the poet is moving in the last two poems of the *Odes*, each dated 1828 and each concerned with an impressionism which is not a feature of the ode as practised so far by Hugo, the principal aim of which had been the propounding of ideas by a discursive eloquence. 'Pluie d'été', while keeping the ten-line octosyllabic stanza, a traditional form of the French ode, is an imitation of the *Bergeries* of Remi Belleau. 'Rêves', using a lighter measure with a preponderance of feminine rhymes, is an attempt to catch the freer movement of the 'muse envolée' in what proves to be a stereotyped piece in praise of meditative solitude remote from the city.

But another type of poem had made its appearance as early as 1824, in the edition of *Nouvelles Odes* and in the form of three *ballades*, inserted among the odes. In the definitive edition of 1828, the *Odes et Ballades* keep the two types separate, the *ballades* forming to some extent, a progression from the manner of the last odes. Hugo's *ballade* derives from Millevoye and exploits the strain of fantasy, particularly of the fairy-tale sort made popular by Nodier, which is a feature of this period. The fixed pattern of the traditional *ballade*, with its *dixain* or *huitain* with an *envoi*, is abandoned. The stanza form is variable, sometimes within the same piece, with the verse of five or six lines predominating. There are also experimental or unusual metrical forms. The eight-line verses of 'Le Pas d'armes du Roi Jean' are in three-syllable lines; 'La Chasse du Burgrave' produces its main effect through the use of echo in each of its fifty quatrains. The themes and figures are the product of conventional fantasy and, apart from the individual pieces on the fairy, the sylph and the witches' Sabbath, represent the current preoccupation with medieval subjects, not in themselves of great importance, and treated as exercises in pastiche, but composed with verve and virtuosity.

Vigny's development as a poet is initially associated, as in the case of Lamartine and Hugo, with the renovation and advancement of an older form of poetry. His concern was principally with the *poème*, a form which, in the later eighteenth century, had been used to signify a short epic or heroic poem, and Vigny's intention was to adapt it to the ideas and style of his time. His experiments with the *poème* lasted between 1820 and 1829, during which period he also turned, more briefly, to another form, the *mystère*, probably from the examples given by Byron in *Cain* (1821) and *Heaven and Earth* (1822). Two other forms, the *élévation*, with which he experimented for a short time around 1830, and the *poème philosophique*, which preoccupied him from about 1839 to the year of his death (1863), were designed to permit the expression of ideas in a more complex way than was possible with the *poème* and the *mystère*.

It was probably his intention to form individual volumes from sequences of these individual types of poem. In the event, his first major volume of verse, *Poèmes antiques et modernes*, slowly built up in stages (*Poèmes*, 1822; *Poèmes antiques et modernes*, 1826; *Poèmes*, 1829; *Poèmes antiques et modernes*, 1837), combined *poèmes*, *mystères* and *élévations*, the unity of the book being obtained from the arrangement of the pieces in a historical order, twenty in all in the 1837 edition.

Of these twenty poems, thirteen bear the subtitle *poème*. One or two, such as 'Le Cor', were originally written as experiments with the *ballade*, giving a lyrical tone and a medieval configuration and colouring, without too much concern for authenticity, to a heroic episode, in this case the stand of Roland and Oliver at Roncevaux. 'Madame de Soubise', though published as a 'poème du xvie siecle', has all the marks of a *ballade* in the manner of Hugo: interesting stanza and metrical forms permitting both a heroic and lyrical interpretation of the subject (an event from the Saint Bartholomew massacre) and an attractive simulation of some mannerisms of the older language. The difference occurs in the intention of the poet. Vigny goes beyond historical fancy towards the sense of events and the performance of the figures involved in them.

His *poème* is a historical genre. It is relatively short, rarely exceeding 200 lines in length, and presents a concentrated episode shown in its effect on one or two figures. The figures themselves represent varied human types, ranging from men of spiritual or political power (Moïse, Charlemagne) to representatives of the code of military service and honour (Roland and Oliver, the soldier–monk of the Trappist order, the Captain of the frigate *La Sérieuse*). The list extends further, to the victims of political persecution (the prisoner in the iron mask), to women capable of tragic action through passion (Dolorida), and to beings capable of surmounting physical frailty through acts of courage (Madame de Soubise; Emma, the young 'princesse de la Gaule' of 'La Neige'). His use of known events to provide perspectives for human action is, of course, not new, and Vigny's starting point is, typically, a familiar episode from the Scriptures ('Moïse', 'La Fille de Jephté', 'La Femme adultère'), a historical or contemporary event ('La Prison', 'Le Trappiste'), or even a *fait divers* of the period ('Dolorida'). His treatment of his subjects is original in the variety of the colour and tone of the episodes and in the evocation of personality in the human figures. Though some of the earlier pieces, such as 'La Neige', subscribe to the fashion of a fairly cursory local colour, others, particularly those founded on biblical episodes, combine imaginative reconstruction with a remarkable degree of detail in allusions. The four major themes of 'Moïse' are centred on four books of the Bible. Moïse's recall of the migration from Egypt to the promised land and the establishing of his leadership derives from twelve chapters of Exodus; his triumphs, miracles and final weariness of responsibility are presented by references to eight chapters from Numbers; his last acts and his death outside the promised land are based on seven chapters from Deuteronomy; the elegiac theme of complaint is a compound of allusions to eight chapters of the Book of Job. A similar technique, though less dominant in the poem, is found in 'La Femme adultère'. The most important features of Vigny's *poème* are found, however, elsewhere than in the external techniques. Although the control of the structure of individual pieces is impressive, their best achievement is found in the use of a spectacle to suggest important ideas concerning the human condition. The interaction of the characters and the situation in which they are found is dramatic (at times, as in 'La Prison', Vigny uses passages of dialogue). The characters react through gesture, which takes on a ritual and symbolic significance, and through action, which shows the disproportion between the individual human will and impulses on the one hand, and the ordering of events on the other, whether these events are determined by natural or providential forces. Each figure is shown at grips with a dilemma occurring either as the consequence of an action or the working of an unseen process. Occasionally, as in 'Le Bal', where the glamour of the ballroom is contrasted with the tribulations that inevitably lie ahead, the dilemma is left vague and inescapable. In most cases, it is a trial that engages the responsibility and courage of an individual: hence the action of Moïse in seeking to confront Jehovah, the unavailing effort of the priest to make contact with the mind of the dying prisoner in the iron mask, the tragic jealousy of Dolorida, the fate of the 'femme adultère', saved but not redeemed by the intervention of Christ in the processes of the Judaic law, the Christian love of Mme de Soubise, stronger than the fanatical conflicts of her century. Over this whole sequence of *poèmes* broods a general question concerning human responsibility and fatality: to what extent can moral strength counter the play of unpredictable forces that threaten human life?[5] The sombre picture is relieved by one thing, the presence of sexual love, which is painted in the suave tones of amorous pleasure ('Dolorida', 'La Femme adultère') and shown briefly in its more innocent and elevated forms as a force able to illuminate and sublimate life ('La Neige', 'Madame de Soubise').

The *poème*, as conceived by Vigny, is valuable for its power of illustrating an idea in heroic and sentimental terms, and its symbolic capacity is considerable, since the actions and speeches of the characters are left, within the context of the events, to carry the import of the larger ideas with which he is concerned. But its objectivity is also a limitation, in that it makes the elaboration of an idea more difficult, when the poet is not free to comment directly upon it. This fact may explain to some extent his early interest in the *mystère*, not so much in the form of the medieval play, as met with, for example, in Gringoire's ill-fated *mystère* in *Notre-Dame de Paris*, but in a rather more modern guise. Reference has been made to the examples given by Byron, which are written in the form of plays. Vigny's two *mystères* are narrative pieces, combining several different techniques, of which dramatic effect is one of the most striking. 'Éloa' and 'Le Déluge' figure among seven *mystères* listed on the first page of his journal, under the date 1823. The heading, *Les Mystères, Poèmes*, shows some hesitation between the two forms, but seems to indicate a decision to keep within a strictly poetic frame. 'Le Déluge' does not differ superficially from the form of 'Moïse' or 'La Femme adultère' ('Éloa' has its own form, being written in three cantos, with ornamental devices such as simile). The difference is found in the nature of the ideas, which are more specifically concerned with the divine ordering of the world and divine intervention in the course of human history. The figures are divine or semi-divine beings. As in Byron's *Mysteries*, a modern and personal interpretation is given to events drawn from the Judaeo-Christian tradition. Éloa, the female angel of pity, is largely a creation of Vigny himself, though the name occurs in a passage by Klopstock quoted by Chateaubriand in *Le Génie du christianisme*. The figure of Satan is probably influenced by Milton's depiction of the fallen angel, but distorted by Vigny by the prominence given to the sensual theme in the description of the ensnaring of Éloa. Both poems depict the conflict between human virtues and supernatural power. Éloa, created by God from a tear shed by Christ over the body of Lazarus, is enslaved by Satan and becomes part of fallen creation, unable to do more than strive to console a suffering world. In their meeting in the depths of Chaos, the divine innocence of Éloa stirs Satan almost to repentance:

> Ah! si dans ce moment la Vierge eût pu l'entendre,
> Si la céleste main qu'elle eût osé lui tendre
> L'eût saisi repentant, docile à remonter . . .
> Qui sait? le mal peut-etre eût cessé d'exister.

The value of Christ's ministry in the world is ultimately in question here. The theme will appear again, in less symbolical terms, in Vigny's later poems. But at this stage his views seem dominated by a belief in a divine will, the principles and consistency of which remain concealed at all levels of creation.

'Le Déluge' is constructed on the account given in Genesis of the destruction of the world by the Flood as a divine punishment following the forbidden mingling of human beings and angels. The poem focuses on two beings – Emmanuel, half man, half angel, and Sara, of human stock – who put their human love before their lives, which could be saved by separation, and perish on Mount Ararat in the last moments of the Deluge. The Flood, frequently treated in painting and in literature, offered an opportunity for original treatment of descriptive effects, for a poignant lyricism intrinsic to the situation imagined by Vigny, and for a strong message universalising the theme. The descriptive effects of the poem are conceived in the form of a violent disruption of harmony: glimpses of the last moments of the 'perfect order' of the antediluvian landscape are followed by visual shots of the destruction of this order by the storm and the Flood, and of the behaviour of animals and men in the rising of the 'implacable sea', until the moment of ironic calm signalled by the rainbow. The lyricism is in the doomed innocence expressed in the dialogue of the lovers. The message of the poet is conveyed in a speech attributed to the angel, father of Emmanuel, who interprets the divine judgment:

> La pitié du mortel n'est point celle des Cieux.
> Dieu ne fait point de pacte avec la race humaine:
> Qui créa sans amour fera périr sans haine.

By 1829, Vigny's *Poèmes antiques et modernes* had almost taken their final shape, although the title was not yet firm. The philosophical groundwork of the collection was already laid; the historical intention was apparent, but not yet developed as completely as Vigny wished. The poems were arranged as individual fragments of a sequence designed to reflect stages of moral development from the beginnings of Judaism to the formation of modern Europe. Despite the presence of 'Le Bal', 'Dolorida' and 'La Frégate la Sérieuse', Vigny was still looking for a form which would permit a more detailed presentation of the values of the modern world. An entry in his journal dated 20 May 1829 notes the difficulty of finding suitable forms of expression for modern subjects; he appears to have been thinking about the possibility of a new form from about 1827, calling it *élévation*. Two poems of this type were written: 'Les Amants de Montmorency' (1830) and 'Paris' (1831). Vigny defined the *élévation*, referring to these two pieces, in a letter to Camilla Maunoir in 1838: 'partir de la peinture d'une image toute terrestre pour s'élever à des vues d'une nature plus divine'. Both were published separately and brought into the *Poèmes antiques et modernes* of 1837 as the last two poems of the collection. 'Les Amants de Montmorency', based on a newspaper account of the suicide pact of two lovers, is a lyrical projection of their state of mind during the last three days of their lives; it extends the theme of condemned or tragic love, to which he gives a special place in his vision of the complex forces that assail human life. 'Paris', in which Vigny gives a detailed elaboration of his thoughts inspired by the modern capital city, starts with the 'image toute terrestre' of Paris viewed by night from a tower by the poet and a traveller. Abandoning the narrative formulation of the *poèmes*, he constructs this *élévation* on a dialogue between himself and the companion who is unfamiliar with the city. The dialogue arises from two images suggested to the traveller by the sight of its lamps and the smoke of its fires: a glowing wheel and a furnace. The poet develops the sense of these images. The wheel is the representation of the motive force transmitted by Paris to the nation, and of the radius of action of the capital. The idea of new things being forged is elaborated chiefly by reference to ideas. The work from which the shape of the future will emerge is the work of 'des Esprits', and the lamp is the symbol of their efforts. Vigny has in mind the action of four thinkers or schools of thought. Three of these, representing contemporary attitudes to religion (Lamennais), politics (Benjamin Constant) and doctrines of society (Saint-Simon), he sees as exponents of limited systems. Above them he places the effort of independent thinkers, presumably like himself, uncommitted and disinterested:

> Des hommes pleins d'amour, de doute et de pitié,
> Qui disaient: *Je ne sais*, des choses de la vie,
> Dont le pouvoir ou l'or ne fut jamais l'envie.

There is no more than a hint here of the values which he himself will seek to elaborate. Such elaboration will require long reflection, not only upon ideas themselves, but on the form and expression in which the ideas can take the most permanent shape.

For the present, Vigny's poetry remains a poetry of isolated ideas on moral and theological problems, and experiments with form appear to be his chief concern: 'Concevoir et méditer une pensée philosophique; trouver dans les actions humaines celle qui en est la plus évidente *preuve*; la réduire à une action simple qui se puisse graver en la mémoire et représenter en quelque sorte une statue et un monument grandiose à l'imagination des hommes, voilà où doit tendre cette poésie épique et dramatique à la fois' (*Journal d'un poète*, 20 May 1829). Nevertheless, the qualities of his poetry are already clearly established. Statuesque and grandiose according to his own formulation, his heroic verse is distinguished from near-contemporary examples such as Théveneau's *Charlemagne* (1816) and La Harpe's *Le Triomphe de la religion* (1814) by the vitality of the effects and the adjustment of technique to the formulation, without didacticism, of an individual idea. The features of that technique are to be found in the variation of tone and perspective (this is probably the dramatic intention referred to by Vigny), and the organisation of images of physical action in such a way as to evoke both a moral crisis and a significant historical moment ('Éloa', for example, to all appearances purely symbolic in its action, also marks the destined role of the compassion brought by Christ to the world).

The 1820s therefore saw the resurgence in France of the three universal forms of poetry, the lyric, the ode and the epic, each in the hands of a poet who had manifested, or promised, greatness in his art. Lamartine had given a new lyrical formulation to religious, philosophical and political themes, as well as to subjects drawn more directly from his own life. Vigny developed the stages of a major work through the decade, and brought a new complexity to poetry based on heroic narrative. Hugo had demonstrated his mastery of the ode by his inventive brilliance in the sustained development of a theme, and in the variation of tone and imagery in accordance with the wide range of his subjects. But the constraints of the form are apparent in the successive stages of Hugo's *Odes*, and he is concerned with the idea of poetry itself rather than with the development of an individual form.

At this remove, it is not easy to appreciate fully the originality of these poets, which is to be found in·the modernity of their work, if by modernity we mean the installing of procedures which are recognisable as features of recent periods, and not simply the handling of contemporary subjects. For, while there is nothing innovatory in the style and language used (Hugo's work is, however, relatively free from the classical cliché and periphrasis still used by Lamartine), there is one recognisably modern trait present in their work from the outset: the discovery or development of a form adapted to the individual needs of the writer, as against the adaptation of the writer's expression to a form and style consecrated by long usage. Romanticism in French poetry starts with this experimentation, from which the composite art of Symbolism and the twentieth century will derive.

TRIUMPH

The years 1829 to 1833 mark the triumph of Romanticism in French poetry. It is the period during which Romanticism was at its strongest as a rallying-point, and at its most exuberant in terms of the number of poetic talents subscribing to a common programme, which was the free exercise of fantasy and imagination. But the poet who made the running at this time was Hugo. Two collections of verse, *Les Orientales* (1829) and *Les Feuilles d'automne* (1831) established his dominance in this art as well as in the theatre. The two works form a diptych, displaying in separate volumes the two trends which had emerged from the *Odes*: a poetry based on external event and a poetry of inward reflection. As with the successive editions of the *Odes*, Hugo adds a preface to each volume as it appears, and this will be his habit, volume by volume as the formidable total of the poetic works increases. Taken together, the two prefaces show Hugo at the centre of a polemic on the function of a poet at a time of political unrest. Should the poet use the power of his art in an attempt to influence opinion, or should he, as Hugo had done earlier in the decade during the *classique–romantique* controversy, maintain his right to freedom and detachment? In both prefaces, he argues for the artist's right to choose his subjects in his own time and according to his own vision of things, which, of course, is not the same as refusing all political commitment. In fact, by the direct presence of a political subject in his *Orientales* (the fight for Greek independence) and by his reference, in the preface to *Les Feuilles d'automne*, to a collection of 'poésie politique',[6] to be published at a less politically charged moment, he is attempting to keep open to the poet as wide a field as possible. In both prefaces he uses the same formula: 'ce livre inutile', but the defensiveness is an appearance only. Poetry based on Near and Middle Eastern cultures, much of it in the form of fantasy, was justified by the topicality of Greece and Turkey and the growing public familiarity with Eastern countries through the work of specialists. The range of subjects of universal interest opened to the mind of a poet in his day-to-day experience is elaborated as a poetic programme in the preface to *Les Feuilles d'automne*.

In order to exploit the topicality, or popularity, of Eastern subjects, Hugo uses the *ballade*, separated from its medieval trappings and equipped with an impressive range of effects. The manner of the ode is rarely found, although 'Navarin', celebrating the naval battle of October 1827, combines both forms. The war of Greek independence and Hugo's enthusiasm for the Greek cause are the clearest themes of the *Orientales*, but the pro-Greek sentiments are balanced, possibly for artistic reasons, by a more vaguely inspired enthusiasm for the warlike nature and primitive sensibility of the Ottoman rulers and leaders ('Cri de guerre du Mufti', 'La Douleur du Pacha'). Battle scenes, viewed in highly poetical terms, provide Hugo with opportunities to create effects of two kinds: colourful images of action, and macabre commentary on death and desolation. 'Navarin' is carefully centred on a presentation of the sea fight, with bombardments, boarding of vessels and the burning of ships. 'Canaris' gives an inventory of the emblems and colours of the powers engaged in the war. 'Les Têtes du sérail' is a visionary lament for the fall of Missolonghi, and 'L'Enfant' a symbolical piece on Greek resistance, seen as rising afresh out of Turkish destruction. Beyond these effects of violence in war, Hugo imagines other scenes of violence, arising from the code of the harem ('Clair de lune', 'La Sultane favorite'), and follows the theme of oriental love into its sentimental and sensual registers. The imagined beauties of Smyrna are evoked by the voice of a captive Spanish girl ('La Captive'); 'Lazzara' combines an attempt to evoke the charms of a Middle Eastern beauty with an ironical and unpoetical conclusion, supposedly in the Turkish manner; 'Sara la baigneuse', less controlled by an artificial *couleur locale*, combines the visual theme of the *baigneuse* with the inner monologue of the *ingénue* and, by subtleties of form (a seven-syllable quatrain with lines of three syllables echoing the feminine rhyme), suggests the way towards an impressionism that will be developed by poets later in the century. At its best, that is to say at its freest, Hugo's fantasy creates poems of a symbolical kind in which ideas about the poet's state are embodied in vigorous narrative and rapidly moving images of action ('Mazeppa', 'Les Tronçons du serpent'). A symbolical significance is given also to Napoleon, evoked in his Middle Eastern legend ('Bounaberdi'), and permitting Hugo to end his collection with a lofty view of the conqueror's presence ('Lui').

Attempts at producing an appearance of authenticity, by frequent use of Turkish names and by reference to sources (Hugo received notes from an orientalist, Fouinet, in the form of translations of Arabic, Persian and Malayan poems), are far less successful than in the case of *Notre-Dame de Paris*, written two years later and where Hugo contrives to give a remarkably clear configuration of medieval Paris. The success and importance of *Les Orientales* are found in the concept of the poem as a self-contained structure rather than as a feat of eloquence. The *ballade* is of benefit here, since its residual qualities are those of a relatively direct mimetic kind, avoiding rhetorical development and commentary. The tableaux are concentrated, one action being represented (where more complex events are evoked, the poem is divided into discrete sections). The action, self-enclosed, is an illustration, or an emblem, of the life of the countries represented.

It is in this way, as well as in the theory outlined in the preface, that *Les Orientales* encourages the doctrine of *l'art pour l'art*. The position of Hugo himself is too ambivalent to allow him to break completely from the idea of a political and social programme for the artist, and it is noteworthy that, almost a quarter of a century later, the visual techniques of *Les Orientales* will be invoked for the purposes of political satire in *Châtiments*. In their own time, influenced by the work of painters, some of whom, like Boulanger, were depicting Eastern subjects, and enhanced by an enlargement of the poetic vocabulary to include concrete and technical words, as in the list of vessels of the defeated fleet in 'Navarin', they were powerful incentives for poets like Gautier to leave behind the lyrical and philosophical poetry of Lamartine.

But philosophical themes are inherent in Hugo's writings. Three works (*Marion de Lorme*, *Hernani* and *Notre-Dame de Paris*), written between 1829 and 1831, that is, during the period of the composition of *Les Feuilles d'automne*, treat the theme of the enigma of events, in each case the subject being love tragically thwarted by twists of events which form a pattern of fatality. Personal and domestic circumstances had no doubt inclined him to a sombre view of human life: bereavements (the loss of his mother in 1821, of his father in 1828, of his first-born in 1823); the virtual loss of his brother Eugène, victim of a mental collapse; the crisis in his marital life in 1831 – these were the motives of the introspective survey of his life in his thirtieth year which forms the substance of *Les Feuilles d'automne*.

There is some overlap, possibly deliberate, between *Les Orientales* and the collection of 1831. 'Rêverie' and 'Extase' of *Les Orientales* anticipate the speculative vein of *Les Feuilles d'automne*, while 'Bounaberdi' and

'Lui', fantasies on the Napoleonic legend, correspond to the purely personal recollections of poem xxx of *Les Feuilles d'automne*. In the same way, poem xxv, 'Contempler dans son bain sans voiles', takes up a theme from *Les Orientales*, as does in a more general way the visual fancy of 'Soleils couchants' (xxxv). But the programme of the book is as laid down in the preface: love, domestic life, recollected events, are the eternal subjects of poetry and as such are to be defended against the exclusive claims of political events. The last poem, 'Ami, un dernier mot', will safeguard Hugo's position in this respect, by its assertion of the power of the 'muse indignée' against oppressive régimes, and by the reference to the 'corde d'airain' that the poet can, when necessary, fit to his lyre.

'Des vers comme tout le monde en fait ou en rêve': this modest formulation is presumably intended to set the tone of the collection. It is hardly in phase with the gamut of the verse, which includes an *art poétique* based on intuitivism ('Pan') and the hallucinatory conclusion of 'La Pente de la rêverie'. But the aim is a kind of unity, which is achieved by a prevailing atmosphere, already prepared by the artificial conclusion ('Novembre') of *Les Orientales*. This pensive atmosphere is carried mainly by the moral tenor of the poems. It is true that a number of them derive directly from personal recollections (Hugo's mother: 'Ce siècle avait deux ans!'; his father's house at Blois: 'A Monsieur Louis B.'; a landscape: 'Bièvre'; his wife, seen in tears: 'Oh! Pourquoi te cacher?' and through the nostalgia of old love letters: 'O mes lettres d'amour'). But the recollections are discreetly handled and merge into more general themes: the passing of youth, the chastening effects of time, reflections on human destiny. These reflections determine also the movement of poems of a more speculative character, such as 'Où donc est le bonheur?', dominated by the same pessimism which is visible in the more world-weary elegies of Lamartine. From the evidence of the texts, the source of this pessimism in Hugo's case is to be found in the poet's marriage and in the controversies of his artistic life. The verses addressed to his wife ('O toi qui si longtemps . . .') evoke an image of progressive darkness relieved, no longer by a radiant companionship, but by a shared faith in the remote designs of God. Gallant verses, probably written for Charles Nodier's daughter, are included, no doubt to lighten the tone of the love theme, which nevertheless remains sombre. The shadow of time hangs also over the inspiration of the artist. The poem 'Un jour vient . . .' reflects the price paid in creative energy for the successes of the past few years. 'Dédain', originally dedicated to Byron, shows the case of the English poet as representing Hugo's own reaction to envy and denigration. This poem, like the preceding one ('Un jour au mont Atlas . . .'), contrives, by rhetorical means, to defend the task of the poet and his creative power.

The theme of creative power, instinctive in Hugo, is ultimately too strong for the constraints of a poetry ostensibly confined to the theme of fallen leaves, reminiscences and discouragement. The poem to 'M. David, statuaire' is a homage to an artist in another medium, one which powerfully affects the consciousness of nations and the appearance of cities. The stanzas to Lamartine are based on an elaborate metaphor of a double voyage of discovery, and, in the description of the ocean journey and the discoveries made by Lamartine, Hugo is able to give something like full rein to his imaginative powers.[7] The famous image of the 'écho sonore', used in the opening poem 'Ce siècle avait deux ans!', is intended to convey the vigilance of the poet, receptive to all the forces of life. One of these forces, celebrated at some length in the collection, is the impact of children on the imagination of the young poet. The fund of innocence and primitive energy discovered in his children, though it produces over-sentimentalised verses ('Lorsque l'enfant paraît . . .'), is beneficial in that it liberates his own imagination and protects him from the solitude of his calling ('Laissez. – Tous ces enfants . . .'). The consciousness of children suggests new paths for the investigations of the poet, as in 'Dans l'alcôve sombre . . .' where the five-syllable lines carry impressions of the dreams of a sleeping child. In 'La Prière pour tous' (the first of the poems to his daughter Léopoldine, who is later to be the tragic centre of Les Contemplations), the innocence of the child is used as a surface theme for the religiosity of the poet, already drawn away from Catholic orthodoxy by pantheistic intuitions. 'Rêverie' itself, the dominant mood of Les Feuilles d'automne, proves in the end too passive a state, and Hugo's exploratory imagination is led, notably in 'La Pente de la rêverie',[8] towards the area where day-dream melts into vision or hallucination. The expanding vision, which finishes with the blank awareness of the continuum of space and time, is carefully controlled, and the poet's main concern seems to be to find adequate expression for his experience. But the poem marks the first stage in a long series of efforts to give explicit form to the limits of consciousness. It could have formed the conclusion of this collection, but the poet preferred to finish on a more climactic note with 'Pan', a strong, dithyrambic piece on artistic inspiration (it is placed third from the end, but the two final pieces are in the form of postscripts). In this poem, Hugo reaches the furthest point of reaction against the factions and polemics of the capital and the artificial notions of poetry which are still current. The truest poetry now seems to him to be that which draws on the instinctive powers of the imagination, which are at their strongest when in direct contact with the forces of nature. So the poet, his subjects, action, intelligence and inspiration are under the aegis of Pan, the deity of nature, and the most natural poetry arises from the interchange between the visible universe and the mental world of the poet.

> C'est Dieu qui remplit tout. Le monde, c'est son temple.

This Lamartinian expression (it is almost certainly drawn from *Méditations poétiques*: 'L'Immortalité') is a sign of Hugo's position in 1831. His reputation made, his imaginative powers have still to find their full development, and he is straining towards a form outside the codified structures of traditional prosody. It is interesting that, in his poem, 'A M. de Lamartine', he evokes himself and his distinguished senior, in their imaginary single-handed ocean voyages, 'échevelés dans la brume, / Chantant plus haut dans l'ouragan'. The idea presented is of songs, powerful, solitary, free, but heard against the din of the hurricane, which presumably stands for the opposition encountered by new poetry; and, from the general sense of the verses to Lamartine, Hugo would seem to be suggesting that the discoveries Lamartine had made lay in the power of symbolising the ideal. For the moment, he seems to accept a vision of the world which is fundamentally that of the Lamartine of 1820.

But Lamartine, from the end of 1825 on diplomatic service in Florence, and back in France on indefinite leave in 1828, the star of the salons when he appeared in Paris, was himself passing through a crucial stage in his relationship with his art. The epic poem, the 'Grand Poème' that he longed to write, while fearing that his time and his powers would not permit him to complete the vast design – the slow movement of a spirit towards redemption through many incarnations – was hardly taking shape. He fell back on a less ambitious enterprise, the composition, from about the spring of 1826, of a series of religious lyrics which he first called 'modern psalms'. A volume of these lyrics took shape over four years, appearing in 1830 under the title of *Harmonies poétiques et religieuses*. About half were written in a period of relative tranquillity in Italy, the others in the two years preceding the abdication of Charles X. The 'harmonies toscanes' were of more purely religious inspiration, those written in France reflect some of the unrest of the second crisis of his life. His political views were changing, and with the change the direction of his life was called into question. In his speech to the Académie Française on his reception in 1829, he publicly underlined his growing liberalism. During 1830, his decision was probably made to seek election as a *député* in the new government. But before this, a more immediate ambition remained: a grand tour of the Middle East and the Holy Land, where perhaps his religious doubts might be resolved. His mother's death in 1829 had deprived him of the strongest influence inclining him to Christian belief. He undertook the journey in 1831.

The principal motive for the composition of the *Harmonies* was, however, ambition. The title shows the continuing quest for artistic discovery, a stage beyond the *Méditations*. In a postscript to the Letter introducing his *Harmonies* in the 1849 edition, Lamartine gives a tentative definition in the form of a list of themes virtually coextensive with individual human life, and concludes with the following: 'tous les bruits de la vie dans un cœur sonore, ce sont ces harmonies . . .' Is this the Hugolian metaphor in *Les Feuilles d'automne*, of the poet's 'âme de cristal' echoing in unison with the world ('écho sonore')? Whatever the significance of the similarity may be, the ideas differ in one important respect. Lamartine's *harmonies* appear to be the transcription of the affective life of an individual and not concerned with external events in themselves. The realities on which they are based are the inner realities of the poet's mind, whether musing on the past, or on the prompting of impressions from the outside world, or (which is most often the case) on the disproportion between the evidence of life as lived in the world and the desire to savour the assurance of an unseen divine order. No clear sense of the term *harmonies* emerges from Lamartine's explanation, but the poems themselves suggest two levels of interpretation, corresponding respectively to the thought and the technique. At the first level, the poems invite interpretation as the blending of dissonant themes to achieve a final expression of elevation and hope. At the second, they can be taken, by virtue of their form, as analogous to musical compositions. In using the word 'psalm' to describe them, Lamartine was presumably thinking of the musical nature of the psalm, as well as of its inspiration, guided between songs of distress and paeans of praise and deliverance. In style and imagery, as well as in the handling of this great double theme, Lamartine follows the manner of the Psalms, but prefers labels such as *hymne* and *cantate*. These *hymnes* usually have the strophic variety of the ode, but the term is no doubt used by Lamartine to indicate a less complicated form, adapted to the celebrating of one theme, without the ornamental devices of the ode. Not all the poems follow this formula. The religious tension is relieved by shorter pieces developing immediate impressions: on sadness; to a nightingale; a woman singer. One great poem ('Novissima Verba') is a development of the *méditation*, moving retrospectively over the surface of the poet's life and illustrating the transient beauty and inconclusiveness of man's passage through the world.

In the *Avertissement* to the 1830 edition, Lamartine, in stressing the naturalness of his process of composition, describes his *Harmonies* as 'quatre livres de poésies écrites comme elles ont été senties, sans liaison et sans suite, sans transition apparente'. The mastery of form and the appearance of effortless development do indeed suggest the presence of a natural poet. But the volume is carefully prepared and carefully ordered. The seventy-two poems of the original edition[9] are distributed more or less equally over the four books referred to. Books I and II are forms of reflection on a missing reality and on the means of stirring the human consciousness to awareness of the Creator. These are suggested through symbols, subjects of meditation for the solitary mind: the solar cycle ('Hymne de la nuit'; 'Hymne du matin'); the lamp in the sanctuary ('La Lampe du temple'); a moonlit landscape ('Poésie, ou Paysage dans le Golfe de Gênes'); the destruction of a famous Roman landscape ('La Perte de l'Anio'); images of time and change ('La Source dans les bois d'***'). A sequence of four powerful odes on the idea of God conveys, through sets of images, a historical and, in some respects, evolutionary view of religious consciousness, combining modern attitudes with a range of poetic effect, from recitative based on the Old Testament ('Jehova'), to the demonstrative stanza of the traditional ode ('Le Chêne'), and to a more personal lyrical style ('L'Humanité', 'L'Idée de Dieu'). These four poems, presenting a view of the progressive nature of religions and a vision of man caught between two mysteries, mortality and immortality, form the centre of the first two books. In Books III and IV, Lamartine concentrates pieces in a more familiar style, tracing reminiscences and impressions of his personal life ('Milly, ou La Terre natale' is one of his best-known poems in this descriptive and reflective register). These are grouped round two poems, in each of which the poet sets down an aspect of his credo. 'Hymne au Christ' is an affirmation of his attachment to the Christian faith in an age of doubt and conflicting doctrines. 'Novissima Verba' is a survey of the values of his life, now seen as dominated by tokens of mortality and fragments of truth. Such tokens and fragments are the substance of short pieces of Books III and IV ('Le Tombeau d'une mère' is written on the death of his mother; 'Le Premier Regret' evokes memories of Graziella and Italy more than fifteen years before).

The religious theme, basically the conflict of doubt and faith and the quest for evidence from human experience that might abolish doubt, is continued from the *Méditations*, where it had found its most dramatic expression in 'Le Désespoir' and 'La Providence à l'homme'. The central conflict is no nearer resolution in the *Harmonies*. The 'Hyme au Christ' is largely about the growing challenge to the values brought to the world by Christ. The religious elevation of Books I and II is a form of idealism whose associations range over religions in general. In Lamartine's eyes, no doubt, this poetry was modern and original in that it brought the historical perspectives of contemporary thought into the same lyrical framework as the sacred songs of the Old Testament. It also marked a stage in the development of the long tradition of biblical paraphrase by French poets. Further, the adaptation of techniques and style to the variations which the religious theme demands is at a level probably not reached before. The fixed forms of individual poems keep largely to the alexandrine or octosyllabic line; but there are also short experimental pieces in a melodic style ('La Tristesse', 'Le Rossignol'), in which already something of the tone of Verlaine is heard. But it is in the *hymnes* and the odes that the control of form is at its finest. Within the long poems of free construction, the modulations are obtained by striking metrical variety (lines of seven or five syllables are used to particular effect) marking the stages of the theme.

This inventiveness is part of the Romantic renewal of poetry, and has its counterpart, at another level, in Hugo's *Orientales*. But Hugo's verse marks also an advance towards modernity in the enlargement of poetic vocabulary for greater precision in pictorial effect. Lamartine, despite his awareness of the need for change, did not follow in this direction. While his syntax is mainly free from the inversion and periphrasis of the style of the previous century, his vocabulary is marked by influences from the Old Testament and by the persistence of stylised classical elements. This is one reason why his *Harmonies*, where his artistic powers are at their height, did not have any decisive effect on the course of lyrical poetry in France. Another, and more cogent, reason is that attitudes were changing. Liberalism and scepticism were replacing, among the literary generation of 1830, the Catholicism and royalism that Hugo had confidently predicted for the society of the Restoration. Nerval, in the first chapter of *Sylvie*, recalls the 1830s as a period when young writers could neither find their way among the conflicting religious and philosophical doctrines of the time, nor accept the race for honours in an increasingly materialistic society. Lamartine himself saw fit to orientate his book more closely towards the contemporary world by adding to the 1832 edition an important ode: 'Les Révolutions', on the theme of progress, and in which he castigates the instinct of peoples and rulers to perpetuate an existing order, and summons them to accept change, however violent or unpredictable, as part of an ordained movement towards a more perfect state. But other issues occupied the minds of younger writers in 1830, and Lamartine's lessons of idealism and lyricism, appreciated as they were by the public of the time, drew him few disciples.

Sainte-Beuve was certainly not a disciple but, to some small extent a follower, of Lamartine in his *Vie, Poésies et Pensées de Joseph Delorme*. 'Je suis resté avant tout un Élégiaque et un rêveur'; but the elegiacs and reveries of Sainte-Beuve do not attempt to imitate the elevation or the pessimism of Lamartine. They pursue the personal theme into the private corners of daily life, where the mind can find an enclave of freedom. The short poem is what is needed to keep pace with the 'incomplet génie' of Delorme, who uses poetry of fixed forms, quite often sonnets, to express snatches of intimate thought: timorous love fantasies, reflections set down for friends, thoughts on reading *Adolphe*, elegiac landscapes. The mood is autumn, a flat calm inhibits the flights of the mind. Imagining his muse, Delorme sees her, not as one of the Nine in full panoply, but as a shy country girl living in a remote spot and caring for an aged father; frail and consumptive, escaping sometimes by night with the poet, and beautiful in the moonlight. The manner of other poets preoccupies him: Ronsard, Wordsworth, Kirke White. But the style of this eclectic poetry is direct, unemphatic, precise, often prosaic. Paradoxically, Lamartine learned from the *musa pedestris* of Sainte-Beuve, as passages of familiar lyricism in *Jocelyn* will show, and Delorme's blend of introspection, realism and aesthetic reference will have its repercussions through the century (Gautier, Coppée, Verlaine, Baudelaire).

The master of the new generation of poets was Hugo, but the Hugo of *Les Orientales* rather than of the grander manner of the *Odes*. These poets, Gautier, Musset, Petrus Borel, for example, exploited the current mode of fantasy and the doctrine of artistic freedom. Gautier begins, in his small volume of *Poésies* published in 1830, with short pieces, mostly covering familiar ground: elegies, *ballades*, discreet landscapes, a 'méditation'. The aim is aesthetic pleasure, whether produced by impressions of a sunset, a springtime love fantasy suggested by a line of Joseph Delorme, or by the adjusting of a subtle theme to a delicate form, as in the attempt to describe the flight of the dragonfly. To these early pieces, which passed almost unnoticed in the political upheavals of 1830, he adds additional short poems within the same range, together with a lengthy extravaganza entitled *Albertus* (1832), apparently written in twelve-line stanzas, but actually forming a sequence of *terza rima*.

Albertus was described by Gautier as 'semi-diabolique, semi-fashionable', by which he meant a combination of the mock-gothic and a Byronic dandyism. The poem is a parody of both of these. Ostensibly a narrative, it lacks a narrative sequence, and this is part of the design. The practice of digressions is an integral part of the technique, as is the prevailing tone of bantering familiarity. But there are two points on which Gautier's intention remains sincere, and these points are the poles of Albertus's character. One is a profound scepticism arising from the spectacle of mortality, the other is the veneration of art. In Gautier's story, Albertus is destroyed gratuitously by a crude machinery of witchcraft and *diablerie*. His cynicism and attitude of disdain, the marks of a disabused idealist, are used only to a superficial degree to motivate his end, which occurs after a passionate sexual encounter with the sorceress who procures his soul for the Devil on a quibble, taking literally his protestation that he would give his soul for a night of love with her. If an adolescent morality about love and the primrose way to the everlasting bonfire hovers over the poem, the devotion to art provides its true purpose.

The painter Albertus embodies Gautier's ideas on art, and specifically the role of art as compensation for the realities of human life and human nature. This is found both in the poem and in the preface of 1832. In this context, art refers to the object created, and to the universe suggested, by the skill of the artist; it presumably refers as well to the aim and purpose of the artist, which is to idealise the world through representation. A conflict arises here between the need for realism (depiction according to appearances and probabilities) and the desire to transcend reality. Gautier does not pursue the question at this stage, but the principles of what Baudelaire will later call 'sorcellerie évocatoire' can be seen already. A second series of ideas is found in *Albertus*, not illustrated through the character, but exemplified in the fabrication of the poem. These concern the subjects and techniques chosen by the artist. Here, the apparently wilful digressions, the change of tone and theme, the adjustment of vocabulary and style to the depiction of various locations, the courage to tackle new or risky subjects, such as the explicit description of a sexual act followed by the macabre evocation of lascivious young flesh turning into a scrawny bag of bones, the experimental 'transposition d'art' (the depiction in verse of a painting or sculpture), are examples of the theory of artistic freedom put into action. Hugo had laid down the law in the preface to *Les Orientales*: 'il n'y a, en poésie, ni bons ni mauvais sujets, mais de bons et de mauvais poètes', and this, coupled with the idea, promulgated in the *Préface de 'Cromwell'*, of the need for the grotesque as well as the sublime in art, had provided a programme which, largely through Gautier's influence, would lead away from the main preoccupations of Romanticism, towards the theory of art as an end in itself, to be judged by the perfection of its form and the beauty of its effect.

For the moment, Gautier's attention was largely on the new effects to be achieved in verse, following the victories achieved by the Romantic school in the theatre and the novel. With all distinctions abolished between the vocabulary of poetry and the vocabulary of prose (but, as Hugo had warned, with no liberties taken with syntax),[10] he was able to score some remarkable successes with eccentric stanzas formed principally of flamboyant catalogues of objects (the description of the painter's studio, in stanza LXXVII, or the inventory of night birds and menacing creatures, with attendant sound effects, in stanza CX). Secondly, by his use of parody and by a kind of satirical whimsy offsetting the extravagance of the supernatural events, Gautier brought a welcome touch of humour into the surface areas of the Romantic imagination.

Humour was also an attractive part of Musset's early work. Introduced into the *Cénacle* at the age of eighteen, distinguished by Sainte-Beuve as 'un enfant plein de génie', he saw his first volume of verse, *Contes d'Espagne et d'Italie*, through the press in 1830. The praise from his fellow poets of the *Cénacle*, who saw him as a brilliant exponent of Romantic themes, was echoed in the press, where he scored a *succès de scandale* with another aspect of his talent, a relaxed and irreverent wit. A disciple of the Romantic school in his adaptation of its theatrical fashions to narrative verse ('Don Paez', 'Portia') and in his cycle of Spanish romances based on the *ballade*, he becomes the parodist of its mannerisms in 'Mardoche' and 'Ballade à la lune'. Don Paez derives from Othello; and Dalti (the hero of 'Portia') from Hernani. Both act out a drama of passion, and both act according to a form of honour which is determined by the power of love rather than by a social code. In concentrating upon the tyranny of passion and the ravages of its effect, Musset, notwithstanding the derivative nature of his material, found at the outset the inspirational centre of his writing, and the art with which this theme is developed is expertly contrived to bring out gradations of feeling and tension. By contrast, 'Mardoche' appears to invert all the values of romantic love. Mardoche's enslavement to his passion for Rosine is measured by the broken ankle he sustains in jumping from a bedroom window when surprised by the enraged husband in the cynically contrived seclusion of his uncle's presbytery. The flimsy narrative is spread over fifty-nine ten-line stanzas, in which the action is liberally interspersed with passages of reflection, mostly satirical. Racy, immoral, irreligious,stuffed with allusions to fashionable life (Mardoche is depicted as a dandy), the poem none the less rejoins the more serious design of Musset in the analysis of the sexual relationship concerned, based as it is on egoism and insincerity. In the same way, the 'Ballade à la lune' parodies the serious Romantic *ballade*, presenting itself as an updated version of the form, while at the same time harking back to an older tradition, that of the burlesque poetry of the seventeenth century, which deflates grandiloquence by caricature. Musset's poem, a sequence of fancies and conceits prompted by the sight of the moon over the rooftops of Paris, offers groups of images exploiting different styles or manners through pastiche or parody (funeral meditation, classical allusion, stereotyped lyrical reactions),[11] but contrives to produce an effect which is strikingly modern.

Modernity is the main impulse in Musset's writing, as it was in the case of the other major innovators. But, in Musset's case, there is a growing impatience with the political and historical perspectives which seem to threaten to take art on a false trail towards forms of external realism. In the *Dédicace*, written in 1832, for his poetic play, *La Coupe et les lèvres*, he explains to his friend, Alfred Tattet, his view of the crucial choice that faces the artist: whether to opt, like Calderón or Mérimée, for a realism that works from the outside, or whether, like Racine or Shakespeare, to depict the working of the human mind ('le cœur humain'). His choice is the art that illuminates the inward nature of men and women, though he appears to view with some scepticism the rewards of clear insight into human minds. Other personal choices emerge in the same *Dédicace*: his reservations on large themes and notions currently exploited by writers – concern for the nation; orthodox Catholicism; nature – preferring, as he explains, the arts and the inspiriting force of love as the basis of his own work, which he seeks to make entirely original, avoiding imitation and plagiarism.

Until about 1833, however, Musset followed the formula of *Contes d'Espagne et d'Italie*: songs or romances, narrative pieces and the digressive parody. After 1830, he began to distance himself from his Romantic models, not merely for the sake of pastiche or irreverent commentary, but in order also to treat his themes with greater independence. A singleness of aim becomes apparent, whatever the form or techniques may be: to concentrate his verse upon the one subject which seems to him of ultimate value, which is human love, and specifically the analysis of the motives of sexual conduct. 'Qctave', a 'fragment' leading to a surprising denouement of the jealousy motif, finds its originality in the blending of two manners, the manner of the poetic drama and the manner of an uncommitted observer. 'Suzon' adds to the mechanics of unnatural death through love a bitter commentary, implied rather than spoken, on male depravity and on the degeneracy of the Church. 'Rolla' (1833), the last of the heavy Romantic narratives by Musset, uses the Byronic figure of Rolla to motivate reflections upon the contemporary state of religion and society. The analysis is summary, carried as it is by two emotional passages, one lyrical and nostalgic on the death of the old religions and the collapse of faith in the modern period, the other declamatory, on the decline of the social and moral values, attributed by the poet largely to the work of the eighteenth century, which is epitomised in his view by Voltaire. Rolla represents the type of the *déclassé* aristocrat, exaggerated in the interests of the melodramatic action, but drawn according to the way in which Musset saw the effects of the new social order on individuals of his own generation. A similar diagnosis is used in his *Confession d'un enfant du siècle*, drawing the causes of this social inadaptability from the so-called 'maladie du siècle', while the aesthetic of personal freedom laid down in 'Les Vœux stériles' (1831) and 'Les Secrètes Pensées de Rafaël, gentilhomme français' (1831) is based also on the loss of an aristocratic independence, which leaves the artist, in Musset's judgment, too much in conflict with the dictates of literary fashion, the opinions of critics and the favour of the public.

This independence is reflected in Musset's nostalgia for the art of Ancient Greece and of the Italy of the Renaissance, personal enthusiasms not widely found in the reigning literary school, and by his adoption of a casual and dilettantish manner out of keeping with the high sense of the poet's responsibility advocated by the leaders of that art. In the group of songs or romances written between 1830 and 1833, a bantering tone runs under the charm of the love lyrics, while in 'Namouna' (1832), Musset again achieves an impressive feat of diversionary tactics, under the guise of an oriental tale which he cannot get under way. 'Namouna' is an *art poétique*. The techniques of discontinuity are not used, as in 'Mardoche', to suspend and elaborate the events, but to probe some of the problems of writing and to give a rather disillusioned sketch of the poet in his relation with his art and in his modest expectations of contact with readers. Frustrated idealism, vulnerability, the effort to describe the deepest promptings of the quest for happiness, the inconclusive pursuit of art, these are the values on which 'Namouna' is constructed, and they are the values of Musset's mature writings.

The informality of style found in 'Namouna' and 'Mardoche' marks a rapid advance in the direction already indicated by Hugo,[12] but Musset's technique of constant intervention requires direct and familiar language which, in the case of 'Mardoche', serves the purposes of the dialogue also, and in 'Namouna' as exploited for the sake of contrast with the highly wrought literary passages. In the same way, the Romantic enthusiasm for varied verse forms and for evocative and sonorous rhymes is exploited by Musset quite often for his own ends rather than from adherence to agreed practice. 'Namouna', for example, is composed of twelve-syllable lines in six-line stanzas based on two rhymes, masculine and feminine. There is no fixed rhyme pattern, and Musset's practice throughout the poem is almost uniformly to use *rime suffisante*,[13] avoiding the more elaborate and sonorous effects of *rime riche* in order not to impede the natural progression of the syntax over the lines. Some rhymes of little poetic quality (*voici/ainsi; a tous/avant vous; une rose/on cause*, etc.) are used deliberately to produce a casual or throw-away effect. It is noteworthy also that Musset makes little use of the enlarged resources of the alexandrine,[14] introduced mainly through the influence of Hugo, who refers already in his *Préface de 'Cromwell'* (1827) to the need for a more supple form. In the narrative pieces, the sense respects the binary division of the line. In the informal poems, the effect of spoken language, of a conversation carried on with the reader, is achieved mostly through the fragmentation of the line by strong pauses and by playing down the role of rhyme.

DIVERGENCE

By 1833 the Romantic movement in French poetry had done its work. Starting with the regeneration of poetic forms, the search for a new immediacy of expression and the adaptation of verse to public as well as private themes, it had produced, in something over a decade, an enlargement of poetry which enabled it to cover religious, philosophical and historical subjects in a highly individual manner, largely free from didacticism. This was made possible by three developments of technique. First, discoveries were made, principally by Lamartine and Hugo, about the increased impact of imagery once freed from the formality of classical reference and made a necessary part of the poet's invention. Secondly, by exploiting areas of familiar and technical language hitherto closed to writers of verse, the Romantics greatly increased the scope of poetry by putting it on a direct footing with contemporary life. In this respect, the special nature of Musset's contribution needs to be underlined. Whereas Hugo, Sainte-Beuve and Gautier, in seeking changes of style or an extension of vocabulary, worked strictly within the literary language, Musset achieved, particularly in 'Namouna', a loosening of syntax, a conversational ease and a style capable of a remarkable range of effects, which put this work, whatever its intrinsic merits, well ahead of its time. Thirdly, the renewal of the expressive power of poetry needed a wealth of stanza forms and a verse instrument better attuned to modern syntax and language. The modifications brought to the alexandrine, discreet enough in themselves, provoked much opposition in their time but, once accepted and integrated, lasted without much further change until the Symbolist experiments of 1886.

The brilliant coalescing of views and talents was now over, as far as the major figures were concerned. Lamartine, elected as a *député* for Bergues in 1833,[15] contrived to live a double life as poet and politician until the end of the decade, when his work as a poet virtually came to an end, his public career and reputation continuing to rise until his crushing defeat in the presidential elections of 1848. Vigny, preoccupied with the novel and the theatre, did not return to poetry until the end of the decade, when he turned to the slow composition of the poems forming his *Destinées*. Hugo's poetic output continued without interruption to the end of the decade, showing a progressively ambitious view of the function of the poet. Subsequently caught up in public life, given a peerage, with the title of vicomte by Louis-Philippe in 1845, he published no poetry until the period of his political exile during the régime of Louis-Napoléon, when the great works of his maturity were composed.

The two younger poets, Gautier and Musset, continued, however, to develop within the Romantic formula during the 1830s, Gautier by design, *La Comédie de la Mort* (1838), being a delayed publication of verses which follow on from *Albertus*, Musset more or less by accident, his famous *Nuits* (1835–7) being the outcome of the dolorous affair with George Sand, which was ended in 1834.

Gautier's poem derives from the graveyard and Satanic schools, the models being mainly English and German (Young, Ann Radcliffe, Byron, Hoffmann), and its theme is death, treated in the mode of macabre fantasy. Musset's quartet of poems is based on the elegy, but is distinguished from the work of other elegists (Catullus, Propertius, Ronsard, Chénier, Parny) in that it concentrates on the bitterness and psychological disturbance brought by unhappy sexual involvement.

Gautier sets himself at the centre of an All Hallows vision of charnel life-after-death, and of the ghosts of Faust, Don Juan[16] and Napoleon. These three Romantic stereotypes represent three forms of the human drive towards ultimate fulfilment (through necromancy, love and political power), all thwarted by the conditions of life. Enriched, as in the case of *Albertus*, by the addition of a number of short lyrics which are among the ornaments of Romanticism, too easily disregarded among the imposing works of the leaders of the school, *La Comédie de la Mort* stands as a series of illustrations of ideas about the relationship of the artist to his work (Gautier's examples are most frequently drawn from the visual arts). An essential pessimism colours his imagination and intensifies the sense of disproportion between the idealised constructions of the mind and the life lived by the artist with few material resources. The glory of the artist is his obsession with his art, in which the sole consolation of his life is found, since the aim of his life is the realisation of beauty. This beauty can be macabre, as in the treatment of death and decay, aesthetic, as in the interpretation of *objets d'art*, or elegant, as in the presentation of decorative or sentimental subjects. These values, arising from an art of apparently limited pretensions, and mostly visual in its procedures, proved to be one of the most vital aspects of Romanticism in its impact on poets of the future, particularly Baudelaire and Mallarmé.[17] After the publication of *España* (1840), a collection of *poésies diverses* in which, under the colouring of the Spanish subjects the main themes persist, Gautier's poetry changed fundamentally in range, form and technique. His *Émaux et Camées* (1852) move out of Romanticism into a different period and help to shape the artistic values of *Le Parnasse*.

The *Nuits* derive entirely from Musset's own experience, and the artistic value of this experience, grief and resentment at sexual betrayal, has had its detractors as well as its apologists; so has the intensity with which the emotional state is expressed. No doubt the particular way in which Musset stages his private drama has appeared to many readers as artificial and over-theatrical. However, no less than the gothic scenery of Gautier, the Muse of Musset's poems is an accepted part of the conventions of this time, even for such a parodist of mannerisms. Superficially, the title evokes the work of Young, and it is true that the supernatural dominates 'La Nuit de décembre', and is presumably present in the dialogues of the poet with the insubstantial Muse. But the night setting of the poems is probably no more than an elegiac convention, of less importance than the months named in the titles. These represent the four seasons of the year and, symbolically, the four phases of the poet's period of mental distress and recovery. Three of the poems, 'La Nuit de mai', 'La Nuit d'août' and 'La Nuit d-octobre', form a sequence consonant both with the passage of the seasons and the progressive state of mind of the poet. The fourth, 'La Nuit de décembre', a soliloquy, stands apart from the others. The key to this poem, which gives a series of descriptions of a ghostly visitant in the shape of the poet himself, at crucial stages of his life, is in the last line: 'la Solitude'. The prior stage of the experience recounted in the *Nuits* is therefore this uneasy and haunted winter solitude. The remaining three poems treat the problem of the poet's recovery, which is seen, not in terms of a restoration to health, but of fitness to resume the practice of his art. In 'La Nuit de mai', the regeneration of nature finds no counterpart in the renewal of inspiration in the poet, too close to the upheaval of his emotional life. In 'La Nuit d'août', the poet, caught up in the euphoria of a new love and finding assurance of the renewal of life around him in the high summer, has not recovered his poetic gift. Before this is possible, he has to come to terms with the experience of betrayal and breakdown. The symbolic autumn setting of 'La Nuit d'octobre' is the background to a reappraisal of his life, and there are fine passages, varied in form and tone, which fluctuate between painful memories, imprecations, and recall of the privileged solitude of the poet's study.

In the three dialogues, Musset assigns to the Muse a defence of poetry which does not necessarily correspond to his own view. The idea of escape into literary subjects, and the view that

Les chants désespérés sont les chants les plus beaux,

are not accepted by the poet in 'La Nuit de mai', at a moment when he is trying to come to terms with an overwhelming experience, and when any attempt to communicate his thoughts in verse would be like writing in the sand when the violent north wind is blowing. The stilted simile of the pelican and the poet, in the same poem, is part of the discourse of the Muse. In 'La Nuit d'août', the fragility of a poetic talent is stressed in the speeches attributed to her. In 'La Nuit d'octobre', the claims of poetry appear to be centred on a state where the gusts of passion have subsided and a more reflective art is possible.

The theme of the capacity of poetry to carry the immediate quality of passion, particularly dramatic and tragic passion, was implicit in Musset's earlier poetry but, up to the composition of 'Le Saule' (1833),[18] he used more and more elaborate devices of narrative and commentary. In the *Nuits*, Musset found a vehicle for a direct lyrical expression of the emotions of betrayed love, demonstrating a powerful development of the line suggested by Lamartine's personal poetry in 1820. Romantic lyricism will not advance further in this direction. Hugo's love lyrics of his final period, richer and more varied, are, in Wordsworth's phrase, 'emotion recollected in tranquillity', with all the mastery of a lifetime's practice of the art. Musset's *Nuits* embody the energy and instinctive talent of a maturing artist still looking for new departures. But they are his last major contribution to poetry. His other serious lyrics, 'Lettre à Lamartine' (1836) and 'Souvenir' (1841) are artificial or derivative by comparison. 'Souvenir' has been given a spurious representative significance by comparison, out of context, with 'Le Lac' and Hugo's 'Tristesse d'Olympio', and with attendant implications of a Romanticism based on sentimental reverie.[19]

To some extent, this surface appearance of a poetry of impressions, based on shifting sentiments according to the changing pattern of the days or seasons, was encouraged at this time by the poets themselves. Hugo's three collections following *Les Feuilles d'automne* have titles which suggest elegiac, introspective or descriptive verse: *Les Chants du crépuscule* (1835), *Les Voix intérieures* (1837), *Les Rayons et les ombres* (1840). But each title has an underlying sense. The *crépuscule* is intended to represent the indistinct light towards dawn as well as the dusk of evening, and also signifies the uncertain period after the 1830 insurrections as well as private uncertainties. *Les Voix intérieures* are the promptings received by the poet from his experiences of domestic life, the natural world and public events, and this is part of the programme set out in the prefaces to the three works. *Les Rayons et les ombres* is a title covering disparate reactions to experiences, which the poet tries to synthesise in a vision of universal life. A progression is apparent through the three books, partly in the political attitude reflected, partly in the treatment of the personal theme which, in *Les Rayons et les ombres*, tends to express the more abstract sense of the experiences described, and in the attempt to combat doubt and uncertainty by accepting the poet's duty, which is to embrace the totality of the experience of an individual in the modern world.[20]

Concerned to keep abreast of events and of the expectations of his contemporaries, Hugo devotes half of *Les Chants du crépuscule* to political subjects. The range is curiously wide – at a moment when he appears to have taken a firm stand in support of the Orleans monarchy ('Dictée après juillet 1830'): it includes two poems on Canaris, recalled to memory as a man of action on behalf of Greece; verses on Poland, subjugated by Russia after emulating the French uprisings of 1830; and two pieces on the Napoleonic legend ('A la Colonne', 'Napoléon II'). Three themes emerge from this grouping: confidence in the future of France; the denunciation of oppressive régimes; admiration of Napoleon and the period of the Empire. These persist, not only throughout this trilogy, but also in the post-1850 period of Hugo's work. For the present, the major accomplishment of the cycle of political poems is the epic vision of 'A l'Arc de triomphe' (*Les Voix intérieures*). Rising above its immediately circumstantial nature (the completion in 1836 of Napoleon's *arc de triomphe* begun in 1806), it provides an archaeological vision of Paris in a remote future, in which the monument survives along with Notre-Dame and the Column of the Place Vendôme, and with the monument survive the exploits of the Empire.

> Je garde le trésor des gloires de l'empire
> (*Les Rayons et les ombres*: 'A Laure, Duch. d'A.')

The enthusiasm for the Napoleonic era outweighs the enthusiasm for the immediate future of the new monarchy, to which little space is devoted in *Les Voix intérieures* and none in *Les Rayons et les ombres*. Instead, Hugo's intention appears to be to trace an evolving attitude of political independence.

> Et maintiens-toi superbe au-dessus des partis,

he wrote to the sculptor David d'Angers in a speculative poem of *Les Rayons et les ombres*, and this is the attitude recommended also in 'Fonction du poète' in the same volume, where the avoidance of political commitment is redeemed by a commitment to the larger values of an improved society.

Stages of pessimism and uncertainty are traced in all three collections. A significant development is the appearance of the theme of social concern, satirical in *Les Chants du crépuscule*, where one poem (XIII, partly written in 1831) anticipates 'Rolla', moral and sentimental elsewhere. The theme of deprived children in 'Rencontre' will find its prolongation in a number of subsequent texts (*Les Contemplations*, *Les Misérables*, *La Légende des siècles*). Allusions to thorny passages in his private and artistic life are countered by the fabrication of a persona, Olympio, the poet who seeks a total vision of life. Recollected episodes of his childhood at Les Feuillantines in Paris, and others concerning his own children, are presented as privileged enclaves, and the love theme, closely attached to the realities of his life, is used for effects of joy and consolation.[21] The cycle of poems to Juliette Drouet begins in these three volumes, and will find its fuller development in *Les Contemplations*. In *Les Rayons at les ombres*, love is already treated in its more abstract aspects. The famous elegy, 'Tristesse d'Olympio' combining notations of a scene revisited with reflections inspired by the absence of the mistress, is found here.

Through all three volumes, bringing an underlying coherence to the poems, runs the theme of the slow formation of the poet, expressed in more sombre forms in poems of doubt,[22] and arriving at suggestions of a total vision in *Les Rayons et les ombres*. In this work, the mind of the poet dwells on the secret affinities in nature ('A une jeune femme') and on 'l'œuvre indéfinie et sombre / Qu'avec le genre humain fait la création' ('Matelots! Matelots!'). A provisional answer is reached in 'Sagesse'. The view of the place of man in the universe is, however, still nearer Lamartine's 'L'Homme' than the ideas of 'Ce que dit la bouche d'ombre', and the view of the poet's mission is based on commitment as well as on the practice of an attitude leading to visionary detachment, as the three 'voices' of the poem show in their guidance of his progress. Anger, love, religious consciousness: in the sequence of the text, the voices suggest conflict or a supplanting of attitudes. The religious attitude has evolved towards deism. The idea of the separation of the human intelligence from God, and of the need to enhance intuitive awareness, is the idea on which the book closes, and with it Hugo's cycle of poems of the 1830s.

Hugo's programme was based on the lyric. All the forms with which he experimented in the two decades of the Romantic movement are brought into the area of lyricism. His conception of the book of poetry was, from about 1829, of a fragmentary work in which short poems, given a coherence by their arrangement and by unifying themes, were designed to imprint the poet's message on the mind of the public by the impact and variety of many individual pieces. On the whole, this was the prevailing conception of the Romantic poets. Lamartine, who appeared in some respects to follow tradition by suggesting in his titles poetry of a single type, may well have influenced subsequent developments by the range and variety of his *Méditations*. In his last lyrical work, *Recueillements poétiques* (1839), where no new formula or experimental writing is involved, it is noticeable that his aim is to please his readers by a diversification of forms and techniques already familiar to them, the sense of familiarity being heightened by a number of occasional pieces and echoes of earlier works.[23]

But not all the poets of the period conformed to this pattern. Vigny's *Poèmes antiques et modernes* is a work where the epic intention predominates, although the forms of his poems are too complex to fit within a single category. Nevertheless, in his 'Éloa' he reaches the most authentic epic level in French Romantic poetry, and 'Le Déluge', 'Moïse', and 'Le Mont des oliviers' (this last written probably in 1839, but published posthumously with *Les Destinées*), with their identical symbolism of isolation on the mountain, provide an epic perspective of the Judaeo-Christian eras, which is not sustained, because Vigny's concern is ultimately not with the epic itself but with the conveying of ideas about the modern world.

In the *Préface de 'Cromwell'*, Hugo ruled out the epic as being a form which ended with the period of pagan antiquity, superseded in the Christian era by the lyric and drama; and he noted, in passing, the inaptitude of the French for the epic poem. It remains, however, that Vigny considered this form, although with important modifications, as part of the programme of the new poetry of the 1820s, and that a number of lesser poets had swollen the list of epic writers of small or moderate talent. In the Romantic period itself, the works of Quinet deserve mention: *Ahasvérus* (1833), in prose and mainly dramatic in form; *Napoléon* (1836) and *Prométhée* (1838), in verse. Ménard, Soumet, Bouilhet, Laprade, with widely differing subjects, classical, national, scientific, etc., prolonged the cult of the epic into the Parnassian period, the master himself, Leconte de Lisle, preferring the relatively short, densely written form of the 'étude' as found in the *Poèmes antiques* (1852).

Lamartine's concern with the epic has already been noted. His 'Grand Poème', conceived in a burst of visionary fervour as early as 1821, was to have been an immense work providing a scenario of human progress. Preliminary fragments written between 1823 and 1829, and partially published by Lamartine in 1851 in his *Nouvelles Confidences*, indicate something of the visionary and episodic intentions of the work. The theme was to be one already treated, notably by Byron and Vigny, and the line of the narrative was to be determined by the stages of the redemption of the spirit of a fallen angel through successive reincarnations. The ending of *La Chute d'un ange* indicates that nine such episodes were envisaged.

In the event, only two were carried through as far as publication: *Jocelyn* (1836) and *La Chute d'un ange* (1838). Published in this order, as separate volumes, the two works could have given little idea of the plan on which they were based. *Jocelyn*, deliberately pitched at the human level, recounts the sacrifice of the life's happiness of two beings thrown together in the solitude of a mountain refuge during the Revolution. The plot, straining credibility at times, follows the movement of the poem over nine *époques* covering seventeen years (1786–1803): a love idyll (*époques* 1–4); a crucial event (*époque* 5 – Jocelyn's enforced ordination before the execution of his bishop); the years of austere and humble dedication (*époques* 6–9), with the theme of the embittered and fallen life of Laurence as counterpoint, but redeemed by religion and by the hope also of the spiritual union after death of the soul-mates, separated in their lives. The poem is given further amplitude by passages of religious lyricism, descriptions of the changing seasons in the mountainous region of France known to Lamartine, and evocations of the humble rustic life shared by the priest.

The episode of redemption therefore precedes the initial account of the Fall. *La Chute d'un ange* is a fictionalised interpretation of the verses of Genesis describing the world before the Flood. Lamartine's angel, Cédar, obsessed by the human beauty of Daïdha, assumes human shape to rescue her from a group of giant pillaging barbarians. The fifteen *visions* into which the poem is divided recount the doomed idyll of this pair, a girl of the race of Cain and a semi-divine but primitive being unversed in human lore. Their wanderings take them to the cave of a prophet who, in the seventh and eighth *visions*, reveals to them the fundamentals of a divine code set down in a 'fragment du Livre primitif'. The doctrine is drawn from Lamartine's own brand of deism, idealism and enlightened rationalism, which is presented as the essential basis of true religious belief. The tribulations of the pair continue in Nemphed's city of giants and demi-gods, from whose barbaric violence they eventually escape only to perish in the desert, Cédar burning on a pyre of his own making, with the bodies of Daïdha and their twin children.

Epic in its conception and in the main lines of its action, *La Chute d'un ange* is a sadly imperfect work, largely through the haste and inattention with which it was composed, partly through the incongruities occurring in the attempt to prepare a biblical epic for popular consumption. The level of the action is mainly that of a sensational adventure story. Cédar's Homeric combat with the six giant cavemen in the second *vision* has all the ingredients of a Hollywood fight sequence. Yet there is a ferocity of imagination, in the monstrous prison scenes for example, which surprises and suggests a range of resources never exploited in any measure by Lamartine. In any case, the 'épopée métaphysique' was a forlorn venture at this stage of his life. His ideas on progress based on a religious rationalism, which he had hoped to communicate to a large section of the French people, were absorbed into his political life, or diverted into works of fiction such as *Geneviève* (1850) or *Le Tailleur de pierres de Saint-Point* (1851).

Vigny also, though for different reasons, did not pursue the attempt at an epic formulation of his views on progress, though he never departed from his opinion, reaffirmed in 1839 in the *Journal d'un poète*: 'Il y a plus de force, de dignité et de grandeur dans les poètes *objectifs*, épiques et dramatiques . . . que dans les poètes *subjectifs* ou élégiaques.' But his principal intention was to use verse forms in order to express aspects of a fundamental question: how far had the Christian era freed itself from the superstitions of the ancient world, particularly from the notion of fatality? The indications are that by the end of the 1830s he had established his answer: Christ's mission in the world remained inconclusive; Christianity was a failed religion; and the modern world had to establish its own values that would lead it towards civilisation. From this period, his poetry concentrated mainly on this third point, and in elaborating his ideas, Vigny found it necessary to develop new techniques. These are the techniques of the *poème philosophique*, a term used by him to categorise his poems written from 1838 onwards.[24] Three of these were composed before 1840. They mark a turning point, a state between the *poème* and the *poème philosophique*. 'La Colère de Samson' (1839), with its diatribe against treacherous love, remains within the sentimental range of the *poème*, which it pushes to the limit. 'Le Mont des oliviers' (1839) would seem to belong to the *Poèmes antiques et modernes* by its trappings and by its sentimental formulation, but to another form of poem by the analytical scrutiny of the unsolved enigmas confronting the human mind. 'La Mort du loup' (1838), still within the narrative range of the *poème* with its dramatic and strongly drawn effects, marks a new departure with its foreground use of the wild animals to inculcate an idea about modern societies.

The *poème philosophique* is a freer form of the *poème* in that the author intervenes to develop his own views in greater detail within a context of imagery, but not necessarily controlled by a narrative. *Les Destinées* forms an extended, if fragmentary, meditation on the values of modern civilisation, the two pieces ('Les Destinées' itself and 'Le Mont des oliviers'), 'set at the beginning of the Christian era', being presumably included for the purpose of illustrating the bleak religious situation of the modern world.

This situation is depicted sometimes by means of episodes, but also, and more effectively, by the projection of ideas through symbols, which are chosen to represent the quality of human effort: the bottle with information from the Captain's log sealed in it, returning through the ocean currents from the wreck of an expedition to map the coast of Tierra del Fuego; the diamond and the pearl, illustrating the qualities of poetry; the railway train, representing the progress of mechanical inventions. Fuller tableaux also are used. In 'La Sauvage' and 'La Mort du loup', the young Red Indian mother and the wolf are set in different ways against the values of European life. The symbolic object itself, as in 'La Flûte', can be the centre of a dialogue.

J.C. IRESON

The underlying argument of *Les Destinées* concerns the extent to which human beings have the power to control their lives and the forces confronting them in the world. In individual poems, Vigny celebrates the modern capacity to dominate the environment, complete the exploration of the planet, open new areas for European settlement. He warns, in two apparently opposed sections of 'La Maison du berger', of the need to understand the relationship of man and nature. He is also the satirist of Louis-Philippe, the humanitarian opponent of the absolutist régime of the Tsar, and the pessimistic observer of the slow progress towards civilisation. He defends poetry, which he sees, in the 1840s, as declining in prestige, presenting it as the most powerful form in which language can be used to illuminate the minds of one's fellow citizens. 'La Maison du berger' is a meditation on the poet, on the social and intellectual independence necessary to him, and on the function of poetry. And the function of poetry is the concluding theme of his last poem, 'L'Esprit pur'. Poetry, the expression of an ideal of nobility in both senses of the term, is, as Vigny conceives it, the best symbol of a new era in which the work of the mind will take over from the disorderly conflicts of an age of wars, and in which the written word will remain the repository of the values of a civilisation.

By its themes and techniques, even more than by the late moment of its publication (1864), *Les Destinées* moves out of the Romantic period, although features of the sensibility of the 1820s still remain. Contemporary by its date of publication with the middle years of the Parnassian movement, it overlaps the work of the Parnassians by its quest for intellectual values in religious history and for a strong, disciplined form, which Vigny found in the seven-line stanza, used in five of the eleven poems, and which he made his own: a quatrain followed by a tercet, with a rhyming link provided between the two parts by the last line. The equation of the art of poetry with an ideal of beauty, referred to at a number of points in the *Journal d'un poète*, connects Vigny further with the poets of the succeeding school rather than with the Romantics of 1830, from whose concerted effort emerges the idea of a poetic language designed to increase the immediate communicative power of language, and not to strengthen its hieratic potential.

A new era in Hugo's poetry opened in the 1850s. He came back into poetry through politics, and the motivation of his three works published in that decade (*Châtiments*, 1853; *Les Contemplations*, 1856; the first series of *La Légende des siècles*, 1859) is itself in various ways political. Direct and violent in *Châtiments*, with a wealth of first-hand detail of the *coup d'état* of 1851 and of its prime movers and supporters, the political motivation is expanded, in *Les Contemplations*, to the promulgation of a large doctrine of progress which immerses social and political structures in a religious optimism. In Book 1 of this work, Hugo defines in retrospect the contribution of the Romantic reform of the literary language as having given poetry access to the free expression of ideas and the power to treat social themes. In *La Légende des siècles*, the single theme of progress is traced in various manifestations, but in forms intended to be less esoteric than in *Les Contemplations*, and thus capable of influencing a wide public. Beyond these works, *Les Chansons des rues et des bois* (1865) treats the theme of equality in its universal as well as its social acceptation, and by its form (quatrains in short metrical lines) suggests the type of light verse made popular by Béranger.[25]

The overriding ambition of all these works is the transmission of a social and religious philosophy. In this respect, Hugo can be said to be following the programme laid out in his verse collections of the 1830s, but with an amplitude and a power of absorption of immediate influences that put him outside all specific schools or groupings. His position as a poet in exile no doubt impelled him to amplify his message aimed at France, and it is, for example, from this period that we can date the habit of swelling his verse with muster-rolls of poets, philosophers, villains or tyrants. His ambition now was to assimilate in his poetry the substance of his own life and the evolution of human consciousness. The political message of *Châtiments* goes far beyond the witness of particular events or the satirical demolition of an adversary. The shape of the future is anticipated, in its structure as well as its qualities. The final purpose of *Les Contemplations* is to propound a religious philosophy of expiation and redemption consonant with Hugo's own intuitions of the immortality and transmigration of the spirit.

Such preoccupations require the reworking of myths in order to find poetic equivalents for the ideas ('Le Satyre' in *La Légende des siècles* is a striking example). A tendency to mythologise events is found at all periods of his work, in his treatment of the Napoleonic legend, for example; and the tendency is seen progressively in the handling of the episodes and attitudes of his own life. Olympio, conceived as the representation of a disabused and detached morality, merges into the later figure of the poet as the witness both of sentient life and of supernatural consciousness. *Les Contemplations* combines both in its spread of six books, and is the clearest example of Hugo's ambition, at this late period, to cover life in its totality in a single work of poetry. *Les Contemplations*, sometimes seen as the crowning achievement of Romantic lyricism in France, is certainly built on foundations established in the 1820s and 1830s. But its thought is not that of the *Préface de 'Cromwell'*, or *Stello*, or the *Harmonies*. It is an amalgam of ideas received over a wide area and over a long period of time, and given a personal identity by the intuitions of the poet. Events such as the seances in Marine Terrace between 1853 and 1855 play their part, as does the evidence of occult doctrines. The life of the senses and sentiments, evoked in the shorter lyrics, is almost entirely retrospective, and completed by the theme of bereavement, the image of the dead daughter, Léopoldine, irradiating the poet's earlier life and illuminating the period of exile with the hope of immortality. In its attempt to encapsulate the substance of twenty-five years, coextensive not only with the poet's life but also with the artistic and political life of France, *Les Contemplations* presents a spectrum of life (the word is from Hugo's Preface to the work): that is, prismatic, broken into differing areas and gradations of colour. The final spectacle of the work is of an immense synthesis of perceptions, episodes and single ideas.

This form of presentation is both natural to Hugo's mental processes, based upon a lifetime of observation, noting and docketing, and the manifestation of an individual technique of organisation and arrangement. From the period of *Châtiments* onwards, the structure of the work becomes an integral part of the composition, replacing the concept of tonality which had governed the collections of the 1830s. Demonstrative and satirical in *Châtiments*, chronological in *Les Contemplations*, but contributing, by the arrangement of individual pieces, to a multivalent lyricism, this overall structure takes on a linear form in *La Légende des siècles* in order to follow the theoretical upward climb of human consciousness.

Does *La Légende des siècles* mark the achievement of a Romantic epic, despite the dates of its composition (augmented editions appeared in 1877 and 1883), and perhaps because of the situation of the poet, isolated from literary events in Paris? The answer is no. It is true that the manner in which episodes are staged recalls Hugo's theatrical techniques. But he had the gift of keeping abreast of his time, and the trends and reactions of the 1840s and 1850s, and even later periods, are present in the work.[26] His conception was not of a traditional epic, but of a series of 'petites épopées' which could be extended at will. The final effect was to be one of totality: 'Exprimer l'humanité dans une espèce d'œuvre cyclique' (Preface, 1859). The advance of humanity was to be seen from two viewpoints: the perspectives of nineteenth-century social and scientific thought, and a simplistic moral viewpoint consistent with the idea of popular legends. The individual pieces need to be seen in context in the vast moving show of the poems, which are ultimately subservient to a grandiose design linking history and religious mythology to the metaphysical ideas expressed in *Les Contemplations*. If *La Fin de Satan* had been completed, with its double theme of redemption in the terrestrial and angelic dimensions, the work, as Hugo himself indicates, would have had its epic denouement. By the same token, *Dieu* was to have given an epic formulation to the effort of the human mind to penetrate the final mystery. But the Hugolian verse epic remains incomplete,[27] and curiously immured in the nineteenth century, despite the intention to illuminate the way forward into the new age.

The active values of French Romantic poetry had been left behind, although they are implicit in all subsequent developments. The basis of these values is found in the adaptation of language to expanding and changing ideas, in the direct questioning of the function of poetry in society, and in the tuning of poetry to the imaginative and intuitive life of the individual poet. This last evokes an operation which was carried out more fully and effectively by the Symbolist poets who followed Baudelaire in bringing French poetry more directly in line with aspects of German Romanticism. The French Romantic poets' initial concern was with the modernisation of verse to keep pace with shifts of sensibility affecting the outlook of a particular period. They opened to the individual writer the questions of responsibility and freedom which have remained in the forefront of the issues of the modern period.

NOTES

ABBREVIATIONS USED IN NOTES:

C	*Les Contemplations* (1856)
CC	*Les Chants du crépuscule* (1835)
CRB	*Les Chansons des rues et des bois* (1865)
FA	*Les Feuilles d'automne* (1831)
FS	*La Fin de Satan* (1886)
LS	*La Légende des siècles* (1859, 1877, 1883)
MP	*Méditations poétiques* (1820)
NMP	*Nouvelles Méditations poétiques* (1823)
OCP	*Oeuvres complètes*, Bibliothèque de la Pléiade
OPP	*Oeuvres poétiques*, Bibliothèque de la Pléiade
RO	*Les Rayons et les ombres* (1840)
VI	*Les Voix intérieures* (1837)

NOTES

1. Both were completed in 1856. 'Le Désert' was begun in 1832, during Lamartine's travels in the Middle East.
2. 'Souvenir' appeared in 1841 (*Revue des deux mondes*, 15 February).

J.C. IRESON

3. 'A Elvire' (MP) refers to one of his early conquests, the Italian girl Antonia Iacomino. Lamartine's prose narrative, *Graziella (Confidences,* 1849; in book form, 1852) gives a romanticised account of the episode. She is also, presumably, the female figure of 'Le Golfe de Baya' (MP). An oblique reference to Lena de Larche is made in 'L'Enthousiasme' (MP). 'Ischia' and 'Chant d'amour' (NMP) refer to his marital happiness with 'Élyse'.

4. For a survey of the evolution of Lamartine's religious attitude, towards forms of rationalised belief, see H. Guillemin, *Lamartine, l'homme et l'œuvre* (Boivin, 1940), ch. IV, 'La Pensée religieuse'.

5. A note in the *Journal d'un poète,* dated 1824, summarises Vigny's general position: 'Dieu a jeté – c'est ma croyance – la terre au milieu de l'air et l'homme au milieu de la destinée. La destinée l'enveloppe et l'emporte vers le but toujours voilé. – Le vulgaire est entraîné, les grands caractères sont ceux qui luttent'.

6. The reference is to three political poems, already written. They appear as the first three pieces of CC.

7. See, for example, stanzas 8, 9, 20, 21, all of which prefigure passages of Rimbaud's 'Bateau ivre'.

8. The other meditative poem of FA with aspirations to visionary awareness is 'Ce qu'on entend sur la montagne' ('mon esprit fidèle, / Hélas! n'avait jamais déployé plus grande aile'). But the dual theme of nature and humanity is left undeveloped.

9. A further sixteen were added to the Édition des Souscripteurs (1849–50).

10. 'Guerre à la rhétorique, et paix à la syntaxe!' Hugo uses this formula retrospectively in 'Réponse à un acte d'accusation' (C). He had also written (preface, *Odes et Ballades*): 'Plus on dédaigne la rhétorique, plus il sied de respecter la grammaire.'

11. Nine stanzas, suppressed in the 1830 edition and restored in the later editions, parody the stereotyped association of love with moonlight by showing the moon peering into a bourgeois bedroom on a not very successful wedding night.

12. Hugo begins to use a familiar style in FA. See XXVII, 'A mes amis L.B. et S.-B.'

13. *Rime suffisante*: where the accented vowels and only the consonants following them are identical in sound.
    Rime riche: where the accented vowels and the consonants preceding and following them are identical in sound.
    (Other categories of rhyme in French verse are: *rime pauvre,* where only the accented vowels are identical in sound; *rime défectueuse,* a term used to cover a number of categories considered as unsatisfactory in regular verse, e.g., a word and its composite form (*faire, défaire*); words where apparently identical vowels are pronounced differently (*grâce, place*); rhymes for the eye alone (*mer, aimer*); a vowel and a diphthong (*nuire, désire,* etc.).

14. These are (a) the displacement of the *césure* from the middle of the metrical line; (b) the substitution of three rhythmic groups ('Romantic trimeter') for the four traditionally used (tetrameter), e.g., Hugo, FA XXIII: 'La valse impure, au vol lascif et circulaire'; (c) *enjambement,* i.e., leaving the sense incomplete at the end of a line in order to complete it in the first part of the line following.

15. He was elected in his absence, during his tour of the Middle East, from which he returned in October 1833. His tour, which lasted a little over a year, was marked by the death of his daughter, Julia, in Beirut in December 1832, and by his visit to the Holy Sepulchre in October of that year, which seemingly failed to rekindle his faith as he had hoped.

16. Gautier made of Don Juan an aging dandy, defeated by having set himself an impossible ideal of womanhood. Musset had already used the theme of Don Juan as an idealist in a passage of 'Namouna'.

Poetry

17. Cf. Baudelaire's essays on Théophile Gautier in OCP (1965); Mallarmé's commemorative poem, 'Toast funèbre' in OCP (1945).
18. 'Le Saule', a 'fragment' in the general formula of 'Portia' and 'Octave', returns for its plot and characters to the Romanticism of *René* and Byron, but marks an advance in Musset's work by the attempts to bring a wider range of lyrical effects into the narrative.
19. See, for example, Anatole France, *Les Poèmes du souvenir: 'Le Lac', 'Tristesse d'Olympio', 'Souvenir'* (E. Pelletan, 1910).
20. Cf. Preface to RO: 'L'auteur pense que tout poète véritable, indépendamment des pensées qui lui viennent de son organisme propre et des pensées qui lui viennent de la vérité éternelle, doit contenir la somme des idées de son temps.'
21. Two poems are devoted to conjugal love, seen as a consoling and stabilising force in the poet's life: XXXVI ('Toi! sois bénie à jamais'); XXXIX ('Date lilia'), both in CC.
22. 'Pensar, dudar' (VI), poses the question of whether doubt is an essential part of the human condition or the feature of a particular historical period.
23. There is a variant of the epilogue to *Jocelyn* and a 'fragment biblique', which is from 'Saül', already represented in MP. An important ode on the theme of progress ('Utopie') is also included.
24. In 1843, Vigny published four *poëmes* (Vigny's spelling) in *Revue des deux mondes*: 'La Sauvage', 'La Mort du loup', 'La Flûte', 'Le Mont des Oliviers'. The following year, 'La Maison du berger' was presented as the 'prologue' to the *poèmes philosophiques*, this term having appeared as the subtitle of the four already published. A sixth poem was published, also in *Revue des deux mondes*, in 1854: 'La Bouteille à la mer'. Vigny's final intention appears to have been to publish a volume under the title of *Les Destinées*, with *poèmes philosophiques* as a subtitle. This intention was carried out by Louis Ratisbonne in preparing the posthumous edition. This included five hitherto unpublished poems: 'Wanda' (written 1847), 'Les Destinées' (1849), 'Les Oracles' (1862), 'L'Esprit pur' (1863), and 'La Colère de Samson', which Vigny had left unpublished for twenty-four years.
25. See J.-B. Barrère, *Hugo, l'homme et l'œuvre* (Boivin, 1952), p. 205. As against this, Pierre Albouy suggests that, in CRB, Hugo aimed at rivalling Gautier, the master of *l'art pour l'art* (OPP, vol. III, p. xv).
26. Jacques Truchet, in his introduction to LS (Pléiade, 1967), mentions the influence of Gautier, Leconte de Lisle, Banville, Coppée, Baudelaire and Verlaine (p. viii).
27. FS was begun about 1854 and abandoned in 1860. Various sections of *Dieu* were composed in 1855, 1856 and 1866.

BIBLIOGRAPHY

The general histories of French Romanticism and pre-Romanticism, noted in the bibliography to chapter 1 of this work can be usefully consulted for the information given on the poets. There is no specialised history of French Romantic poetry, and this marks a strong contrast with the poetry of the Parnassian and Symbolist movements, each of which has its historian (M. Souriau, *Histoire du Parnasse* (Spes, 1929); G. Michaud, *Message poétique du Symbolisme* (3 vols., Nizet, 1947). F. Brunetière's *L'Évolution de la poésie lyrique au dix-neuvième siècle* (Hachette, 1895) and E. Faguet's *Histoire de la poésie française de la renaissance au romantisme* (Boivin, 1923–36) are of mainly historical value. In G. Brereton, *An Introduction to the French Poets* (London, Methuen, 1973), individual chapters are devoted to the major figures. Two anthologies are recommended for their choice of texts and the value of the introductory material: A.M. Boase, *The Poetry of France from André Chénier to Pierre Emmanuel* (London, Methuen, 1952); A.J. Steele *Three Centuries of French Verse, 1511–1819* (Edinburgh University Press, 1961).

159

J.C. IRESON

Aspects and perspectives: Since about the end of the Second World War, a number of reappraisals have been attempted by bringing into focus neglected or more remote aspects: G. Poulet, various essays on Romantic poets included in *Études sur le temps humain* (Plon, 1950), *La Distance intérieure* (Plon, 1952), *Les Métamorphoses du cercle* (Plon, 1961), *Mesure de l'instant* (Plon, 1968); J.P. Houston, *The Demonic Imagination: Style and Theme in French Romantic Poetry* (Baton Rouge, Louisiana State University Press, 1969); J.-P. Richard, *Études sur le romantisme* (Seuil, 1971); H.B. Riffaterre, *L'Orphisme dans la poésie romantique* (Nizet, 1970); B.V. Juden, *Traditions orphiques et tendances mystiques dans le romantisme français, 1800–55* (Klincksieck, 1971).

Genre studies: There is one work specifically on the Romantic epic: L. Cellier, *L'Épopée romantique* (Publ. de la Faculté des Lettres, Grenoble, 1954). See also, L. Cellier, *L'Épopée humanitaire et les grands mythes romantiques* (SEDES, 1954); H.J. Hunt, *The Epic in Nineteenth-Century France* (Oxford, Blackwell, 1941); B. Wilkie, *Romantic Poets and Epic Tradition* (Madison, U. of Wisconsin, 1965). A recent study throws a modern light on three forms revived or created by the Romantics: L.M. Porter, *The Renaissance of the Lyric in French Romantism: Elegy, 'Poëme' and Ode* (French Forum, Lexington, Kentucky, 1978).

Immediate influences and background: E. Estève, *Byron et le romantisme français* (Hachette, 1907; Geneva, Slatkine Reprints, 1973); B. Ladoué, *Millevoye (1782–1816)* (Perrin, 1912); Paul Van Tieghem, *Ossian en France* (2 vols., Rieder, 1917); R. de Souza, 'Un préparateur de la poésie romantique' (article on Delille) in *Mercure de France*, 285 (July 1938).

Poetic theory and language: M. Gilman, *The Idea of Poetry in France from Houdar de la Motte to Baudelaire* (Cambridge, Mass., Harvard University Press, 1958); A. Cassagne, *La Théorie de l'art pour l'art en France chez les derniers romantiques et les premiers réalistes* (Dorbon (Hermann), 1959; first published, 1906); F. Brunot, *Histoire de la langue française des origines à nos jours*. Vol. XII, *L'Époque romantique (1815–52)* is by Ch. Bruneau (Colin, 1948).

Versification: H. Morier, *Dictionnaire de poétique et de rhétorique* (PUF, 1961); Th. de Banville, *Petit Traité de poésie française* (first published, 1872); M. Grammont, *Le Vers français. Ses moyens d'expression, son harmonie*, revised edn (Delagrave, 1947); M. Grammont, *Petit Traité de versification française* (Colin, 1965).

Lamartine: The standard edition of Lamartine's poems is *Lamartine: Œuvres poétiques complètes*, ed. M.-F. Guyard (Gallimard, Bibliothèque de la Pléiade, 1963). See also, F. Letessier, *Méditations poétiques*, critical edn (Garnier, 1968). An earlier critical edition of the *Méditations poétiques* by G. Lanson (Hachette, 1915) includes Lamartine's essay, *Des Destinées de la poésie*. For the life and work, see Marquis de Luppé, *Les Travaux et les jours d'Alphonse de Lamartine* (Albin Michel, 1942) and H. Guillemin, *Lamartine, l'homme et l'œuvre* (Boivin, 1940). See also, W. Fortescue, *Alphonse de Lamartine: A Political Biography* (London, Croom Helm, 1983). For general studies of the works, see H. Guillemin, *Connaissance de Lamartine* (Fribourg, Librairie de l'Université, 1942); M.-F. Guyard, *Lamartine* (Éditions universitaires, 1956); J.C. Ireson, *Lamartine: A Revaluation* (University of Hull, 1969); N. Araujo, *In Search of Eden. Lamartine's Symbols of Despair and Deliverance* (Brookline, Massachusetts; Leyden: Classical Folia Editions, 1976). Among studies of specific works, see H. Guillemin, *Le 'Jocelyn' de Lamartine* (Boivin, 1936); P. Jouanne, *L'Harmonie lamartinienne* (Jouve, 1927).

Poetry

Hugo: The edition used for the purposes of this chapter is *Victor Hugo: Œuvres poétiques*, vols. I, II, and III, ed. P. Albouy (Gallimard, Bibliothèque de la Pléiade, 1964, 1967, 1974), and *Victor Hugo: La Légende des siècles, La Fin de Satan, Dieu*, ed. J. Truchet (Gallimard, Bibliothèque de la Pléiade, 1950). The two best editions of the complete works are: *Victor Hugo: Œuvres complètes* (4 vols., Pauvert, 1961–4) and *Victor Hugo: Œuvres complètes* (18 vols., Club Français du Livre, 1967–71). Biographies: A. Maurois, *Olympio ou La Vie de Victor Hugo* (2 vols., Hachette, 1954); P. Flottes, *L'Éveil de Victor Hugo (1801–1822)*; (Gallimard, 1957). See also, H. Guillemin, *Victor Hugo par lui-même* (Seuil, 1951); J. Richardson, *Victor Hugo* (London, Reinhardt, 1976). For a general survey of Hugo's writings, see P. Berret, *Victor Hugo* (Garnier, 1927); J.-B. Barrère, *Hugo, l'homme et l'œuvre* (Boivin, 1952). For the development of ideas, see H. Peyre, *Hugo* (PUF, 'Philosophes', 1972); J.-B. Barrère, *Victor Hugo* (Desclée de Brouwer, 'Les Écrivains devant Dieu', 1965); G. Venzac, *Les Origines religieuses de Victor Hugo* (Bloud et Gay, 1955); M. Levaillant, *La Crise mystique de Victor Hugo (1843–1856)* (Corti, 1954); D. Saurat, *Victor Hugo et les dieux du peuple* (La Colombe, 1948); Ch. Villiers, *L'Univers métaphysique de Victor Hugo* (Vrin, 1970). Aspects of Hugo's imaginative life are studied by J.-B. Barrère, *La Fantaisie de Victor Hugo* (3 vols., Corti, 1949, 1950, 1960); L. Emery, *Vision et pensée chez Victor Hugo* (Les Cahiers Libres, 1939). For more specialised studies of the poetry, see B. Guyon, *La Vocation poétique de Victor Hugo: Essai sur la signification spirituelle des 'Odes et Ballades' et des 'Orientales'* (Gap, Éd. Orphrys, 1953); J. Gaudon, *Le Temps de la Contemplation: L'Œuvre poétique de Victor Hugo des 'Misères' au 'Seuil du Gouffre'* (Flammarion, 1969); S. Nash, *'Les Contemplations' of Victor Hugo* (Princeton University Press, 1977).

Vigny. The Pléiade edition, *Alfred de Vigny: Œuvres complètes*, ed. F. Baldensperger (2 vols., Gallimard) gives Vigny's poetic works in vol. I (1950). Other editions for reference are: *Poèmes antiques et modernes*, ed. E. Estève (Droz, 1914); *Les Destinées*, ed. E. Estève (Droz, 1924); *Les Destinées*, ed. V.L. Saulnier (Droz, 1946). See also, *Les Destinées*, with commentary by P.-G. Castex (SEDES, 1964); P. Moreau, *'Les Destinées' de Vigny* (Malfère, 1936). General studies of the life and work: P.-G. Castex, *Vigny, l'homme et l'œuvre* (Boivin, 1952); E. Lauvrière, *Alfred de Vigny, sa vie et son œuvre* (2 vols., Grasset, 1945; B. de la Salle, *Vigny* (Fayard, 1939); H. Guillemin, *M. de Vigny, homme d'ordre et poète* (Gallimard, 1955). Ideas and sources: E. Estève, *Alfred de Vigny, sa pensée et son art* (Garnier, 1923); P. Flottes, *La Pensée politique et sociale d'Alfred de Vigny* (Les Belles Lettres, 1927), G. Bonnefoy, *La Pensée religieuse et morale d'Alfred de Vigny* (Hachette, 1944); M. Citoleux, *Alfred de Vigny: Persistances classiques et affinités étrangères* (Champion, 1924). The dominant literary study of Vigny is by F. Germain, *L'Imagination d'Alfred de Vigny* (Corti, 1961).

Musset: The Gallimard edition (Bibliothèque de la Pléiade) is in 3 volumes, ed. M. Allem. The *Poésiés complètes* form vol. I (first published 1957). There is a one-volume edition of the *Œuvres complètes* (Seuil, 'L'Intégrale', 1963). The nine-volume (*Œuvres complètes*, ed. E. Biré (1907–8) has been reproduced in a facsimile edition. Of the numerous biographical studies, the best is by M. Allem, *Alfred de Musset* (Arthaud, 1948). See also, P. de Musset, *Biographie d'Alfred de Musset* (Charpentier, 1877); Y. Lainey, *Musset ou La difficulté d'aimer* (SEDES, 1978). General literary studies: P. Gastinel, *Le Romantisme d'Alfred de Musset* (Imprimerie du Journal de Rouen, 1933; Philippe Van Tieghem, *Musset, l'homme et l'œuvre* (Boivin, 1945); Ph. Soupault, *Alfred de Musset* (Seghers 'Poètes d'aujourd'hui', 1957) (literary study with anthology). On the poetry: J. Cassou, *'Les*

J.C. IRESON

Nuits' de Musset (Émile-Paul, 1930); V. Brunet, *Le Lyrisme d'Alfred de Musset* (Toulouse, Imprimerie régionale, 1936). An analytical bibliography is given in S. Jeune, *Musset et sa fortune littéraire* (Ducros, 1970).

Gautier: For the collected poems, see *Théophile Gautier: Poèmes complets*, ed. R. Jasinski (3 vols., Nizet, 1970). Apart from *Émaux et Camées*, few separate editions of individual works have appeared. Exceptions are, *L'España*, ed. R. Jasinski (Vuibert, 1929); *Poésies* (1830), ed. H. Cockerham (Athlone Press, 1973). Life and works: A. Boschot, *Théophile Gautier* (Desclée de Brouwer, 1933); J. Richardson, *Théophile Gautier, his Life and Times* (Reinhardt, 1958); P. Tennant, *Théophile Gautier* (Athlone Press, 1975) (section III gives an excellent brief survey of Gautier's poetry); B. Delvaille, *Théophile Gautier* (Seghers, 'Poètes d'aujourd'hui', 1968); S. Faucherau, *Théophile Gautier* (Denoël, 1972). Special aspects: R. Jasinski, *Les Années romantiques de Théophile Gautier* (Vuibert, 1928); L.B. Dillingham, *The Creative Imagination of Théophile Gautier* (Princeton 'Psychological Monographs', 37, 1927).

Sainte-Beuve: G. Antoine, *Vie, poésies et pensées de Joseph Delorme: Établissement du texte, notes et lexiques* (Nouvelles Éditions Latines, 1958); G. Antoine, *Vie, poésies et pensées de Joseph Delorme* (Nouvelles Éditions Latines, 1957) (critical study); A.G. Lehmann, *Sainte-Beuve: A Portrait of the Critic, 1804-1842* (Oxford, Clarendon Press, 1962).

V · *Prose fiction*

D.G. CHARLTON

INTRODUCTION

Prose fiction was published by every leading Romantic literary writer, even Lamartine in his later years. This was not the case with either poetry or drama, and yet those are the genres above all associated with the movement. In literary–historical surveys, by comparison, 'le roman romantique' usually appears in a belated chapter, even, as with Thibaudet, under the title of 'le roman des *poètes*' – to which he added a judgment many twentieth-century readers might reiterate: 'Aucun n'a marqué profondément dans le genre.'[1] For the past half-century and more, in fact, scholars have largely neglected their prose fiction, with only isolated exceptions: *Adolphe*, *Les Misérables*, the 'short fiction' of the movement, occasional studies of other works. Amongst historians of the French novel the last to give substantial attention to the Romantics were writing before 1939.[2] More recent works – by M. Raimond, R.-M. Albérès, Winifried Engler, and even Gaëtan Picon – give far shorter space to them; typically of a wider disregard, an American study in 1972 on fictional techniques in France since 1802 allocated them only a single chapter – entitled, moreover, 'Minor genres: romance and confession novel'. As to specific forms of their fiction it is startling to note that almost all the principal critical studies were published several decades ago. Le Breton in 1901 on Romantic fiction as a whole (and even so ending with *Cinq-Mars*); Merlant (1905) and Hytier (1928) on the *roman de l'individu*; Maigron (1898) on the *roman historique*, with a work by Lukács (written 1936–7) as a less than wholly admiring supplement; Johannet (1909), Brun (1910) and Evans (1930) on the *roman social*: these remain the latest secondary authorities, some recently reprinted, failing newer works, to meet what may at last be a modest revival of attention. Pierre Salomon's *Le Roman et la nouvelle romantiques* (1970) was only a short, but perhaps symptomatic, book of extracts. More substantial have been colloquia volumes in particular: to take France alone as illustration, *Roman et société* (1971), a special double issue of the *Revue d'histoire littéraire de la France* (*RHLF*) in 1975 on 'Le Roman historique', and collective surveys of individual Romantics, notably Mme de Staël and George Sand amongst previously neglected *prosateurs*.

All the same, we are still far from rediscovering most of the Romantic novels that were so deeply admired in their own century. We remain disconcerted that the critics of the 1830s and beyond should so promptly have added to their lists of outstanding European novels, alongside *Don Quixote*, *La Princesse de Clèves*, *Gil Blas*, *Tom Jones*, *Clarissa Harlowe*, and *La Nouvelle Héloïse*, not only *René*, *Ivanhoe* and *Adolphe* but also *Cinq-Mars*, Mérimée's *Chronique*, *Notre-Dame de Paris* and *Volupté*.[3] And whilst that might be explained away by reference to the unreliability of critics in evaluating their contemporaries – so many now forgotten novels once awarded the Prix Goncourt, to give a single instance – the praise of the Romantics' fellow practitioners is less easily dismissed. For Dostoevsky, for example, Hugo's *Dernier Jour d'un condamné* was a 'masterpiece' that haunted his mind and work[4] – and he also admired as 'almost unique' the novelist of them all who best illustrates the contrasts of critical appreciation as between then and our own time: George Sand. She was admired not only by her French contemporaries: Sainte-Beuve, who wrote in 1840 of her 'purs chefs-d'œuvre du roman', Hugo, Flaubert, or Renan, for whom she was 'le plus grand écrivain du siècle'. Her reputation with fellow writers in England and America, as well as Russia, was equally high.[5] For Elizabeth Browning she was the 'true woman of genius', for Charlotte Brontë distinguished by a 'wondrous excellence'; her novels were the first since *La Nouvelle Héloïse* to be 'of a high value or of a philosophic tone', Henry James declared, amongst such others as George Eliot and G.H. Lewes – with yet more 'admiration for your genius' – and Matthew Arnold, who even travelled to France especially to meet her. We today are unable for the most part to recapture or explain her outstanding fame in her own time; certainly, at least, the present writer has failed to do so. Yet such evidence as this should all the same lead us to a closer attention to the Romantics' prose fiction than it has normally been given for many years.

It cannot be assessed in even a basic, literary–historical way unless we appreciate the situation in which the Romantics were writing. Twentieth-century critics have retrospectively described a serious tradition in the French novel prior to the early nineteenth century, from Rabelais to Marivaux and Laclos, from the *Heptaméron* and *La Princesse de Clèves* to the fiction of Voltaire and Diderot. As the Romantics came to maturity, however, there was then little sense of a distinctively French heritage in regard to the novel as opposed to theatre and poetry. Even in England, freer of classicist authority, Jane Austen would complain in 1798, in the preface to *Northanger Abbey*, that 'no species of composition has been so much decried' as the novel and deplore 'almost a general wish of decrying the capacity and undervaluing the labour of the novelist'. In France even more the novel remained a largely despised form, 'la littérature facile', described by critics even in the 1820s as 'un genre léger'. Boileau's condescension in his *Art poétique* 150 years before was still widely shared:

> Dans un roman frivole aisément tout s'excuse:
> C'est assez qu'en courant la fiction amuse.

And more conservative theorists still appealed to the distant authority of his contemporary Huet's *Traité de l'origine des romans*, published in 1670 as an introduction to Mme de la Fayette's *Zaïde*. Still in the 1830s traditionalist critics like Nisard and Nettement continued to discount a novel as 'un ouvrage frivole' (Boileau's very word), and greatly deplored the moment in 1831 when, for the first time, more novels were published in France than volumes of poetry. The very term 'roman' was often felt to be in itself derogatory, and it is not surprising that an intellectual and man of politics like Constant should clearly have felt the need to dismiss *Adolphe*, even after its first success, as a mere 'anecdote' written to see if some interest could be given to a book with only two characters and who are always in the same situation.

The reasons behind the critics' contempt are not far to seek. First, the novel lay outside the still-prized literary heritage of the Ancients and of French classicism. Secondly, the novel's main readers (and, indeed, majority of authors) throughout the seventeenth and eighteenth centuries had been women – and also, in suitably moralising form, from the later eighteenth century on, children. And if that were not enough to exclude serious consideration, the first half of the nineteenth century saw a gradual but cumulatively vast increase in the production of popular fiction for mass consumption. This occurred first in the aftermath of the Revolution – in drama and poetry also but above all in fiction. The *romans populaires* of Pigault-Lebrun, in the erotic, libertine tradition; the *romans noirs* of Ducray-Duminil in particular, imitating the English 'gothic' novels of Ann Radcliffe, 'Monk' Lewis, and Walpole's *Castle of Otranto* earlier; the sentimental, moralising stories of mainly female novelists such as Mmes Cottin, de Krüdener and Souza: these were the immediate predecessors in fiction to the young Romantics. The conservatives' deduction that fiction belonged to 'l'infralittérature' was to be further confirmed, moreover, by a still greater explosion in publishing terms thereafter. One listing, for example, notes an increase from 142 novels produced in 1816 to 231 in 1826 and 338 in 1836 (though with a decline to 238 by 1846).[6] The reasons behind this hardly encouraged the novel's opponents to reconsider their dismissive views, though these were increasingly countered by opposite arguments, from the Romantics amongst others. Changes in the printing industry and in paper-making led to much reduced production costs, and so did the use of 'stereotyping' and of steam power for the rotary press.[7] The brilliant, if baleful notion in the mid 1830s of including advertisements in newspapers and periodicals lowered their price even further. The French population was simultaneously rising – by some 30 per cent between 1800 and 1850 – and though the literacy rate rose much less, the outcome was a marked increase in the size of the reading public for interesting and entertaining fiction. This development was, by the late 1830s, to be symbolised and all the more hastened by the introduction of serialisation, of the *roman-feuilleton*, a form in which many of the Romantics' later novels would be first published.

It is hardly surprising if the Romantics were influenced by these various factors. It has been argued, for example, that their historical novels were affected by such works as Ducray-Duminil's *Cœlina ou l'Enfant du mystère*, with ghosts and masked brigands roaming in underground passages or on the battlements of ancient castles, and their *romans personnels* by sentimental novels like Mme Cottin's *Claire d'Albe* and *Malvina*, with their suicidal 'âmes de feu' tearing their breasts or gnawing the ground in their distraught passion. The resemblances cannot be denied, yet what they observed or imitated in such popular writing, most of them surely transcended; as one instance, editors of *Adolphe* from Rudler on have correctly noted similarities with earlier personal novels, and yet Constant far surpassed them. Nor should we overlook the fact that certain elements in Romantic writing which we may register as sentimental, melodramatic or too declamatory, belonged to a longer, more esteemed cultural tradition that we have currently forsaken – to that 'sentimental revolution' illustrated by the novels of Richardson, Rousseau and others, by the *comédies larmoyantes* and moral *drames* of eighteenth-century theatre, and by wider attitudes in daily life whereby even strong men felt no shame in weeping publicly. Sympathy for the Romantics may be hindered for us by the limits of our own tastes as much as theirs.

However that may be, the primary task facing them in their own day was not to seek liberation from the classicist heritage, as it was in poetry and drama; the novel's independence of such constrictions was the compensating advantage of its lowly reputation. The need was to fight for the novel to be taken seriously at all and to explore its potentialities as a literary medium for more than women, children and popular mass consumption. It would be wrong to suggest they were the first French writers to attempt this, but not wrong to claim that they were more successful in changing the views of others, that, in Picon's words, 'le romantisme a donné au roman ses lettres de noblesse littéraire'.[8] Certainly a variety of social and economic factors independent of them favoured their success – and they themselves argued that the novel was peculiarly apt for the expression of modern society – but that does not detract from it.

Their commitment to win for the novel equality with poetry and drama is evident in a preliminary way from the numerous theoretical claims they advanced for the genre, from Mme de Staël's *Essai sur les fictions* (1795) onwards, in the prefaces to their own novels and elsewhere. Chateaubriand's prefaces to *Atala* and *René*; Staël's preface to *Delphine* and passages on the future of the novel in her *Considérations* as well as the *Essai*; Constant's third preface to *Adolphe*; Vigny's 'Réflexions sur la vérité dans l'art' added to a re-edition of *Cinq-Mars*; Hugo's introductory 'notes' to *Notre-Dame de Paris* and *Les Misérables*; George Sand's prefaces to such novels as *Indiana* and *Lélia*; and – arguing a different view but no less seriously – Gautier's *Préface de 'Mademoiselle de Maupin'*: all these and other statements show the high goals they set for the novel. Even if one concluded that their own novels did not fully reach those goals, the sincerity of their aspirations would still be difficult to deny.

Their most evident achievement, cumulatively, was to open up as serious matter for literature possibilities in fiction which their successors would utilise. Their output covered a range of forms that mirrored the eclecticism of their intellectual and literary interests alike, and a single chapter can obviously not survey all they attempted. Still less can it hope to analyse afresh individual novels, and the aim here has to be limited to the major aspects of their collective contribution to French prose fiction. By this criterion their social novels and short fiction will be given markedly less space (for reasons suggested later) than their *romans de l'individu* and their *romans historiques*.

THE 'ROMAN DE L'INDIVIDU'

'Novels of the individual' were written by more of the Romantics than any other fictional form and their production spanned the whole movement. Their historical novels, by comparison, were mainly published between 1826 and 1831, with only isolated later examples, and their social novels and short fiction mainly came a little later still. Chateaubriand's *Atala* (1801) and *René* (1802), Mme de Staël's *Delphine* (1802) and *Corinne* (1807), Constant's *Adolphe* (1816) and its incomplete companion story *Cécile* (only published in 1951), and Senancour's *Obermann* (1804) as well, if one disregards his own denial that it was a novel at all: these came in the first phase of the movement, to be followed distinctly later by such early George Sand novels as *Indiana* (1832) and *Lélia* (1833), Sainte-Beuve's *Volupté* (1834), and Musset's *Confession d'un enfant du siècle* (1836), to which one could arguably add Gautier's *Mademoiselle de Maupin* (1835). Such a list (and also aspects of several Romantic plays) clearly suggests a common and persisting preoccupation. This section will attempt to interpret its significance and to offer a way of reading these novels that somewhat differs from more prevalent approaches; to that end, indeed, other major aspects will have to be neglected for lack of space.

In all these novels, clearly enough, attention is focused upon the experience of the individual less in his relationship to society, though that is certainly not irrelevant or excluded, than in regard to the inner life, the 'existential' dilemmas, of an intelligent and sensitive personality. Some have likened them to the German *Bildungsroman* or to Stendhal's *Le Rouge et le noir* and Thackeray's *Henry Esmond*, in which we see the 'sentimental education' of a young man or woman under the moral and social pressures they experience,[9] but many others have interpreted them as closer to works of introspective examination. Consequently, they have often been described as above all 'autobiographical' and 'confessional', as 'novels of self-disclosure', and numerous commentators have slipped into equating Chateaubriand with René, Musset with Octave, and so on, as if they were identical. From that assumption, moreover, has frequently followed another and more far-reaching claim: that the novelist was seeking to justify the values of his main character, to present him as an ideal to be admired and imitated, as a hero not in the sense of principal personage (whether good or evil, as, say, in the plays of Corneille) but, in a different dictionary sense, as a moral hero. Although recent studies have identified not one kind of Romantic hero but several – the poet–prophet, the rebel, the dandy, even the 'unheroic' hero and the anti-hero – no figure has been more often linked with the Romantics than the archetypal 'héros romantique français', the melancholy solitary gripped by 'le mal du siècle', embodiment of the twin Romantic cults, allegedly, of emotion and egocentric individualism.[10]

Here, by contrast, it will be argued that this is a misinterpretation which has tended to obscure certain major aspects of the Romantic *romans de l'individu* (and perhaps of some poetry and drama too) – and, more widely, of the movement as a whole. The Romantics themselves, obviously enough, drew on their own inner experiences in depicting René and his passion-tossed siblings, but most of them in their own lives and concerns were very far from withdrawing into melancholy and social isolation, and in their political and intellectual careers were at the opposite extreme from the withdrawn apathy of René, Octave, or Amaury. Undeniably the Romantics had deep sympathy, in one sense of the term, with their fictional characters, had themselves known their feelings, and experienced their sense of *ennui* and frustrated idealism. Yet sympathy for their characters' dilemmas does not entail approval of their responses to them, and in novel after novel the evidence, to the contrary, is that they were criticising and warning against them. Maurice Barrès, though an antagonist of the Romantics, claimed this many years ago: 'Ces écrivains . . . travaillèrent de leur mieux à reconnaître le mal du siècle, à le dénoncer, à le refouler.'[11] Some readers' assumptions since then about self-disclosure and 'le héros romantique' have served to distract our attention from this aspect of their works.

The Romantics were seeking, first and most obviously, to describe and analyse 'le mal du siècle'. In doing so they were evoking a state of mind that, far from being peculiar to themselves or created by them, was widespread in their own time and had been so from at least the mid eighteenth century. Studies of sensibility and pre-Romanticism in that earlier period – and of the widespread incidence of melancolia, 'the English malady', as a fashionable complaint – make it abundantly clear that one should indeed speak of what has been well-termed 'le mal des *deux* siècles'.[12] What the Romantics were examining was a long-prevalent mental condition, albeit intensified in their own day by the upheavals of the Revolutionary and Napoleonic years and by other social and intellectual factors alike as France moved into the nineteenth century. One can even contend that they were amongst the very first to explore a 'malady' that has become increasingly prevalent since, that today's 'rebels without a cause' and 'drop-outs' are the descendants of René and his fellow sufferers, and that the Romantics (even if their analyses were inadequate in certain ways) remain more relevant than is usually recognised. They were attempting to understand the nature and sources of a complex phenomenon in their age and society, and not merely or primarily within their private experience. Their portrayal was (and was intended to be) not of an idiosyncratic but of a more universal personal situation, of what has been more fully examined by others since as the alienation of the individual in the modern world. As they described it, this alienation was in part from a materialistic society which they felt to be inimical in various ways to individual fulfilment, to be undermining of idealism and aspiration, but it had other origins also, they believed. The individual is alienated at times even from himself, but especially from others. He is possessed by what Canat many years ago called 'le sentiment de la solitude morale' – 'la douloureuse certitude que chaque individu est comme muré dans son moi et que tout ce qui existe lui est impénétrable'; the Romantics, one might say, were amongst the earliest to realise that solipsism was not merely a philosophical theory but a root of private despair.[13] Alienation, as they saw it, also had ideological dimensions that were both philosophical and political (though the Marxist may fairly criticise their limits here). The reforming social optimism of the *philosophes*, the dreams of liberty, equality and fraternity, had turned sour (at least for the Romantics' own upper social class) with the tumbrel realities of the Terror and Napoleon's despotism and defeat, and as they grew to maturity any hopes they placed in the Bourbon Restoration were increasingly disappointed.[14] In terms of religious commitment too the choice could only seem to be between, on the one hand, strict Catholic orthodoxy and, on the other, the deterministic materialism of the *philosophes* and *idéologues*. And underlying and largely deriving from both political and social disillusion and religious doubt there were more personal uncertainties as to purposes and ideals; it is these especially which their 'romans de l'individu' were exploring.

To make such claims is not to project retrospectively: they themselves often stressed the prevalence of this total 'malady'. Chateaubriand, describing it as 'le vague des passions' in *Le Génie du christianisme*, set it in a long historical context: 'Plus les peuples avancent en civilisation, plus cet état du vague des passions augmente.' The contrast in his view almost extends to a gulf between the Ancient and the Christian eras, and certainly he finds it so pervasive in his own time that he can exclaim: 'Il est étonnant que les écrivains modernes n'aient pas encore songé à peindre cette singulière position de l'âme.' For Constant too in *Adolphe* it is 'une des principales maladies morales de notre siècle', and for Musset in *La Confession* '[une] maladie morale abominable' suffered by many of his contemporaries. Vigny paints it in *Chatterton* as 'une maladie toute morale et presque incurable, et quelquefois contagieuse: maladie terrible qui se saisit surtout des âmes jeunes, ardentes . . .' Hugo in the *Préface de 'Cromwell'* reiterates Chateaubriand's comparison over the centuries: 'avec le christianisme et par lui s'introduisait dans l'esprit des peuples un sentiment nouveau, inconnu des anciens et singulièrement développé chez les modernes . . . la mélancolie'. Such declarations make it the more surprising that so many literary historians should have centred their interpretations upon the autobiographical and 'confessional'. Chapter I above noted the movement from the purely personal to the general and even universal which the Romantics aspired to achieve; nowhere is this more central than in their presentation of 'le mal des deux siècles'.

Yet, if they all described what was basically the same complex sickness, they did so from individually different standpoints and stressed quite different aspects of it. In René lack of religious faith is presented as a prime source of his melancholy. In Delphine the causes are in part society's attitude to women and in part excessive intelligence unchecked by good sense and moral principles. In Adolphe there is an intellectual sophistication that leads to cynical relativism and to 'cette fatigue, cette incertitude, cette absence de force, cette analyse perpétuelle . . .' In Sainte-Beuve's Amaury the source is an introspective sensuality, an unprincipled 'volupté' in the novel's title. In George Sand's Indiana it is above all 'le rapport mal établi entre les sexes' created by society's treatment of women through the constraints of marriage in particular, while in her Lélia the prime factor is 'la maladie du doute', the lack of spiritual and religious conviction produced by 'cette ère d'athéisme et de désespoir'. In Musset's Octave – who gives a classic analysis of the malady in the second chapter of *Confession* – it is a mixture of contempt for society and religious nihilism.

The variety of these diagnoses has perhaps been too little appreciated, but few readers will deny the vividness with which they are presented – with a discernment and a stylistic impact alike that others have discussed and that must here be merely acknowledged. Whatever else they achieved, these novels – and such plays as *Hernani*, *Chatterton* and *Lorenzaccio* also – cumulatively created a symbolic figure of anguished alienation which was as potent for their contemporaries as, say, Sartre's Roquentin or Camus's Meursault would prove for a later generation. They perhaps succeeded too well – to the point, it seems, that many a reader was himself converted to 'le mal du siècle'! Most famously, Chateaubriand was forced to acknowledge of *René*: 'Il a infesté l'esprit d'une partie de la jeunesse, effet que je n'avais pu prévoir, car j'avais au contraire voulu la corriger.'[15]

It is ironic that they should so often have been interpreted as commending in some way 'le mal du siècle'. This is an allegation against which, even then, Charles Nodier amongst others protested, as when he asserted that truly Romantic literature should not be confused with 'le genre frénétique': 'On appelle, en France, cette poésie *maladive* la poésie romantique, mais à faux.'[16] Their explicitly stated intention was not only to describe and analyse but roundly to condemn 'le mal du siècle'. This had been true earlier, at the same explicit level, of the two influential prototypes of its victims, Rousseau's Saint-Preux in *La Nouvelle Héloïse* and Goethe's Werther. Rousseau was recommending the morality of Julie against her lover's passions. Goethe was likewise condemning (as his revision of the novel's ending reaffirmed) the melancholy that had led Werther to suicide – as Mme de Staël would recognise in praising *Werther*, in *De la littérature*, as 'un livre qui rappelle à la vertu la nécessité de la raison'. Undoubtedly they were analysing, under the guise of Saint-Preux and Werther, elements in their own nature, but they were doing so in substantial part in order to exorcise them.

This was comparably true of the Romantics in their novels. '[L'auteur] a voulu dénoncer cette espèce de vice nouveau, et peindre les funestes conséquences de l'amour outré de la solitude': thus Chateaubriand of *René*, itself included in his apologia for Christianity. In the novel itself criticism of his attitude comes from René himself as he looks back on his past, from his sister Amélie, and finally from the Catholic priest Souël. Delphine is certainly critical of social attitudes to the liberated woman, but Staël also stresses a quite different and primary 'but moral': 'Je n'ai jamais voulu présenter Delphine comme un modèle à suivre . . . je blâme et Léonce et Delphine' – a point she develops at length, claiming to have shown the immorality of her heroine's suicide and also, 'comment, avec un cœur généreux et sensible, l'on se livre à beaucoup d'erreurs, si l'on ne se soumet pas à toute la rigidité de la morale'. Constant is no less emphatic in declaring his moral aims in *Adolphe*: to condemn both insincere and casual liaisons and a moral malady, '[un] affaiblissement moral', that is expressed not only in private relations but in the political and religious spheres as well. 'La fidélité en amour est une force comme la croyance religieuse, comme l'enthousiasme de la liberté. Or nous [a use of 'we' that underlines the wide reference he gives his work] n'avons plus aucune force. Nous ne savons plus aimer, ni croire, ni vouloir.' His novel, he claims, 'prouve que le caractère, la fermeté, la fidélité, la bonté, sont les dons qu'il faut demander au ciel . . .'

The following generation declared the same purpose. Sainte-Beuve's preface to *Volupté* claims: 'Le véritable objet de ce livre est l'analyse d'un penchant, d'une passion, d'un vice même, et de tout le côté de l'âme que ce vice domine . . .' And it is noteworthy that contemporary reviewers judged he had achieved this end, discerning in it 'une haute moralité', '[une] confession écrite d'un point de vue chrétien', 'un dénouement catholique', even praising it as '[le] seul roman d'utilité spirituelle qui ait paru en France'.[17] Likewise, Musset's *Confession* gives a critical presentation of Octave, and, to cite a theatrical case, Vigny protests about his comparable depiction of Chatterton and his suicide that, though he is also highly critical of society, 'le suicide est un crime religieux et social' that he has never sought to justify. Only George Sand's personal novels, amongst all the others, are uncritical of their heroines – of Indiana, victim of 'la fausse morale par qui la société est gouvernée', of Lélia, afflicted by religious unbelief.

So many declarations of this kind lead to a clear conclusion: the Romantics intended their depiction of their suffering 'heroes' to be the embodiment of a problem and not the embodiment of a moral ideal; their 'heroes' were in each case individuals who have failed to find any solution to the problem. In dwelling upon it so often they had a triple purpose. They wished, first, to emphasise the reality of the spiritual, intellectual and social dilemmas underlying 'le mal du siècle', to insist in an age they saw as materialistic and profoundly unspiritual that man needs more for his fulfilment than bread and social order. Secondly, they wished to explore the full range of those dilemmas in order to understand the disease for which they were seeking a cure. For, thirdly, their novels were not only critical of the submissive passivity of their 'heroes'; they were also probing for new reasons for hope and action, for an alternative personal morality in a period when the traditional certainties were crumbling.

The extent to which these novels were works of ethical debate has tended to be cloaked by two common interpretations in particular. The first, already discussed, sees them as confessional self-disclosure, even self-justification. The second, however, identifies in their work a quite different moral hero, creative, positive, energetic – 'le héros sauveur', as Simon and others have called him, 'the passionate and dominant man' presented as 'model type', in Shroder's words, a French equivalent of the figure of the 'Heroic Redeemer' discerned by Peckham in other European writers of the age.[18] Yet the dangers of simplification are as great here as in regard to 'le héros mélancolique'. There are Promethean moments in the French Romantics' writings, notably with Hugo, and some of them were at times attracted by the myths of Icarus and Faust and by other symbols of creative energy such as Byron and Napoleon. But their attitude was critical rather than admiring in most instances. Trousson's thorough study of *Le Thème de Prométhée dans la littérature européenne* finds little evidence, other than in Ballanche and Quinet, of a cult of Prometheus by the French Romantics (as contrasted, say, with the Shelley of *Prometheus Unbound*), and the same is true of Černy's earlier *Essai sur le titanisme dans la poésie romantique occidentale*. Recent studies of the Napoleonic cult tend in the same direction. Descotes finds in Romantic literature not one but two 'légendes de Napoléon'. The first of these idealised Napoleon as the friend of liberty and of the principles of 1789, and it was as such that he appealed to Balzac, to Stendhal, and to Hugo – in whom Descotes finds 'une curieuse alchimie': 'l'utilisation du mythe de l'ex-Tyran pour le service de la cause de la Liberté'. But the majority of the Romantics – Chateaubriand, Mme de Staël, Constant, Lamartine, and, for the most part, Vigny – embraced the contrary view of the Emperor as a brutal, self-seeking tyrant.[19]

If, in contrast with many other interpreters, we abandon the supposition that their aim was to present a moral hero, whether energetic or melancholy, we can more readily see in their personal novels the central role of moral contrast and appreciate that they are above all dialogues, not monologues from a single character or the author himself.

Moral debate is present in their works in various forms. It may exist, quite consciously, as between successive works from their pen. An example seen earlier is between Senancour's *Obermann* and his *Libres Méditations*, and a similar contrast is found in George Sand. Whereas the first version of *Lélia* in 1833 was a study of scepticism and despair, the revised edition of 1839 contained two major innovations: Lélia gains religious faith and takes her vows as a nun, eventually becoming abbess; Trenmor, serenely inactive previously, becomes a man of action. Doubt has proved a stepping-stone to belief (as Sand noted in her Preface of 1839), and this later *Lélia* declares Sand's new-found faith in God, progress and humanity, as did her *Spiridion* in the same year.

Secondly and far more frequently, the dialogue is conducted through the juxtaposition of characters within a given work. Again and again the melancholy solitary is contrasted with others around him who react in quite different ways. Amélie and Chactas are set over against René in their responses to the despair that they too have known, and this adds a further dimension to père Souël's explicit strictures. And in *Atala* the different attitudes of père Aubry, René, the younger Chactas, his beloved, and her mother are similarly contrasted. Likewise, as Mme de Staël herself stressed of her first novel, 'le caractère de Mathilde sert à faire ressortir les torts de Delphine' – a contrast of which she asked: 'Est-il possible de mieux montrer la souveraine puissance de la morale?'

Her *Corinne* presents a double comparison: between the melancholy of Oswald and the creative 'enthusiasm' of Corinne, and, secondly, between Corinne as liberated woman and the values of domestic happiness represented by Lucile.

Similar moral oppositions abound in the works of later Romantics – in plays as well as novels. Vigny's Chatterton is contrasted with the Quaker and Kitty Bell, Musset's Lorenzo with both Alexandre and the Strozzis, Hugo's Ruy Blas with don Salluste and don César, as Hugo himself stressed. George Sand's *Lélia* offers a further example. As she noted, its characters are in part allegorical: Pulchérie embodies sophistical epicureanism and Magnus a corrupted religiosity, whilst Sténio illustrates 'un enfant du siècle' rather different from Lélia herself, showing (in Sand's words) 'l'enthousiasme et la faiblesse d'un temps où l'intelligence monte très-haut entraînée par l'imagination, et tombe très-bas . . .' Musset's *Confession*, likewise, sets Octave over against Brigitte, Smith, Desgenais and the morality of his own home, as we shall see. In Vigny's *Cinq-Mars* the idealism of de Thou and Cinq-Mars himself contrasts with Richelieu's power politics, and in his *Daphné* the religious intellectualism of Julien and Libanius is explicitly evaluated against the religious needs of the masses. The clash of characters is, obviously enough, at the heart of most fiction and drama, but it has not always been noted how often it is used by the Romantics as a vehicle for ethical discussion.

Finally, the underlying debate in their work is often carried on within the mind of a single main character, in the conflict between different aspects of his personality. René vacillates, we observe, between idealism and apathy, repentance and melancholy, and Eudore in Chateaubriand's prose epic, *Les Martyrs*, provides an even clearer instance, as he progresses from self-questioning and uncertainty to a positive affirmation of values pursued to the point of martyrdom. Earlier in the work he shows numerous resemblances with René (and even more so in the original version, *Les Martyrs de Dioclétien*), but thereafter he passes through repentance to religious conviction and heroic action; his martyrdom is portrayed as the triumphant climax of a protracted searching for self-mastery – illustrated in the same work by Cymodocée also. Staël's Corinne is no less a divided mind, and Adolphe is the arch example of a constant vacillation that ends in tragedy for Ellénore. Likewise, in the later generation's works, Musset's Lorenzo is torn within himself between corruption and purity, scepticism and idealism, and so too is his Octave. Vigny's *Servitude et grandeur militaires* depicts the struggle within the Captain of *Laurette* to resolve the anguished clash of duty and conscience and to achieve redemption through his self-abnegating care of Laurette, and a similar inner conflict in Capitaine Renaud is explored in *La Canne de jonc*.

Yet a major question remains if one accepts the reading of these novels that has been sketched: why have most of them (*Adolphe* being a salient exception) been so often interpreted rather differently, and in particular as self-justifying monologues? Certainly, as numerous critics have made clear, they draw upon their authors' perceptive introspection; certainly too they utilise a wealth of language and stylistic command – but this only serves to highlight the question all the more: how can works intended as a warning against 'le mal du siècle' have been so often read, both at the time and since, as praising it? To attribute insincerity and hypocrisy to the author of *René*, as Sainte-Beuve and others have done, might be plausible for a single instance but hardly for so many of his fellow Romantics.

The answers will differ from text to text: all require separate detailed analysis. But perhaps the underlying explanation should be sought in their deep awareness of the conflicting claims implicit in each individual's situation: they knew the 'anguish' of moral 'choice' well before the existentialists – unless one includes Pascal, whom certain of them so much admired. The very centrality of moral dialogue and contrast in their works suggests that they were exploring even more than concluding, and that any finalities were hard-won. Again and again, whilst clear at the explicit level (and the same is true of *La Nouvelle Héloïse* and *Werther* too), below the surface their novels reveal ambiguity – not self-contradiction (as occasionally alleged by their critics) but often conscious ambivalence.

A full analysis of the Romantics' ambivalences – the plural being required – would have to examine dilemmas of class and society, especially so since the interpretations of Pierre Barbéris, and also other sources of the kind explored by Mario Praz.[20] Here, remaining with their general attitude to 'le mal du siècle', their essentially double-sided view of melancholy is especially relevant. For in reality, far from seeing it as a transitory mood, they respected it as a deep-seated and in some ways justifiable response to the human condition. At the same time, however, they believed that though it might too often lead to inactive, listless despair, it need not do so but could be transcended, subsumed in a wider reaction to the situations that provoked it.

Mme de Staël provides a first and emphatic illustration of such a view in *De la littérature*. She especially connects melancholy with 'la littérature du nord', as the outcome of not only the sombre landscape and climate of northern Europe but also its sombre Protestant religion, and she makes high claims for it on four counts. First, it conduces to a more imaginative literature: 'Les peuples du nord sont moins occupés des plaisirs que de la douleur, et leur imagination n'en est que plus féconde.' Secondly, she argues – somewhat unpersuasively perhaps but with evident conviction – that it favours a love of liberty and makes servitude 'insupportable'. Thirdly, it represents a truer, deeper view of life: 'La poésie mélancolique est la poésie la plus d'accord avec la philosophie. La tristesse fait pénétrer bien plus avant dans le caractère et la destinée de l'homme, que toute autre disposition de l'âme.' And at the same time, fourthly and most relevantly here, it leads to great and heroic action: 'Ce que l'homme a fait de plus grand, il le doit au sentiment douloureux de l'incomplet de la destinée.' This 'disposition de l'âme', 'source de toutes les passions généreuses, comme de toutes les idées philosophiques', inspires alike 'l'héroïsme de la morale, l'enthousiasme de l'éloquence, l'ambition de la gloire'.

Chateaubriand identifies Christianity as a whole – not Protestantism alone – as a primary source of modern melancholy, of that 'vague des passions' which he was to evoke in *René*.[21] Civilisation and the influence of women have played their part in provoking 'cette inquiétude secrète' but above all (as we saw earlier) the Christian teachings, unlike the religious beliefs of the Ancients, have inspired dissatisfaction with this life and a preoccupation with the after-life. 'C'est dans le génie du christianisme qu'il faut surtout chercher la raison de ce *vague* des sentiments répandu chez les hommes modernes.' And by 'modern' he understands a far longer period than his own age; this 'science de la tristesse, des angoisses et des transports de l'âme que les anciens n'ont jamais connus' has inspired Christian literature, art and life over the centuries – 'le merveilleux de la position d'Héloïse', the tragedies of Racine as compared with Euripides and Seneca, and much else.

Other Romantics postulated similar connections, and most emphatically Hugo, as noted earlier.[22] The Gospel has revealed 'l'âme à travers les sens, l'éternité derrière la vie' – in sharp contrast, we saw, with the outlook of the Ancient world: 'De ce sentiment, qui avait été pour Caton païen *le désespoir*, le christianisme fit *la mélancolie*.' This major distinction is not developed further here, but two aspects can be deduced from the context. First, Hugo sees melancholy as more profound and spiritually conscious than despair. Secondly, whereas the latter is passive and may lead to apathy, melancholy can be the springboard for social action; far from encouraging pure other-worldliness, the Christian's sense of the vicissitudes of this life leads him to 'prendre en pitié l'humanité', so that

D.G. Charlton

his faith becomes 'une religion d'égalité, de liberté, de charité'.

Hugo's juxtaposition offers the clue to the Romantics' ambivalence about melancholy. If it leads to stultifying apathy it becomes a malady, as with René and his fellows, a sterile alienation, widespread in their own time, which they both understood and deplored. Yet, on the other hand, its origins lie in truths and in a personal inwardness that are far superior to facile optimism or mere materialism, and it may result, no less desirably, in positive, more realistically-based consequences beyond itself. For Chateaubriand it is the gateway to Christian faith, as he himself had found; hence his seductive presentation of melancholy in *René* is closely linked with his wider apologetic aims. René's sadness is so described that the reader is led to feel it is an appropriate reaction to the human situation: 'Le chant naturel de l'homme est triste, lors même qu'il exprime le bonheur.' But the sadness should not be final: true for man's life without God, it is inadequate for life with God. Amélie has moved through and beyond despair; René remains trapped within it, even conscious of the contrast in himself: 'J'étois plein de religion, et je raisonnais en impie.' For Mme de Staël, comparably, it not only favours 'l'esprit d'un peuple libre', but above all a creative outlook, 'l'enthousiasme': 'Le sublime de l'esprit, des sentiments et des actions doit son essor au besoin d'échapper aux bornes qui circonscrivent l'imagination.' The later Romantics provide further examples. Melancholy and idealistic action are combined in Hernani and Ruy Blas themselves, and Vigny's Capitaine Renaud moves through anguish to acceptance and resolution. In Musset's *Confession*, rather differently, Octave is contrasted with Brigitte.[23] She, like him, has been deceived in love and suffered disillusionment, but whereas he remains in a state of passive despair, she has moved through her sickness (in her own word) to an ethic of self-giving love. Nor are this novel's moral explorations limited to this single contrast between melancholy transcended and untranscended, or to what can be seen, when closely examined, to be a detailed and comprehensive analysis of 'le mal du siècle', ranging from the social to the religious and intellectual and centred upon the ethical. In addition, Musset's work embodies more positive values. The same is true of most of the other *romans de l'individu*; here the *Confession* must serve as one example of an element of moral affirmation present in them as well.

In the earlier Parts of his study Musset had given a critical presentation of the bored 'enfant du siècle' and of a corrupt, sceptical society (and the criticisms themselves obviously have ethical implications). In Part III and thereafter he draws the contrast with an older,

more constructive morality. He had originally thought to end the novel
by showing Octave's redemption through love – 'amour, ô principe du
monde! flamme précieuse . . .' – but in the outcome Musset shows us
that even love can be ineffective and be soured by the sick mind. In
contrast, he depicts not only Brigitte's victory over despair but also,
from the start of Part III, Octave's own father and the ethical world in
which he has lived. 'Sa vie avait été, d'un bout à l'autre, un modèle de
vertu, de calme et de bonté' – a judgment reinforced by his papers, as
Octave acknowledges when reading them: 'Ton dévouement pour tes
amis, ta tendresse divine pour ma mère, ton admiration pour la nature,
ton amour sublime pour Dieu, voilà ta vie.' And linked with this sense of
'la douce sérénité de l'âme de mon père' goes a perhaps sentimental but
certainly emphatic sense of the morality of rural as opposed to urban life,
symbolised again by the servant Larive, 'peut-être, après mon père lui-
même, le meilleur homme que j'aie jamais connu'. Even Octave himself,
when living in his father's country home, attains at last 'une vie calme et
régulière': 'pour la première fois de ma vie j'étais heureux'. In the final
Parts he will lose his happiness, but these moral attitudes will not be
renounced. The values of his father and servant are exemplified further
in both Smith and Brigitte. Octave has earlier noted of the latter that 'la
douce sérénité de son front n'était pas venue de ce monde, mais qu'elle
l'avait reçue de Dieu . . .' (a close parallel to his view of his father). By
her attitude to Octave Brigitte continues to symbolise the redemptive
possibilities of love, and she also defends the traditional values of her
family too, justifying them to Octave as they seek to recall her 'à la
raison, au monde, que je respectais jadis, et à l'honneur que j'ai perdu'.
Smith is likewise presented as an unselfish and almost improbably
admirable (not to suggest priggish) young man – 'le plus noble
caractère', marked by 'sa bonne foi et sa simplicité'. Octave continues to
acknowledge that 'Smith est brave, bon et honnête', and his own
admittedly over-dramatised parting from Brigitte suggests that he
himself is struggling to return to their values. Towards the end, indeed,
even the Christian faith can speak to him, as when despite his intellectual
unbelief he is restrained from killing Brigitte by the sight of her crucifix,
and afterwards affirms: 'Qu'importent le nom, la forme, la croyance?
tout ce qui est bon n'est-il pas sacré? Comment ose-t-on toucher à Dieu?'
And we leave him – though the scene is melodramatic – thanking God
that, in effect, moral justice has triumphed since only he remains
unhappy. The novel can thus be seen to juxtapose traditional morality
and contemporary immorality, to set the values of Octave's rural family
background, of Brigitte and Smith, and of a self-giving love, against the

corrupt, bored attitudes of nineteenth-century Parisian society and thought.

This summary certainly does not exhaust the moral content of the novel; notably, it explores also the tension between ideal and real, private aspiration and public life, and the character and outlook of Desgenais add another major dimension to the debate. A fuller analysis would help us to appreciate why admirers like Taine could rate Musset so highly as a moral thinker – in this instance utilising the 'novel of the individual' to embody, juxtapose and probe alternative responses to personal dilemmas.

The other Romantics were similar in greater or lesser measure, and were often similar too in their conclusions, in so far as these were firm in their case or in his. These were less dramatic than more apocalyptically minded interpreters have sometimes implied: often supportive of social involvement and commitment, of kindliness and love, of self-giving. It is striking to note, in particular, how often approval appears in their works to go to women. Chateaubriand's Amélie and Cymodocée; for Mme de Staël a composite, it would seem, of Corinne and Lucile; Musset's Brigitte; Vigny's Kitty Bell; Sand's heroines: these are illustrations amongst others of an empathy with the 'feminine' that marks almost all of them. It is seen elsewhere in their support for women's liberation and in their interest in the 'myth of the androgyne'[24] – of the male complemented by the female (or vice versa) in a completer human being – but it is manifested most inwardly in their depictions of their fictional female characters. If the discussion above is correct (and some critics would no doubt contest it), the practical ethic of many of the Romantics, expressed in their novels as well as in actual social and political involvement, was neither that of the withdrawn solitary nor that of the melodramatically energetic Promethean but lay, with refreshing normality, in straightforward moral goodness. Read in the way outlined, their *romans de l'individu* give discerning, moving confirmation of such a claim.

SHORT FICTION AND SOCIAL NOVELS

The Romantics' contributions to short fiction and the social novel will be only briefly discussed here – and not only for lack of space. Neither, one may think, warrants the same emphasis as their personal or historical novels in what has to be a selective survey of their most notable achievements, although the reasons for this conclusion differ in the two cases.

The first half of the nineteenth century saw a major development of short fiction. The *conte* and the *nouvelle*, two genres which became ever more confused with each other at this time,[25] now attained wide popularity, especially when published in periodicals and newspapers after 1830, and even gained a literary respectability they had largely lacked before. Yet the striking fact appears to be that the major Romantics made only a slight and incidental contribution to this change. *Atala*, *René* and *Adolphe* should surely not be treated as *nouvelles*, still less as *contes*, and whilst Mme de Staël wrote a few short stories, they appeared early in her career and are of minimal interest. What of the second generation? All its leading members wrote short stories. Yet not only did they not theorise about the form, compulsive theorists though they were on all other genres, but these were few in number and were all after 1830, later than their first major works in poetry, drama and novel. As regards the marked rise of the *conte fantastique* at this time, under the influence of Hoffmann and of Jacques Cazotte earlier, only Nodier and Gautier practised the form (unless one were to include Balzac as a Romantic), apart from Mérimée where a different consideration applies.[26]

The short stories they did write fell into one of two categories. Most were produced, as entirely subsidiary to their main literary aims, at a belated stage and for the popular press. Lamartine's two *récits villageois*, *Geneviève, histoire d'une servante* (1850) and *Le Tailleur de pierres* (1851), and his two autobiographical stories, *Raphaël* (1849) and *Graziella* (1852), all came, obviously enough, after both his main literary works and his political career. Likewise, Musset wrote such stories as *Emmeline* and *Les Deux Maîtresses* (both 1837), *Frédéric* (1838) and *Mimi Pinson* (1845) at a late stage and reluctantly, for financial reasons. Dumas *père* tried his hand in the genres somewhat earlier – his unsuccessful *Nouvelles contemporaines* appeared (and sold just four copies) in 1826 – but his later attempts were clearly overshadowed by his novels. The same was true of George Sand's few short stories, and of Hugo's two short fictions the medieval *Légende du beau Pécopin* was only included in letter XI of *Le Rhin* (1842). Stendhal and Balzac are not here classified as Romantics, but even if they were and even though their achievements in short fiction were of higher quality, it has been persuasively argued that they turned it into 'a dehydrated version of the novel';[27] for them too it remained a secondary form.

The only remaining texts are Hugo's *Claude Gueux* (1834) and the stories in Vigny's *Stello* and *Servitude et grandeur militaires*. The tales of Gilbert and Chatterton in *Stello* and the stories in the latter work did indeed appear separately, but their re-publication in book form soon after indicates that Vigny considered them not as self-sufficient but as part of wider works – works that are social novels of a kind and not collections of short stories. In these instances, and in Hugo's plea against the prison system and the death penalty in *Claude Gueux* likewise, the short story is being utilised (in no bad sense) for ulterior ends and as a vehicle for ideas – much as Voltaire and others had previously developed the *conte philosophique*.

It is hard not to conclude, in short, that the major Romantics had only a passing interest in short fiction as a distinctive literary form. This is perhaps surprising, since they much admired one of its leading initiators at this period, Charles Nodier, and his *Smarra* (1821), *Trilby* (1822), and other stories. Yet, in reality, his influence in this respect seems to have been limited to mainly younger writers; it was they who achieved for the short story what their elders had attempted for the novel: Petrus Borel, Xavier Forneret, Gérard de Nerval, to whom must be added Gautier, from *La Cafetière* (1831) and the stories of *Jeunes-France* (1833) on. As regards the authors with whom this chapter is concerned, A.J. George seems justified after his thorough survey of short fiction over this period in concluding that it 'received little aid and comfort from the great generation of French romantics'.[28] There is one outstanding master of the genre, as no reader will need to be reminded: Mérimée. Yet even he serves to confirm the basic contention. His first collection of tales was *Mosaïque* (1833); *Colomba* and *La Vénus d'Ille* appeared in 1841 and *Carmen* in 1845, and he continued to write stories even during his unhappy retirement in Cannes; his *Dernières Nouvelles* were published in 1873, three years after his death – including *Lokis*, a further example of his major, even if unbelieving, contribution to the *conte fantastique*. These dates reveal that his writings as *conteur* come after his earlier affiliation with the Romantics had markedly weakened and when he was occupied by his archaeological and architectural career. His *Chronique du règne de Charles IX* can reasonably be treated as illustrative of the Romantic movement; his short stories, notwithstanding certain affinities, are independent of it and should thus not be invoked as part of its collective achievement.

The major Romantics wrote so much over so wide a range; it is perhaps reassuring to conclude that they largely neglected at least one literary genre – albeit one can obviously read with pleasure such stories as Musset's *Histoire d'un merle blanc*. If one seeks the reasons, it may be ungenerous but not irrelevant to recall a comment upon George Sand that was hardly less true of her friends: 'brevity was not her virtue'.

The Romantics' social and political involvement was expressed in numerous ways. Liszt's playing at the Saint-Simonian receptions in Paris or his *Lyon*, a work for piano in protest at the massacre in the city's rue Transnonain; Delacroix's vast depiction of liberty on the barricades; the political poems of Hugo and Lamartine; Vigny's attack on capitalism in *Chatterton* and Musset's wider portrayal of power politics in *Lorenzaccio*: these and much else, alongside their explicitly formulated ideas, reflect one of their major concerns, as other chapters in this work confirm. Their prose fiction is characteristic in this respect, including their personal and historical novels. *Delphine* and *Corinne*, for example, are concerned with the place of women in society, as are George Sand's *Indiana* and *Lélia* later, and *René* with the individual's relation to the call for action in society expressed by père Souël. *Adolphe* is in part a critique of a corrupted society and above all analyses a mental state which, we saw Constant stress, has political and religious as well as personal consequences, and *Volupté* later has even been termed 'un roman politique'.[29] Their historical novels (and dramas) have numerous intended references too to nineteenth-century France and to contemporary issues; in some ways it may be misleading to differentiate them too sharply from the social novel, not least those like *Les Chouans* which dealt with the more recent past. None the less, despite uncertainties of definition, the distinction is real between novels evoking the society of the past, with whatever current references, and those which depict the society of the present. This is the more relevant since the history of the nineteenth-century novel in France and elsewhere was to be dominated by the realistic novel of contemporary society; we are thus bound to consider the relation of the Romantics to this major literary phenomenon. If Balzac and Stendhal were treated here as 'French Romantics' the answer would not be far to seek. Since they are not (for reasons good or ill) it is more difficult to find, and this is especially so since 'le roman social des romantiques' has been largely neglected by literary critics in our own time, or at least until very recent years. It is surprising, for instance, that two surveys of 1909 and 1910 should have needed reprinting in 1973 for lack of later studies, and even one of these, by Brun, had been dismissive of the Romantics' social novels in general and denounced their outlook as 'simplette'; as to Evans's more sympathetic study, that largely concerned lesser novelists than the Romantics.[30] Now there are signs of reviving attention, illustrated by major editions and studies of Hugo and Sand in particular and wide-ranging colloquia such as those on *Romantisme et politique* in

1966 and *Roman et société* in 1971. And yet even now an understandable priority continues to go to the great tradition of Stendhal, Balzac, Flaubert and Zola – and not only in such outstanding but necessarily selective works as Auerbach's *Mimesis* and its inheritors but also in terms of current research. The Romantics remain overshadowed by these masters, with the sole but even so contested exception of Hugo.

Such reactions are not unjustified even from other viewpoints. Of the Romantics as here defined only very few wrote novels about contemporary society, and beyond that there is a further consideration. Whereas *Le Rouge et le noir*, many of Balzac's novels, and *L'Éducation sentimentale* analyse society in its wide, complex realities, almost all the Romantics' social novels were centred on the remedy of specific abuses, on campaigning for some explicit cause. Brun proposed a distinction between 'le roman à thèse' and 'le roman social'; many later critics have implicitly accepted it, and with the same firm preference for the latter. This value-judgment may not be a necessary one: many highly-valued works are propagandist, as the cases of Voltaire, Rousseau and others illustrate. Yet most of us remain critical, and perhaps justifiably so, of didacticism and philosophising in the novel, and this sets a limit on our evaluation of most of the works concerned.

This is most evidently true with Vigny's *Stello* (1832) and *Servitude et grandeur militaires* (1835). The former consists of a dialogue between the poet Stello and his more rationalising, sceptical interlocutor, 'le docteur Noir', which is interspersed with three case-histories. Each is used to show that the poet is disregarded under any government – Gilbert under Louis XV, Chatterton in late-eighteenth-century Britain, and Chénier during the French Revolution. All three episodes are economically and movingly recounted, but the only unity of the total work lies in its limited, almost axe-grinding thesis. Vigny's ideas remain dominant and are rarely assimilated into concrete, lived experience; there is, in one critic's words, 'a kind of bifocalism of thesis and narrative, to the detriment of the latter'.[31] The three stories of the later work are similarly intended to illustrate a thesis, as developed in the first and final chapters. As a former army officer himself Vigny seeks to show the plight of the French soldier or sailor: forced to obey inhuman orders in the case of the merchant captain in *Laurette*; killed by an accidental but self-caused explosion in the case of Mathurin in *La Veillée de Vincennes*; led to slay a child during a Napoleonic battle in the case of Capitaine Renaud in *La Canne de jonc* (and himself shot by a child in 1830). Unfortunately, not only do the second and third stories inadequately bear out the thesis but the characters are in large part allegorical representations of Vigny's ideas, and their portrayals seem simplified and implausible illustrations of (for example) the self-seeking tyrant (Napoleon) or the process of redemption through suffering and the moral status of obedience (the two captains). In both works, despite their merits, we are thus conscious of special pleading and an intellectualisation that prevent any wider-ranging depiction of society.

George Sand's earlier novels have already been mentioned as *romans de l'individu*. Under the spur of her increasing social concern and the influence of Lamennais and Leroux in particular, she wrote a number of socialistic novels in the second phase of her career: *Le Compagnon du Tour de France* (1840), *Consuelo* (1842), *Le Meunier d'Angibault* (1845), and *Le Péché de M. Antoine* (1847). The events of 1848 disillusioned her and undermined what had been close to revolutionary fervour. She withdrew increasingly to her estate in the tiny Berry village of Nohant, where she presided as 'mistress' over what in her mind was an idyllic rural community. It is this pastoral dream that is also evoked in her *romans champêtres*: *La Mare au Diable* (1846), *La Petite Fadette* (1849), *François le Champi* (1850), and *Les Maîtres sonneurs* (1853) – novels of memorable charm for all of us who read them in our youth and which have also been seen as precursors of the *roman rustique* and the *roman régionaliste* later in the century and since.

'Le grand romancier social du romantisme, c'est, incontestablement, George Sand': thus Roger Picard.[32] We noted the deep admiration of both French and foreign writers in her own time, and today French critics in particular seem to be rediscovering her merits – as special issues of both the *RHLF* (1976) and *Romantisme* (1977), marking the centenary of her death, have shown as well as other evidence. Others of us have to confess our reservations, even though not dismissing her work with Guillemin as 'un désert d'ennui'.[33] The novels concerned with the dilemmas of woman in society have a first-hand, realistic vigour deriving from her own experience and powers of observation. Her socialistic novels seem, by comparison, to offer far less a picture of contemporary society (other than the obvious facts of poverty and oppression) than a utopian sketch of some future reconciliation of the classes to be based, it seems, on love and intermarriage. Hers is, as Johannet remarked, 'une espèce vague de socialisme champêtre et édénique',[34] hesitant to the point of indecision on the hard issues (for reasons entirely to her credit[35]) and thus led to indulge in hopeful emotion. Only in depicting rural life does she equal Balzac; a recent comparison with *Les Paysans* seems right to find her peasants 'plus diversifiés et placés dans le cadre de leurs travaux saisonniers, de leur vie quotidienne', and to question the disparaging view that they are merely 'des êtres idylliques'.[36] By contrast, the urban works in *Le Compagnon* or in a later novel like *La Ville noire* (1861) seem more distantly observed. The unconvinced reader may at least welcome current reassessments of this novelist of once international reputation – and should meanwhile pass on.

The greatest social novelist amongst the Romantics is, *pace* Picard, surely Hugo, who was characteristically both first and last. He was first with his attack on the death penalty in *Le Dernier Jour d'un condamné* (1829), followed by *Claude Gueux* (1834), and last with *Les Misérables* (1862) and other novels such as *Les Travailleurs de la mer* and *Quatre-vingt-treize* in so far as they have an explicit social or contemporary dimension. The first two briefer works are clearly centred on a particular cause: reform of the penal system. Yet to treat them, and especially *Le Dernier Jour*, as limited to a 'thesis' would be quite inadequate: it transforms its theme into a vibrantly conveyed human experience – in marked contrast with Vigny's stories – that still has the power to haunt us as it did Dostoevsky. Nor is that its only significance: in terms of the novelist's art it was in its time, arguably at least, the equivalent of a *nouveau roman* in ours – 'par le refus de la narration suivie, par l'introduction du monologue intérieur, par une série de déplacements . . . entre le rêve et la réalité, par toutes sortes d'expérimentation'.[37] *Les Misérables* defies brief treatment. Its aspects include the historical, as with the famous evocations of Waterloo and the Insurrection, and the philosophical, including themes of fatality, redemption and providential justice, as well as the social – or, rather, these elements are interfused in the most comprehensive and powerful novel of the century. It is in some ways a *roman à thèse*, concerned with what its preface identifies as 'les trois problèmes du siècle': 'la dégradation de l'homme par le prolétariat, la déchéance de la femme par la faim, l'atrophie de l'enfant par la nuit'. One may think its themes are vaguely dithyrambic: historical optimism, a spiritualism based on providence, progress to be achieved through education, redemption through repentance – and its critics have linked its popularity with the banality of its ideas. Hugo's specific economic or political proposals are, moreover, 'even more nebulous than those of George Sand' (or so it can be claimed[38]): 'Ajustez mathématiquement le salaire au travail . . .; développez les intelligences tout en occupant les bras . . .; démocratisez la propriété, non en l'abolissant, mais en l'universalisant . . .; en deux mots: sachez produire et sachez répartir.' And yet what Lamartine despised as 'l'épopée de la canaille' transcends all its failings and continues to reveal to modern criticism new richness and meaning within its exuberant, imaginative epic realism.

Yet Hugo's novels alone, even with Sand's added, do not allow us to attribute to the Romantics in general a major part in the development of the social novel. Strikingly enough, their attempts to observe and evoke in their novels a whole society – as opposed to campaigning for particular causes – are related less to their own age than to earlier times. Just as they developed the fictional form of the *roman de l'individu*, so too (we must now note) they contributed very significantly to the rise of the historical novel.

THE HISTORICAL NOVEL

Their historical novels were concentrated for the most part within a short period: from Vigny's *Cinq-Mars* (1826) to Hugo's *Notre-Dame de Paris* (1831), albeit with later examples like Gautier's *Le Capitaine Fracasse* (1863) and Hugo's *Quatre-vingt-treize* (1874). But that should not mislead us into under-rating the intensity of their concern with the historical or into accounting for it as primarily escapism into a colourfully dramatic past. On the contrary, these novels (and several of their dramas also) reflect the vast expansion of historical studies during and after the French Restoration. Numerous official innovations were promoted – chairs of history, learned institutes, archaeological missions, protection of historical monuments, and the like – but above all works of scholarship and vast compilations of chronicles and documents were published in greatly increased numbers. One estimate for 1825 alone, for example, counted 40 million pages of historical work (whereas only 3 million in 1811), compared with 30 million pages of *belles-lettres*: such was the dimension of what Renan would later call a 'revolution'.[39]

Our novelists were keenly aware of it. Not only did they draw much of their literary material from such scholarly editors as Petitot. Several of the major French historians were their friends and themselves members of the Romantic groupings of the 1820s: Thiers, Barante, Guizot, Rémusat and others. And literary and historical writers shared many of the same underlying preoccupations. These were naturally varied: patriotic concern with French history in particular, intensified after Waterloo by the wish to recall more glorious times; political motivations as the Liberals sought to weaken the alliance of monarchy, aristocracy and clergy; a growing awareness of historical relativities and the differences between societies and peoples; a determination also to seek for the causes of recent national misfortunes by study of the past. There was a near obsession, indeed, with revolutions and the analysis most particularly of the origins of the French Revolution. It is noteworthy how many of the Romantic plays and novels concern times of historical crisis: the fall of the Roman Empire in Chateaubriand's *Les Martyrs*; medieval revolts, as in Mérimée's *La Jacquerie* and Hugo's *Notre-Dame de Paris*; Renaissance conflicts, as in the Florence of Musset's *Lorenzaccio* (and a prior work by George Sand) or the French wars of religion, as with Mérimée's *Chronique* and a number of dramas also; the Fronde in Vigny's *Cinq-Mars* and *La Maréchale d'Ancre* and Hugo's *Marion de Lorme*; the Cromwellian period in England with Hugo and also Mérimée; the French Revolution itself in Balzac's *Les Chouans* and Vigny's *Stello* as well as Hugo later. Certain of them also wrote historical analyses on the revolutionary phenomenon, parallel with the writings of Guizot on English revolutions and of Mignet, Thiers and Michelet on French revolutions. Chateaubriand's first published work was his *Essai sur les révolutions* and Staël's last was her *Considérations sur la révolution française*; Mérimée would produce an *Essai sur la guerre sociale* and Lamartine his *Histoire des Girondins*.

The Romantic novelists and dramatists – and the epic poets too – were, in short, motivated as much by intellectual, social and political concerns as by purely personal or literary factors in their historical works. Undoubtedly the novels of Walter Scott had a major impact upon them – translated into French from 1816 onwards, with a 60-volume edition in the 1820s which sold no fewer than $1\frac{1}{2}$ million copies within six years. Yet the vogue for Scott, shared by the Romantics, even if with reservations in the case of Vigny, leaves us with a further explanation to find beyond his influence upon them: why Scott, as opposed to other authors? His example may help to account for various literary features of their own historical novels but cannot explain much more than that. In addition and perhaps above all, the Romantic novelists saw themselves as involved in the same historical movement as their historian friends, contributing to it in a complementary way. Thus Vigny, for example, links his *Cinq-Mars* and the historical genres with 'l'étude du destin général des sociétés' and 'la vérité d'observation sur la nature humaine', and his own novel was planned as only one in a series to be devoted to the fortunes of the French aristocracy down to his own day. Mérimée's *Chronique* contained numerous contemporary references and was clearly inspired by his wider views on religion, politics and human nature. The same was true of Musset's *Lorenzaccio*, and Hugo likewise could refer to 'the philosophical and aesthetic ideas concealed' in his *Notre-Dame de Paris*. One may debate whether such non-literary concerns proved healthy for their plays and novels – Vigny's bias towards the aristocracy, for instance, or Mérimée's religious scepticism – but their centrality in work after work seems hard to deny. It has often been judged that picturesque details and descriptions, at times too much local colour, marked these works, but the Romantics' aspirations, whether achieved or not, markedly transcended such external evocation of past times.

Over and beyond the social and intellectual concerns they shared with the historians, they resembled them in a further way. Guizot, Michelet and their fellows sought to evoke not so much the history of governments, battles, and major public events as the 'civilisation' of previous ages. Typically, Guizot wrote major studies entitled *Histoire de la civilisation en Europe* and *Histoire de la civilisation en France*, and Michelet, even more perhaps, was committed to 'la résurrection de la vie intégrale [du passé]' – amongst the poor and humble as well as the great and powerful. If (as one may think) they anticipated present-day attempts at 'total history' and even 'the history of mentalities', so also did the literary Romantics. 'L'histoire est un roman dont le peuple est l'auteur'; the novelist must present 'le spectacle philosophique de l'homme profondément travaillé par les passions de son caractère et de son temps': thus declared Vigny in his 'Réflexions sur la vérité dans l'art' appended to *Cinq-Mars*. 'Une peinture vraie des mœurs et des caractères à une époque donnée': such was Mérimée's aim in his *Chronique* as declared in its preface. (His attempt to present also 'une insurrection populaire' may even remind us of modern historians of 'the crowd'.) They were not contending that literary and historical works are identical – even though in their own day they were far less clearly differentiated than now. Vigny's *Journal* in 1828 draws a useful contrast. History presents 'le sens philosophique et le spectacle *extérieur* des faits vus dans leur ensemble'; the historical novel, on the other hand, 'donne l'*intérieur* de ces mêmes faits examinés dans leur détail'. The historian takes the wider, more long-distance view and is 'le peintre d'un Panorama sur la plus haute élévation de la terre'; the novelist should descend to the valley, should seat himself 'dans les chaumières et sous les buissons' and enter into the very heart of the age. Their functions are thus, for Vigny, complementary, not opposed: 'après avoir lu l'histoire d'un temps et son roman, on en aura l'idée la plus complète'.

The aim was thus to present not so much the events as the psychology of the men themselves – to draw, in Mérimée's words, 'ces portraits de l'*homme* qui m'amusent et qui m'intéressent' and do so without importing nineteenth-century moral standards. Whereas history deals with 'les vastes destinées de l'*humanité*', as Vigny puts it, literature should depict 'le sort particulier de l'*homme*'. How, and how successfully, one may thus ask, did he and other Romantics fulfil this purpose?

If their historical novels should be understood as part of the wider historical revolution, they also have to be seen within a second, quite different context – and unfortunately so, some may judge. The historical genre was thriving at the popular level before any of the Romantics practised it (*Les Martyrs* and Hugo's youthful *Han d'Islande* alone excepted). The historical dramas of Soumet, Népomucène Lemercier, Pierre Lebrun, Pichald and others were paralleled by a flood of historical novels: some in the manner of the *roman noir* and the gothic novel before it, others imitative of Scott, yet others mere historical romances of the kind still flourishing today on railway book-stalls. It has been calculated that between 1815 and 1832 some 30 per cent of all new novels in France were historical, or, again, that in Paris alone within some fifteen months in 1824–5 over 130 historical novels were published.[40] In short, the Romantics did not invent the historical novel in its nineteenth-century form; they utilised a genre that was proving highly successful, retained or imitated certain of its characteristics (for good or ill), and adapted it in the light of their own preoccupations. 'Dans ces dernières années [wrote Vigny], l'Art s'est empreint d'histoire plus fortement que jamais.' In seeking to effect their own linking of the two, the literary Romantics were affected by two existing approaches. The one was serious, moral and instructional, the approach being currently praised by conservative critics in the novels of Scott, and which they aspired to follow themselves, as we have noted with Vigny. The other, alas, was melodramatic, over-written, and sensationalist and yet was also imitated by some of the Romantics, both for elements in it that appealed to their own temperaments and sometimes also in their eagerness for acclaim. Hugo's early novels *Bug-Jargal* and *Han d'Islande* clearly fall within this tradition, and so, later and rather differently, do the swash-buckling historical fictions of Alexandre Dumas *père*, offering readable entertainment and adventure laced with romance to a very wide public, often serialised in *Le Siècle*. *Les Trois Mousquetaires* (1844), *Vingt ans après* (1845), and others thereafter brought him immense success, and in some ways deservedly so, given his narrative gifts, his imaginative power, his readily enjoyed style. Yet it is hard even for those of us who relished him in our adolescence to accept his claim to have 'elevated history' to 'the dignity of the novel'. The historical content is largely colourful adornment, with little attempt at deeper probing; he uses history, one study judges, 'to confer a semblance of veracity on his fiction'.[41] The literary qualities seem likewise superficial in their appeal, offering easy pleasures with few demands.

What of the novels for which higher claims may be made, however?

Literary historians have broadly agreed on two points. First, they collectively lifted the genre to a level that justifies serious critical attention, especially in comparison with their popularising predecessors. Secondly, their stress on documented and realistic description of past societies encouraged a similar approach to the present age, even though only a few of the Romantics moved from the historical to the social and realist novels. It was on these literary–historical grounds that Maigron, for instance, concluded that Vigny was 'un des fondateurs en France, non pas simplement du roman historique, mais du roman moderne'. Yet such a conclusion, even if well-justified, is basically historicist – linked with the notion of the 'evolution of genres'. So, in a quite different way, are the judgments of Lukács in his celebrated Marxist study of *The Historical Novel*, and both leave us with literary–critical questions to answer (though Lukács might not agree).[42]

On these the specialists have been surprisingly at variance. For Maigron, despite the claim cited above, *Cinq-Mars* has serious defects and is noteworthy only on grounds of literary history, and Lukács has no less fundamental criticisms to make. For Le Breton, by contrast, it is 'incontestablement le chef-d'œuvre [du roman historique]', 'le plus beau des romans historiques', and a later English critic sees it, despite reservations, as 'an excellent illustration' of a novel in the Scott tradition.[43] Likewise, Mérimée's *Chronique* is 'une œuvre bâclée' for Filon, yet is highly regarded by Maigron – 'le chef-d'œuvre du roman historique français à cette période' – and by more recent critics such as Lukács and Clark.[44] Yet again, according to Maigron, *Notre-Dame de Paris* begins the deterioration of the historical genre, and for Lukács it shows 'the same principle of decorative subjectivization and moralization of history' that he has already criticised in Vigny. But Thibaudet judges that Hugo's novel 'réalise un des modèles du genre' and that, despite defects, it is 'peut-être le chef-d'œuvre littéraire de la peinture historique'.[45] Such radical divergences between well-qualified judges are perhaps disturbing: are their standards the same? how far, indeed, do reasonably common criteria for evaluating historical novels exist? This gives all the more reason for diffidence in considering now specific examples of what the Romantics achieved within the two quite distinct and even dissonant 'contexts' that have been sketched.

Vigny's *Cinq-Mars* (1826) depicts the conspiracy around 1639 to depose Richelieu. Its failure and the execution of Cinq-Mars are presented as a significant stage in the struggle between the Cardinal and the aristocracy and, more broadly, in a decline of aristocratic influence in French society over the centuries that Vigny deplored. His view,

presented by Bassompierre, De Thou, even Milton and Corneille, as well
as Cinq-Mars, is that Richelieu destroyed the two main supports against
popular unrest and chaos, the *Parlements* and aristocratic power: hence,
after due time, the French Revolution. Whether historians assess this
thesis as simplistic or not, the general reader will be struck by the defects
it leads to – resulting, ironically, from precisely the author's most serious
aims. First, to justify it Vigny is obliged to centre attention on well-
known historical figures such as the King, Cardinal and Cinq-Mars, with
a consequent loss of imaginative freedom for himself and his reader
alike. He criticised Scott for concentrating upon 'des personnages
inventés que l'on fait agir comme l'on veut', with the great men merely
in the background to suggest authenticity. Yet Scott – and Mérimée
after him – may have realised the disadvantages of Vigny's practice. The
reader knows or believes he knows the characters of major historical
figures and the events that befell them. The novelist thus loses scope for
dramatic suspense and psychological originality; even at the most basic
story-telling level we already know Cinq-Mars will fail and die.
Secondly, Vigny's thesis intrudes as a constant bias that leads to over-
simplified characterisation: Richelieu is implausibly villainous, the hero
implausibly noble, and the impression of objectivity praised in Scott by
his contemporaries is replaced in Vigny by a sometimes strident
exaggeration. Thirdly, it has been argued, this same ulterior preoccupation led him to historical errors and a one-sided selectivity. Vigny
prided himself upon the researches he undertook and stressed the
authenticity of his documentation, notably in the novel's second edition
in the same year, to which he added both a list of his sources and further
lengthy notes derived from them. Yet the sources themselves were
sometimes less reliable than documents that had been recently published
but which Vigny appears to have neglected, and he also makes some
surprising changes of fact. Grandier's trial is moved from 1634 to 1639;
in 1642 De Thou is made to quote Descartes's *Principes*, published in
1644 and in Latin at that; Marion de Lorme discusses Mlle de Scudéry's
famous 'Carte du Tendre' years before its publication in 1654; young
Molière broods on *Les Précieuses ridicules* seventeen years ahead of its
production; Milton – most notoriously – reads from *Paradise Lost* at a
date before it was composed and to a group including Descartes,
Corneille and Molière. Vigny clearly believed such discrepancies were
trivial and were justified artistically to aid both local colour and
compression, and, sensitive to contemporary criticism on this score, he
defended himself in the 'Réflexions' added to the novel's fourth edition.
There is a difference between 'la *vérité* de l'Art' and 'le *vrai* du Fait', he

claims, and the novelist should be free to introduce 'toutes les figures principales d'un siècle' and to 'faire céder parfois la réalité des faits à l'*idée* que chacun d'eux doit représenter aux yeux de la postérité'; one should be less concerned with 'l'authenticité du fait' than with truth about human nature. This self-defence, though over-insistent, is not without plausibility, but perhaps he ignored one consequence for the reader. His factual rearrangements, added to our sense of a special case being pleaded, end by weakening our confidence in the author's reliability as historical guide. The historical novel has to serve two muses: we end uncertain of Vigny's fidelity to Clio. Finally, Vigny, interested above all, given his thesis, in the power conflicts of the time, has markedly less concern with presenting the mentality of ordinary people than Mérimée or Balzac just after or Scott before him. Though seeming to make attempts, he largely fails to evoke the crowd and its passions, thought or even language: his attention goes primarily to the upper classes. His novel is less successful as a result in capturing what he himself claimed especially to have sought, 'le caractère général d'une époque'. Lukács juxtaposes Vigny and Mérimée and praises the latter for aiming at 'an unbiassed exploration of the real life of the past';[46] the accusation against Vigny that is implied on both counts is difficult to counter.

Perhaps Vigny ultimately accepted that he had failed in his primary aims, even if not recognising that the failure followed from those very aims. To Napoléon III much later he acknowledged that the novel was 'vulnérable par un point, le vrai réel des faits' and that therefore he had chosen not to complete his planned series but instead to write his two 'romans philosophiques', as he terms them, *Stello* and *Servitude et grandeur militaires*.[47] And before that, in his *Journal* in 1841, he had made another reassessment: 'C'est la rapidité du récit qui a dû en faire le succès pour le public. Les observations fines, les scènes de détail s'enchaînent très vivement . . .' He was surely correct. *Cinq-Mars* has dramatic action, narrative speed, passages of imaginative evocation, stylistic ease, the story-teller's quality of 'readability', but these achievements fall below Vigny's original high purpose.

Mérimée's *Chronique du règne de Charles IX* (1829) contrasts with Vigny's novel in various ways. It came from a writer apparently more preoccupied with historical veracity and who would later be officially employed on historical monuments and write historical, architectural and archaeological works. Moreover, friend of Stendhal and frequenter of Delécluze's Liberal salon, he was less impressed than Vigny by the aristocracy (though much later he would become a Second Empire

senator and friend of Empress Eugénie). He had already written, as well
as a play on Cromwell, a historical drama, *La Jacquerie* (1828), which
vividly if disjointedly describes a peasant rising against the nobility in
the mid fourteenth century, with stress on violence and cruelty and
sarcastic portrayals of both Church and State. The later-sixteenth-
century French wars of religion offered an apt subject for this sceptical,
pessimistic young man, drawn to passion and energy but cynical of all
establishment values: a time of turmoil and religious intolerance, on
which, moreover, ample new documentation had just been published by
both Buchon and Petitot.

'Tracer une esquisse des mœurs des Français sous le règne de Charles
IX': that was his announced aim, and without judgments by present
standards unlike Vigny. A love story is added – perhaps to parody the
well-worn recipe of his day – but he was not even to tell us how the affair
between Mergy and Diane ends. For his interest was elsewhere, partly in
a neutral presentation of the manners and outlook of a period that
attracted him, partly in demonstrating the follies of religion in particular
and mankind in general. Catholics and Protestants are treated with even-
handed disapproval, excepting only a few Protestants like Coligny and
La Noue and a few Catholics like frère Lubin. Even his interpretation of
the St Bartholomew massacre is neutral, if inconsistent: his Preface
supports the Catholic claim that it was unpremeditated; the novel itself
favours the Protestant view that the King plotted it. The final squabble
of Catholics and Calvinists over the death-bed of the atheist George
illustrates an equal condemnation of all religious fanatics.

His method of 'sketching' the past claims to eschew physical
description of the kind he mocks in Scott in his interpolated eighth
chapter and would later regret in Flaubert's *Salammbô*. He is well able
vividly to evoke the external scene, as his short stories would also show
in later years, but does so for an ulterior end. He gives a series of sharp,
lively scenes – *La Jacquerie* had comparably been subtitled 'Scènes
féodales' – each of which serves to reveal the mental atmosphere of the
age and the war. The hunt, the crowd scene, George and his soldiers, the
burning of a soldier in his armour: these are some examples of narrative
force and economy utilised to give us 'une peinture vraie des mœurs et
des caractères'. And this impressionistic rapidity allows him to range
widely over the social classes and life of '1572' (subtitle of the novel).
The courtiers, with individuals like Vaudreuil, Béville and Comminges
clearly differentiated; the soldiers; the common people, including
villagers, girls of easy virtue, the Paris mob and the inhabitants of La
Rochelle, each distinctively presented; a variety of individual types,

ranging from the innkeeper, comic, aggressive and cowardly by turns, and the boatman to the superstitious woman 'quack' and the both comic and brutal peasant woman: all these and more live for the reader as well as the principal characters, and cumulatively introduce him to the psychology of the time.

In all this, moreover, Mérimée bases himself more firmly than Vigny upon numerous documentary sources, from which he chooses small but significant details and revealing anecdotes ('Je n'aime dans l'histoire que les anecdotes', he alleged) which build up the total picture. Trahard in particular has shown how extensive were his historical references, drawn from Catholic, Protestant and, for preference, neutral witnesses.[48] He is not above using a doubtfully authentic story if it seems apt and revealing: the King shooting at passers-by, La Noue struck on the face during the siege at La Rochelle, the incident of the Queen of Navarre's poisoned gloves. He is also undoubtedly selective in his choice of sources and his use of them. Evidence of courage, heroism, religious commitment and compassion is omitted; it is also significant that in using (say) D'Aubigné, who had fought in the wars, he draws not from *Les Tragiques* but the more ironic *Aventures du baron de Fœneste*. Yet despite inaccuracies and selectivity he does win our confidence in the historical basis of his 'chronicle' in a way Vigny does not. There is truth in the accusations against him of cold detachment, of excluding sincere conviction from his portrayals, of being biased by his own ironic scepticism. Most of his many characters, moreover, are types, representing some particular social group or category, and even Bernard and Diane are simply portrayed; only the unbeliever George is complex and fully rounded. Yet the reason for this may lie not only in the novelist's own sympathies but in possible limits of the historical novel itself. Notwithstanding such reservations, the *Chronique*, praised by conservatives and their opponents alike when first published, remains the best example of Romantic historical fiction. In a historical novel, argues Lukács, 'what matters is that we should re-experience the social and human motives which led men to think, feel and act just as they did in historical reality'.[49] By that criterion Mérimée is to a large extent successful.

By the date of the *Chronique* the vogue for the historical novel was already waning, however: far from creating it, the Romantics came towards its end, though the historical romances of Eugène Sue, Frédéric Soulié and others would be published in the 1835 to 1840 period and prove popular. At a higher literary level the social novel of contemporary life became increasingly dominant with the works of

Stendhal, Balzac and lesser writers. Balzac's *Les Chouans* (1829), the first novel he published under his own name, can certainly be seen as a historical novel, yet even it – prior to all his later novels of modern life – portrays events in the very recent past, the royalist insurrections in Brittany a mere thirty years earlier. Modelled on Scott and with the customary love interest added, it offers a lively description of the period and its manners and of location. Unlike Vigny Balzac avoids well-known historical personages and seeks to capture a wider, more diffuse 'mentality' – biased only by his characteristic stress upon the general desire for loot – and his presentation of events and of crowds and groups like the company captained by Hulot is realistic, vivid and historically more objective than with Vigny. The novel is arguably marred by elements of melodrama and by the emphasis upon externals seen in the numerous passages narrating happenings or describing physical details of scene, manners and costume, but Lukács is surely justified in claiming that, unlike Mérimée, Balzac conveys a sense of 'the real, decisive problems of the people'. However, as he also notes, this novel illustrates in reality the 'extension of the historical novel into an historical picture of the present'.[50] Like *Stello* and *Servitude et grandeur militaires* and, later, Hugo's *Quatre-vingt-treize*, *Les Chouans* is as much a modern as a historical novel and thus did not need to face the problems of recapturing the long-vanished past which confronted Vigny in *Cinq-Mars* and Mérimée in the *Chronique*.

One more obviously historical novel published only two years later remains to be briefly considered here: Hugo's *Notre-Dame de Paris* (1831). It has almost always been highly successful with the general public both in France and abroad, notably in England where, for example, four translations were published between 1833 and 1839 alone and numerous other versions later. Its fortunes with the critics have been more uneven, possibly affected by its very popularity not only as novel but also as film scenario; few Anglo-Saxons over fifty can distinguish Hugo's Quasimodo and Mr Charles Laughton as 'the hunchback of Notre-Dame'. Its melodramatic plot, its emotionalism, its larger-than-life main characters, its exuberant abundance of external detail, its sketchy and sometimes implausible psychology, have all been held against it even as its sales have soared. These charges are not unjustified, and Hugo himself was to remark of the work: 'S'il a un mérite, c'est d'être une œuvre d'imagination, de caprice, de fantaisie.'[51] He even affirmed as well that 'le livre n'a aucune prétention historique' and stressed his architectural preoccupations – to defend gothic building against the depradations of the town-planners, to inspire the nation (as he claimed in a note to the 1832 edition) with a love of its national architecture.

Yet he added that his novel was also attempting, 'avec quelque science et quelque conscience, mais uniquement par aperçus et échappées', to present 'l'état des mœurs, des croyances, des lois, des arts, de la civilisation enfin du XVe siècle'. Furthermore, in the original preface he stressed his preoccupation with the role of 'fatality' in human life, and in the 1866 preface to *Les Travailleurs de la mer* he would claim to have 'denounced' in the earlier novel the fatality of religion and its dogmas, parallel with that of society (treated in *Les Misérables*) and that of nature (in the third novel). In line with such assertions one may interpret *Notre-Dame de Paris* less as an anticipation of Dumas or Hollywood than in terms like those of its best recent editor: 'Le roman historique se fait symbolique et travaille à la constitution d'une philosophie de l'Histoire.'[52] Nor is he alone in inviting us to evaluate the novel afresh: for example, a present-day English translator, of broadly structuralist sympathies, has argued that 'it is something richer and less lowbrow' than a merely 'picturesque' novel, 'much more intelligent and topical' than a purely emotional 'entertainment'.[53] Not that its more 'popular' qualities should be despised. It possesses obvious qualities of dramatic power and action and stylistic vitality, and most readers would acknowledge its vivid evocation of fifteenth-century Paris – of its cathedral and other buildings and of the countryside closeby, of the bustling life of the old city, of a comprehensive range of rich and poor, good and evil, and of social classes, from royalty, gentry and burgesses to clerics, students and the masses. Overdrawn the descriptions may sometimes be, but again and again one feels within the medieval world and its attitudes, as a variety of scenes are used to evoke the spirit as well as the 'local colour' of the age: the performance of the mystery play; Quasimodo on the pillory; the attack on Notre-Dame, and others. But, alongside this characteristic of historical totality, there is perhaps also a greater intellectual resonance in the novel than usually acknowledged. The main characters have a symbolic role, it has been argued: Esmeralda representing the themes of purity and the future, the three men around her, Frollo, Phœbus and Quasimodo, the powers of Church, State and people, equated also with past, present and future. And Frollo in particular embodies the complex psychology of a divided intellectual, 'l'homme de science tout entier tendu à la conquête de l'absolu, et que bouleverse et ruine la brutale découverte de la femme, du corps'.[54] Political preoccupations are no less present. Hugo's democratic beliefs are expressed through the Flemish hosier, Coppenole, for example, as he warns the King that the people will ultimately rule, and, beyond that, Louis XI is being interpreted as the unwitting accomplice of a long historical process that has led, inevitably in Hugo's view, to nineteenth-century democracy: seeking to break aristocratic power, like Richelieu later, the King was initiating the decline which Vigny regretted but Hugo welcomed. His broader social optimism is also reflected, but more hesitantly. His belief in regeneration through knowledge and public enlightenment has been discerned in the portrayal of Frollo as the guardian and reader of manuscripts, but whereas *Les Misérables* would illustrate in the case of Valjean Hugo's hope for social reconciliation and redemption, Quasimodo here remains separated. Hugo himself referred to the novel's 'philosophical and aesthetic ideas', we noted; present-day 're-readings' make it less easy than formerly to dismiss their significance.

The historical genre was to be more neglected by serious novelists for the remainder of the century – prior, indeed, to Anatole France's *Les Dieux ont soif* – excepting only *Salammbô* and Gautier's *Le Capitaine Fracasse*, this latter even so a picaresque novel closer to Dumas than to Mérimée or Scott. This has been related by Lukács to larger social developments. The Romantics mirrored, 'inevitably', 'the great social transformations of modern times', and 'the decisive intellectual struggles round the historical novel' took place in France as a reflection of Restoration power-tensions. *Salammbô* apart, which illustrates 'the crisis of bourgeois realism', the historical novel reawakens only with the Russian Revolution. It has been alleged that Lukács's thesis rests on a travesty of Scott, and it may also be reading too much into these novels. Others may rather attribute the decline of the historical genre to different developments, to the more serious claims being made for both history and literature as the century advanced. History became more professionalised and 'scientific'; after a brief decade or so when narrative history and literary narrative remained in uncertain harmony, the tension between documented fact and novelist's imagination grew more unacceptable. The novel too laid claim to more solemn functions than story-telling, picturesque description, and evocation of the past, and sought a deeper probing of individual psychology and the social realities of the present. The historical novel in the Scott tradition was perhaps outstripped by the higher literary aims which the Romantics helped to affirm and the changed critical attitudes that have followed; perhaps in this respect their historical novels have to some degree been 'hoist with their own petard'.

This may be more broadly true. In retrospect one sees that the

Romantics came at a point of transition in the history of the novel in France – and that they above all made it that. What they inherited was a largely despised genre; they, by contrast, attributed serious purposes to it and in the outcome convinced their contemporaries to rate its possibilities as highly as those of poetry or drama. They explored various of its forms, to differing degrees, but above all – if the arguments above and of pp. 167–80 especially are correct – they made of it a vehicle for high intellectual concerns and especially for their moral preoccupations. If so, it is the more ironic that some observers have thought them primarily emotional, and all the more since some of their defects as novelists may stem from too many ideas, imperfectly absorbed into their novels as with Vigny, rather than too few. However that may be, those who effect transitions – or revolutions – tend to be surpassed, and to some extent this was to be the Romantics' fate as novelists, a few outstanding works excepted. Yet, by all but the most excluding standards, their prose fiction remains rewarding and relevant to this day.

NOTES

1. A. Thibaudet, *Histoire de la littérature française de 1789 à nos jours* (Stock, 1936), p. 248.
2. For these and the following references, see the bibliography below.
3. Cf. the study, of major relevance, by M. Iknayan, *The Idea of the Novel in France, 1815–1848* (Geneva, Droz and Paris, Minard, 1961).
4. Cf. a discussion in V. Brombert, *The Romantic Prison: The French Tradition* (Princeton UP, 1978), ch. VI.
5. Cf. in particular P. Thomson, *George Sand and the Victorians: Her Influence and Reception in Nineteenth-Century England* (London, Macmillan, 1977) and C.M. Lombard, 'George Sand's image in America (1837–1876)', *Revue de littérature comparée*, 40 (1966), 177–86.
6. Cf. Iknayan, p. 185.
7. For a study of the resulting growth of popular literature, cf. J.S. Allen, *Popular French Romanticism* (Syracuse UP, 1981).
8. G. Picon, in *Encyclopédie de la Pléiade: Histoire des littératures*, new edn (vol. III, Gallimard, 1978), p. 998.
9. By Henri Peyre, for example, in D.G. Charlton (ed.), *France: A Companion to French Studies*, 2nd edn (London, Methuen, 1979), pp. 394–5.
10. Amongst numerous instances, cf. especially G.R. Ridge, *The Hero in French Romantic Literature* (University of Georgia Press, 1959).
11. M. Barrès, *Les Maîtres* (Plon, 1927), pp. 283–4.
12. The term is used by A. Hoog, 'Who invented the *mal du siècle*?', *Yale French Studies*, 13 (1954), 42–51. Cf. also Hoog, 'Un cas d'angoisse préromantique', *Revue des sciences humaines*, 102 (1962), 181–97, and R. Mauzi, 'Les Maladies de l'âme au 18e siècle', *Revue des sciences humaines*, 100 (1960), 459–93.
13. R. Canat, *Du sentiment de la solitude morale chez les romantiques et les parnassiens* (Hachette, 1906), p. 32.
14. Cf. in particular the analysis by P. Barbéris, 'Mal du siècle, ou D'un romantisme de droite à un romantisme de gauche', *Romantisme et politique, 1815–1851* (Colin, 1969),

pp. 164–82, and in his *Balzac et le mal du siècle* (2 vols., Gallimard, 1970).

15. Chateaubriand, *Mémoires d'outre-tombe* (4 vols., Flammarion, 1948), II, 43–4.

16. Cited by C.M. Desgranges, *Le Romantisme et la critique: La presse littéraire sous la Restauration* (Mercure de France, 1907), pp. 217–19.

17. Gustave Planche, Cuvillier-Fleury, and Ernest Falconet, cited by M. Allem, *Sainte-Beuve et 'Volupté'* (Malfère, 1935), pp. 227ff.

18. P.H. Simon, *Le Domaine héroïque des lettres françaises* (Colin, 1963), p. 310; M.Z. Shroder, *Icarus: The Image of the Artist in French Romanticism* (Cambridge, Mass., Harvard UP, 1961), pp. 37–9; and M. Peckham, *Beyond the Tragic Vision* (New York, Braziller, 1962), part 3.

19. R. Trousson, *Le Thème de Prométhée dans la littérature européenne* (2 vols., Geneva, Droz, 1964), vol. II, ch. VII: 'Le Prométhée des romantiques'; V. Černy, *Essai sur le titanisme dans la poésie romantique occidentale* (Prague, Éditions Orbis, 1935); and M. Descotes, *La Légende de Napoléon et les écrivains français du XIXe siècle* (Minard, 1967). Cf. also 'The myth of Napoleon', *Yale French Studies*, 26 (1960–1).

20. Cf. Barbéris's writings cited above and M. Praz, *The Romantic Agony* (London, Oxford UP, 1933). In addition to examples discussed below, cf. the analysis given in R. Grimsley, 'Romantic melancholy in Sainte-Beuve's *Volupté*', in *Studies in Modern French Literature presented to P. Mansell Jones* (Manchester UP, 1961), pp. 144–62. This notes not only a movement from subjective towards universal but also Amaury's 'ambivalent attitude towards his "confusion"', an ambiguity perhaps analogous with that found in *René* and other works.

21. The argument here is developed in my article 'The ambiguity of Chateaubriand's *Réne*', *French Studies*, 23 (1969), 229–43.

22. Cf. Hugo, *Préface de 'Cromwell'*, ed. M. Souriau, 5th edn (Société Française d'Imprimerie, n.d.), pp. 186–8.

23. For a fuller statement of the analysis that follows cf. my essay 'Musset as moral novelist: *La Confession d'un enfant du siècle*', in C.E. Pickford *et al.* (eds.), *Mélanges de littérature française moderne offerts à Garnet Rees* (Minard, 1980), pp. 29–46.

24. Cf. A.J.L. Busst, 'The image of the androgyne in the nineteenth century', in I. Fletcher (ed.), *Romantic Mythologies* (London, Routledge and Kegan Paul, 1967), pp. 1–95.

25. Such at least is the conclusion of R. Godenne, *La Nouvelle française* (PUF, 1974), ch. III.

26. Cf. P.-G. Castex, *Le Conte fantastique en France de Nodier à Maupassant*, new edn (Corti, 1962).

27. A.J. George, *Short Fiction in France, 1800–1850* (Syracuse UP, 1964), p. 65.

28. *Ibid.*, p. 135.

29. R. Molho, 'Les Variations de Sainte-Beuve au lendemain de 1830', in *Romantisme et politique, 1815–1851*, p. 248.

30. Cf. bibliography to this chapter.

31. George, *Short Fiction*, p. 150.

32. R. Picard, *Le Romantisme social* (New York, Brentano's, 1944), p. 223.

33. For a brief survey of French praise and criticism cf. C. Chonez, *George Sand* (Écrivains d'Hier et d'Aujourd'hui, Seghers, 1973), pp. 15–20.

34. R. Johannet, *L'Évolution du roman social au XIXe siècle*, original edn, 1909 (Geneva, Slatkine Reprints, 1973), p. 21.

35. She, like her fellow Romantics and Pierre Leroux, recognised the often conflicting claims of personal liberty and social equality; cf. chapter II above.

36. G. Lubin, 'George Sand et la révolte des femmes contre les institutions', in *Roman et Société* (Colin, 1973), p. 43.

37. J. Seebacher, in Hugo, *Notre-Dame de Paris; Les Travailleurs de la mer* (Bibliothèque de la Pléiade, Gallimard, 1975), p. 1050. Cf. also Seebacher's essay in *Revue d'histoire littéraire de la France*, 75 (1975), 308ff.
38. J. and M. Lough, *An Introduction to Nineteenth-Century France* (London, Longman, 1978), p. 303.
39. E. Renan, *L'Avenir de la science*, 23rd edn (Calmann Lévy, 1929), p. 132. Cf. S. Mellon, *The Political Uses of History* (Stanford UP, 1958), p. 1, citing *Revue encyclopédique*, 32 (1827), 679, and, more broadly, P. Moreau, *L'Histoire en France au XIXe siècle* (Les Belles Lettres, 1933) and L. Halphen, *L'Histoire en France depuis cent ans* (Colin, 1914).
40. Cf. L. Maigron, *Le Roman historique à l'époque romantique* (Champion, 1898), still the basic survey.
41. F.W.J. Hemmings, *The King of Romance: A Portrait of Alexandre Dumas* (London, Hamish Hamilton, 1979), p. 123.
42. Maigron, *Le Roman historique*, p. 266; cf. G. Lukács, *The Historical Novel* (London, Merlin Press, 1962). For a critique of their historicism, cf. J. Molino, 'Qu'est-ce que le roman historique?', *Revue d'histoire littéraire de la France*, 75 (1975), 195–234.
43. A. Le Breton, *Le Roman français au XIXe siècle*, original edn, 1901 (Geneva, Slatkine Reprints, 1970), pp. 296 and 308; R.J.B. Clark, in Mérimée, *Chronique du règne de Charles IX* (London, Harrap, 1969), p. 24.
44. A. Filon, *Mérimée* (Hachette, 1898), p. 46; Maigron, book III, ch. v; Lukács, pp. 78–80; R.J.B. Clark, 'Introduction' to Mérimée, *Chronique*.
45. Maigron, *Le Roman historique*, p. 334; Thibaudet, *Histoire de la littérature française*, p. 250.
46. Lukács, *The Historical Novel*, pp. 78–9.
47. Cited in Vigny, *Cinq-Mars*, ed. A. Picherot (Gallimard, 1980), p. 555.
48. Cf. P. Trahard, *La Jeunesse de Mérimée* (2 vols., Champion, 1925), vol. II, appendix 13.
49. Lukács, *The Historical Novel*, p. 42.
50. *Ibid.*, pp. 80–4.
51. *Victor Hugo raconté par un témoin de sa vie* (vol. II, Brussels, Lacroix, Verboecoven et Cie, 1863), p. 300.
52. J. Seebacher, in Hugo, *Notre-Dame de Paris*, p. 1045.
53. J. Sturrock, 'Introduction' to translation of *Notre-Dame de Paris* (Harmondsworth, Penguin Books, 1978).
54. The words are J. Seebacher's (in Hugo, *Notre-Dame de Paris*, p. 1046).

BIBLIOGRAPHY

Romantic prose fiction has been largely neglected in recent studies of the novel in France – in M. Raimond, *Le Roman depuis la Révolution* (Colin, 1967), R.-M. Albérès, *Historie du roman moderne* (Albin Michel, 1962), and even W. Engler, *The French Novel from 1800 to the present*, translated by A. Gode (New York, Ungar, 1969), but G. Picon gives it more attention in 'Le Roman et la prose lyrique au XIXe siècle', in *Encyclopédie de la Pléiade: Histoire des littératures*, vol. III: *Littératures françaises, connexes et marginales*, new edn (Gallimard, 1978), pp. 980–1088. J.P. Houston, *Fictional Technique in France, 1802–1927* (Baton Rouge, Louisiana State UP, 1972) devotes only one chapter to the Romantics (excluding Stendhal and Balzac). Far fuller treatment is found in works of over a half-century ago, notably G. Saintsbury, *A History of the French Novel*, vol. II: *From 1800 to 1900* (London, Macmillan, 1919) and F.C. Green, *French Novelists from the Revolution to Proust* (London and Toronto, Dent, 1931), though both are inevitably outdated in part and the former, despite very detailed knowledge, may seem discursive to a fault to the present-day reader. The general works on the French Romantics noted in the bibliography to chapter I above usually discuss their prose fiction, but often more rapidly than their drama and poetry.

A short book of extracts appeared in 1970, P. Salomon, *Le Roman et la nouvelle romantiques* (Masson), but otherwise the standard works in French date from many years ago. A. Le Breton, *Le Roman français au XIXe siècle (avant Balzac)*, original edn, 1901 (Geneva, Slatkine Reprints, 1970) is an extensive study, though ending in 1827, that retains its value. The different fictional forms are treated in detail in the following: for 'le roman de l'individu' J. Merlant, *Le Roman personnel de Rousseau à Fromentin* (Hachette, 1905) and J. Hytier, *Les Romans de l'individu* (Les Arts et le Livre, 1928), to which can now be added a more restricted study, G. Holmes, *The 'Adolphe type' in French Fiction* (Quebec, Naaman, 1977); for the historical novel L. Maigron, *Le Roman historique à l'époque romantique* (Champion, 1898) and (a distinguished but partial later work) G. Lukács, *The Historical Novel* (London, Merlin Press, 1962); for the social novel (of distinctly lesser value), C. Brun, *Le Roman social en France au XIXe siècle*, original edn, 1910 (Geneva, Slatkine Reprints, 1973) and R. Johannet, *L'Évolution du roman social au XIXe siècle*, original edn, 1909 (Geneva, Slatkine Reprints, 1973) and, still authoritative but largely devoted to minor figures, D.O. Evans, *Le Roman social sous la monarchie de juillet* (PUF, 1930). These are now supplemented by certain essays in far more recent collective works: W. Engler (ed.), *Der französische Roman im 19 Jahrhundert* (Darmstadt, Wissenschaftliche Buchgesellschaft, 1976) (with short bibliography); *Roman et Société* (Colin, 1973); 'Le Roman historique', *Revue d'histoire littéraire de la France*, 75 (1975), a double issue with several major essays, notably by J. Molino, P. Barbéris, C. Duchet, J. Seebacher, R. Desné, *et al.*

Romantic short fiction has received particular attention in recent decades, notably from A.J. George, *Short Fiction in France, 1800–1850* (Syracuse UP, 1964). On one important genre the major authority remains P.-G. Castex, *Le Conte fantastique en France de Nodier à Maupassant*, new edn (Corti, 1962); J. Rettinger, *Le Conte fantastique dans le romantisme français*, original edn, 1909 (Geneva, Slatkine Reprints, 1973) is a far shorter, older survey of only slight interest. R. Godenne, *La Nouvelle française* (PUF, 1974) devotes ch. III to the nineteenth century and its diversity of short fiction.

On a final fictional form, P. Vernois, *Le Roman rustique de George Sand à Ramuz* (Nizet, 1962) can be noted but has only a brief discussion of Sand. Two books in English discuss special aspects: J.S. Allen, *Popular French Romanticism: Authors, Readers and Books in the 19th Century* (Syracuse UP, 1981), an interesting work but centred on popular literature; and P.P. Clark, *The Battle of the Bourgeois: The Novel in France, 1789–1848* (Didier, 1973), the subtitle being misleading.

As regards contemporary ideas about prose fiction, a work of major value is M. Iknayan, *The Idea of the Novel in France, 1815–1848* (Geneva, Droz, and Paris, Minard, 1961). A good selection from the Romantics' own theoretical writings on fiction is H.S. Gershman and K.B. Whitworth, *Critical Prefaces to the Nineteenth-Century French Novel* (Columbia, University of Missouri Press, 1962).

Linguistic and stylistic aspects of the Romantics' fiction have been neglected here, for lack of space; on these, though they concentrate mainly on their poetry, cf. E. Barat, *Le Style poétique et la révolution romantique* (Hachette, 1904) and Ch. Bruneau, *L'Époque romantique* (vol. XII of *Histoire de la langue française*, ed. F. Brunot, Colin, 1948).

In addition to the general studies above there are, of course, numerous works on individual Romantics which discuss their fiction, either in detail or incidentally, and scholarly editions of their novels, notably in the Pléiade (Gallimard) and Garnier collections, are often of great value, as are also articles on specific novels in the collective volumes mentioned above. Within the limits of this bibliography only a few additional

Prose fiction

studies, for the most part specifically concerned with their fiction, can be noted here.
On Chateaubriand, cf. P. Barbéris, *René de Chateaubriand, un nouveau roman* (Larousse, 1973); L. Martin-Chauffier, 'Le romancier: des *Natchez* à l'*Abencérage*', in *Chateaubriand: Le Livre du Centenaire* (Flammarion, 1949); and D.G. Charlton, 'The ambiguity of Chateaubriand's *René*', *French Studies*, 23 (1969), 229–43. On Constant there are numerous studies, of which the most helpful include I.W. Alexander, *Constant: 'Adolphe'* (London, Edward Arnold, 1973); P. Delbouille, *Genèse, structure et destin d'Adolphe* (Les Belles Lettres, 1971); A. Fairlie, 'The art of Constant's *Adolphe*' (3 articles in *Modern Language Review*, 62 (1967), 31–47; *Forum for Modern Language Studies*, 2 (1966), 253–63, and *French Studies*, 20 (1966), 226–42); G. Rudler, *Adolphe, éd. critique* (Manchester UP, 1919); J. Cruickshank, *Constant* (New York, Twayne, 1974), and M. Hobson, 'Theme and Structure in *Adolphe*', *Modern Language Review*, 66 (1971), 306–14. Mme de Staël's novels, often neglected in recent decades, are best discussed by S. Balayé, *Mme de Staël: Lumières et Liberté* (Klincksieck, 1979), ch. IV (with full bibliography); cf. also G. Poulet, '*Corinne* et *Adolphe*, deux romans conjugués', *Revue d'histoire littéraire de la France*, 78 (1978), 580–96; and M. Gutwirth, *Mme de Staël, Novelist: The Emergence of the Artist as Woman* (Urbana, University of Illinois Press, 1978). On Senancour's *Obermann* cf. in particular B. Le Gall, *L'Imaginaire chez Senancour* (2 vols., Corti, 1966) and editions by A. Monglond (3 vols., Grenoble, Arthaud, 1947) and G. Michaut (2 vols., Cornely, 1912, and Hachette, 1913).

The second-generation Romantics' fiction has received less attention than their drama and poetry, even in the case of Hugo. On him, cf. G. Piroué, *Victor Hugo romancier, ou Les Dessous de l'inconnu* (Denoël, 1964); P. Albouy, *La Création mythologique chez Victor Hugo* (Corti, 1963); R. Journet and G. Robert, *Le Mythe du peuple dans 'les Misérables'* (Éditions sociales, 1965); and C. Gély, '*Les Misérables*' de Hugo (Hachette, 1975). On Vigny, cf. F. Germain, *L'Imagination de Vigny* (Corti, 1963) and a helpful edition of *Cinq-Mars* by A. Picherot (Gallimard, 1980). On Musset there is little other than in more general studies of which the best is Philippe Van Tieghem, *Musset, l'homme et l'œuvre* (Hatier, 1944); three recent articles in English on his *Confession d'un enfant du siècle* are by R. Grimsley, *Studies in Romanticism*, 9 (1970), 125–42; R.S. King, *Nottingham French Studies*, 11 (1972), 3–13; and D.G. Charlton, in *Mélanges de littérature française moderne offerts à Garnet Rees* (Minard, 1980), pp. 29–46. On George Sand the most useful starting points are P. Salomon, *George Sand* (Hatier, 1953) and essays in *Hommage à George Sand* (PUF, 1969); *Revue d'histoire littéraire de la France*, 76 (1976), 531–651 (notably on *Consuelo* by S. Balayé, 614–33, and on *Lélia* by B. Didier, 634–51); *Romantisme*, 16 (1977); and *Nineteenth-Century French Studies*, 4 (1975–6). On Sainte-Beuve, cf. M. Allem, *Sainte-Beuve et 'Volupté'* (Malfère, 1935). A recent introduction in English to Alexandre Dumas *père* is F.W.J. Hemmings, *The King of Romance: A Portrait of Alexandre Dumas* (London, Hamish Hamilton, 1979). The best introductions in English to Mérimée, though not centred on *Chronique du règne de Charles IX*, are F.P. Bowman, *Prosper Mérimée: Heroism, Pessimism and Irony* (Berkeley, University of California Press, 1962) and A.W. Raitt, *Prosper Mérimée* (London, Eyre and Spottiswoode, 1970). P. Trahard, *Mérimée et l'art de la nouvelle* (PUF, 1923) is tangentially relevant as well as his 4-volume biography (Champion, 1925–30). The most useful edition of the *Chronique* for English readers is by R.J.B. Clark (London, Harrap, 1969).

DATE DUE